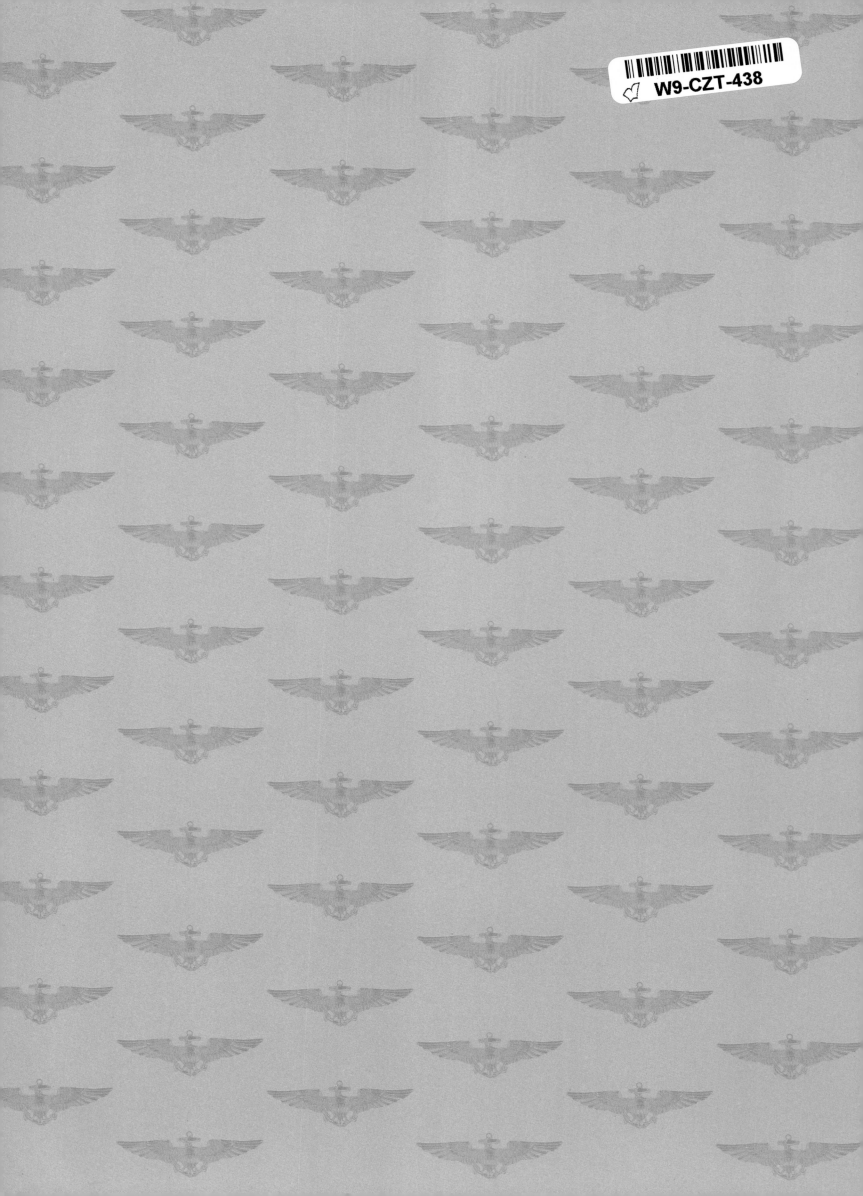

U.S. NAVAL AVIATION

U.S. NAVAL AVIATION

M. Hill Goodspeed, Editor-in-Chief
Rick Burgess, Editor

BARNES & NOBLE BOOKS
NEW YORK

NAVAL AVIATION MUSEUM FOUNDATION

Naval Aviation Museum Foundation

The Naval Aviation Museum Foundation is a nonprofit 501(c)(3) organization that was founded in 1966 to support the development of the National Museum of Naval Aviation in Pensacola, Florida. Through effective fundraising and positive leadership, the Foundation has enabled the Museum to grow from its original 8,500-square-foot facility to become one of the largest aviation museums in the world, boasting almost 300,000 square feet of exhibit space and more than 140 naval aircraft. The Foundation is much more than just a fund-raising organization. From award-winning publications to the annual Naval Aviation Symposium, the Museum Foundation continues to excel in fulfilling its mission to promote and preserve the proud history and rich traditions of naval aviation. With the opening of the Flight Adventure Deck in 1999, the Foundation took on an additional role of education. The program teaches concepts of aerodynamics, aerostatics, gravity, and propulsion to middle-school children in an exciting, hands-on environment. This educational role will be further expanded with the creation of the National Flight Academy—a bold new endeavor that will teach students the concepts of flight and the fundamental core values resident in Naval Aviation in an exciting, week-long program. With a strong sense of purpose, an extraordinary wealth of educational resources, and the strength of more than 11,000 members, the Naval Aviation Museum Foundation enters the twenty-first century as one of the nation's most dynamic nonprofit organizations.

In the National Museum of Naval Aviation's Blue Angel Atrium, A-4 Skyhawks and an F/A-18 Hornet represent the past and present of the Navy's illustrious flight demonstration team. (Chad Slattery)

Naval Aviation Museum Foundation
1750 Radford Boulevard
Naval Air Station Pensacola, Florida 32508
(850) 453-2389; fax (850) 457-3032
http://www.naval-air.org

This edition published by Barnes & Noble, Inc., by arrangement with Hugh Lauter Levin Associates, Inc. 2005 Barnes & Noble Books

M 10 9 8 7 6 5 4 3 2 1
ISBN 0-7607-7116-2
Printed in China

Design: Lori S. Malkin
Project Editor: James O. Muschett

All photography and illustrations are courtesy of the U.S. Navy unless otherwise credited.

Contents

Navy Wings

Navy Wings

Admiral Leighton W. Smith, USN (Ret)

Eager eyes looked up at me as I pondered an appropriate response to a question asked moments earlier. Several young men and women who wanted my advice about serious career choices had just flattered me with a question about their futures. The four bright, aspiring officers wanted to know whether or not they should select naval aviation as a career choice.

Finally, I said, "Absolutely not! Don't even consider naval aviation. Don't give Naval Air Station Pensacola a second thought. Don't, whatever else you do, go down that path—unless," I paused. "Unless you have a

Above: *For those who did not graduate from the Naval Academy or Reserve Officer Training Corps programs, the path to Navy wings begins at Officer Candidate School at NAS Pensacola, Florida. Throughout the course of instruction, the lives of the prospective officers are governed by the omnipotent presence of a Marine drill instructor. (Al Audleman)*

Pages 6–7: *Bathed in blue above a sea of clouds, a trio of F/A-18 Hornets form the centerpiece of a panoramic vista of flight. "Oh I have slipped the surly bonds of earth and danced the skies on laughter-silvered wings."*

Opposite: *Officer candidates scale the wall of the obstacle course at NAS Pensacola, Florida, one rite of passage during the intensive training it takes to transform a civilian into a naval officer. Enduring the crucible of Officer Candidate School and pinning on the gold bars of an ensign is but the first step toward wings of gold. (Al Audleman)*

Left: *A flight instructor demonstrates a maneuver to a pair of prospective naval flight officers, imparting a lesson on the ground that will translate into increased proficiency in the air. Though they will not actually fly aircraft in the fleet, naval flight officers log flight time in T-34C trainers, including some in the pilot's seat, gaining an appreciation for what it takes to fly an aircraft. (Al Audleman)*

Above: *A pair of T-45A Goshawk trainers pictured in close formation over California on 22 November 1996. For aspiring jet pilots the T-45 represents the capstone of their training prior to earning their wings, the aerial classroom in which they learn instrument and formation flying, hone basic air combat maneuvering skills, and make their first attempts at "hitting the boat." (Ted Carlson)*

Right: *A flight student receives a cockpit check from his instructor, who is typically fresh from a tour in a fleet squadron. With the benefit of hundreds of flight hours, the veteran imparts the knowledge that only experience can bring. (Al Audleman)*

Opposite, top left: *A parachute draped over the canopy railing of a T-34C Turbo-Mentor training aircraft is a tangible reminder of the potential danger in flying. The instructor is teaching these flight students the importance of knowing their airplane, which one day may save their lives. (Al Audleman)*

Opposite, top right: *Actually flying the airplane is but one element of the intense training it takes before one can be called a naval aviator or naval flight officer. Many hours of study in subjects such as aerodynamics, meteorology, and navigation supplement time in the cockpit. (Al Audleman)*

Opposite: *A naval flight officer climbs into the rear cockpit of an F/A-18D Hornet of Strike Fighter Squadron 124 to prepare for a flight from Abraham Lincoln (CVN 72) in May 1997. The successful completion of flight training is but the start of a life spent honing combat skills in a constant quest for perfection. (Ted Carlson)*

gnawing hunger for excitement, an unquenchable thirst for challenge, and an eagerness to do things that few men and women on this planet will ever have a chance to do.

"No," I continued, "none of you should start down that path unless you want to experience more excitement in a few seconds than most people will in a lifetime, and unless you want to join a very special organization that is the envy of virtually every fighting force in the world." The initial looks of shock gave way to smiles that betrayed excitement and anticipation. I had their attention.

"Let me tell you a bit about naval aviation," I said. "From the start you will be pushed to what you think are your limits, only to find that there is more in you than you thought. As you begin to learn the basics of flying, both academically and 'hands on,' the best practitioners of an art that requires very special skills will teach you. They will be men and women who have been there, done that. Yes, you will be taught well, but to learn, and learn well, will require a commitment from you the likes of which you have never known or experienced. Know this! Much will be expected of you. But, in return, much will be given.

"You will be challenged, in a measured way, to explore your own possibilities. Unlike other services's flight instructions and regulations, you will be told what you cannot do rather than what you can do. There is an important difference in this philosophy. You see, telling you what you cannot do allows so much more flexibility for you to learn more about what you can do. I caution you, take heed of those maneuvers and actions that are prohibited, for in all probability, the lessons from which they were derived have been written in the blood of your predecessors.

"You will be taught to rely on your own capabilities, develop self-confidence in your abilities, handle the not-so-routine events, and strive for exactness. You see, aviation, no matter what the discipline or service, requires all of those attributes. Oh, you will make mistakes. That is to be expected. But your instructors and your leaders will have done what they could to prepare you for them, demanded that you acknowledge them and insisted that you accept responsibility for your actions. This is how your predecessors learned and grew. It is how you will learn and grow. The richness of thousands of experiences will be used to build upon your natural skills and talents. As this process unfolds you will, without even knowing it, develop a reservoir of knowledge that, one day, may well mean the difference between a successful flight and you becoming a statistic.

"You will come to understand that each type of aircraft has its own unique operational envelope. Similarly, we each have ours. During your training, which really never stops, you will be encouraged to seek the

NAVY AIRCREWMAN'S CREED

I am a United States Naval Aircrewman, member of a combat team. My pilot and shipmates place their trust in me and my guns. I will care for my plane and guns as I care for my life. In them I hold a power of life and death—life for my countrymen, death for the enemy.

I will uphold my trust by protecting my pilot and plane to the absolute limit of my ability. So help me God.

edges of yours. Getting there will take some time, but as you develop confidence and hone your skills, you will move further out from that comfort zone at the center of the envelope to those outer edges. It is there, at that outer edge, where you will extract the most from yourself and your aircraft. Trust me, when that happens you will know and sense it. Exhilarating hardly begins to describe the feeling, but at that moment, you will understand why naval aviation is so very special.

"So why," I ask these eager young aviator aspirants, "is it important to push yourself, to learn as much as you can, to make that total commitment that naval aviation demands?" Answering my own question, I tell them that one day they will know. "It might be on a dark night with you, as pilot in command, working like the very devil to land a cantankerous P-3 Orion that, on that particular night, has decided to test you by allowing you only two of its four engines. Your crew of twelve men and women will be depending on your skills to bring them in safely. And, as the pilot, you must. It won't matter that the crosswinds are out of limits, or that the ceilings are at minimum. What will matter is that you are the one person who is responsible for a safe conclusion to your flight.

"Or it may come as you approach the target, deep in enemy territory, in a strike fighter launched from the deck of an aircraft carrier hundreds of miles from the coastline. You will be in an aircraft that is the best our country can provide, with precision-guided munitions that can be delivered

Above: The blue waters of the Pacific just a few hundred feet below, the crew of a P-3C Orion of Patrol Squadron 91 banks to starboard during an antisubmarine warfare training flight on 22 February 1997. Flying a P-3 is more than a one-person job; the pilot and co-pilot are at the controls and an enlisted flight engineer is positioned between them monitoring engine performance. (Ted Carlson)

Below: A P-3C Orion of Patrol Squadron 22 pictured in flight near Japan. The successor to giant flying boats upon which naval aviation was built, the Orion continues the maritime patrol mission that has been an integral part of fleet operations for nearly a century. (Department of Defense)

Opposite: An F-14 Tomcat of Fighter Squadron 51 passes over Carl Vinson *(CVN 70). The essence of naval aviation, and the aspect that sets it apart from all other air forces, is the fact that operations are routinely conducted from the deck of a moving ship. (U.S. Navy)*

Top: *Lieutenant "Reggie" Hamon, flying an F/A-18C Hornet of Strike Fighter Squadron 146 off John C. Stennis (CVN 74), triggers the release of flares from his aircraft after a training exercise on 16 August 1999. Realistic training often spells the difference between success and failure when the call comes to launch against a target deep in enemy territory. (U.S. Navy)*

Above: *A rescue swimmer leaps into the waters of the Gulf of Mexico through the side door of a UH-1N Iroquois helicopter of Helicopter Combat Support Squadron 16 during search and rescue training. Superbly conditioned, rescue swimmers must be able to perform their duties in the most demanding of conditions, day or night. (Department of Defense)*

within a few meters of your intended aim point. But all is for naught unless you know your stuff. The target, surrounded by surface-to-air missile sites and antiaircraft batteries, every one of which will be doing their level best to destroy you, is critically important to a ground commander's scheme of movement. Simply put, you must succeed.

"Another scenario might include a stormy night at sea with you at the controls of a rescue helicopter hovering over a shipmate whose fate rests in your hands. You will be following the precise directions of your nineteen-year-old aircrewman as he or she guides you into position. You will be expected to—no, you must—hold that position steady as the hoist is lowered to that individual who will, for the remainder of his or her days, understand why your craft is referred to as 'Angel,' and why your predecessors are held in such high esteem.

"In any of these situations, or others like them, you will be severely tested," I tell them. "Sweat will be running into your eyes and down your neck; your flight suit will feel as if you have just worn it through a car wash. In fact, the only dry spot on your body is likely to be the inside of your mouth, which will feel like an entire bale of cotton has been used to absorb every bit of saliva that your body could possibly produce. If I am correct, it is about this time that you will ask yourself two questions: 'What the hell am I doing here?' and 'Can I really pull this off?'

"It is then that you will reach down deep within yourself—into that reservoir of determination, inner strength, and skills perfected over hours and hours of repetitive training—and summon whatever is needed to complete the mission successfully. You will be able to do it because you will

have been taught well. You will do it because you know that others depend on you doing it, and doing it correctly. You will do it because others before you have faced the same dangers and risks and have not flinched in the face of similar adversity. You will do it because you wear wings of gold and because that is precisely what is expected of you.

"As you grow professionally you will, like most of your colleagues, become fiercely independent. But you will also come to realize that, in naval aviation, there is a shared dependence on each other. If you don't believe me now, you will the first time you ever witness air operations on board an aircraft carrier. First-time observers might think the actions that occur during launch and recovery operations are orchestrated mayhem, that the business of carrier operations starts on the brink of disaster and can only get worse. But to those of us who have experienced it firsthand, it is more like a choreographed ballet in which every member of the troupe knows his or her role perfectly. The noise, the intensity, so many moving parts, complex and confusing, the edge of the envelope. That it can be

Top, left: *The foundation of naval aviation's current and future success rests on the accomplishments of those who have come before, including men like Captain Thaddeus Vejtasa. His is a face of battle, one that saw air combat at such hallowed places as the Coral Sea and Guadalcanal. (Rich Pedroncell)*

Top, center: *Dangling from a hoist beneath an SH-2F Seasprite helicopter of Helicopter Antisubmarine Squadron Light 30, a rescue swimmer is pulled from the water during a training exercise. To these intrepid sailors one of the most satisfying sights is seeing a pilot or aircrewman that he has just rescued being pulled to safety. (Department of Defense)*

Above: *Lieutenant Jerry Leekey, an F-14 Tomcat pilot in Fighter Squadron 102, pictured on board* America *(CV 66) prior to launching on a mission during Operation Deny Flight in 1993. The keepers of the flame, beneficiaries of the proud traditions of naval aviation, are the young men and women who man the cockpits of today and tomorrow. (Department of Defense)*

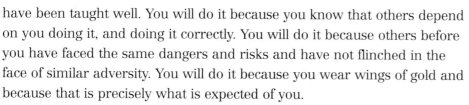

Positioned just a few feet from the spinning propeller of an E-2C Hawkeye, a plane inspector shields his eyes from the sun during flight deck operations on board Carl Vinson (CVN 70) in 1999. The close confines of carrier decks packed with high-performance aircraft are fraught with danger, but highly trained personnel make it look easy. (David Peters)

15

Above: *Fumes generated by an F-14A Tomcat of Fighter Squadron 41 launching from* Theodore Roosevelt *(CVN 71) create a surreal setting on the flight deck of the giant carrier. The scores of men and women who make a carrier flight deck function are a testament to the word teamwork. (U.S. Navy)*

Below: *Combat Aircrewman Darrell Weiss peers out at the seemingly endless expanse of the Pacific Ocean through the side door of a UH-3 Sea King helicopter of Helicopter Combat Support Squadron 85 during a May 1999 flight. Naval aviation and the Navy of which it is a part are tasked with the mission of patrolling the waters that make up most of the earth's surface. (Ted Carlson)*

Right: *A plane handler uses hand signals to direct an aircraft on the flight deck of* Carl Vinson *(CVN 70) during flight operations in 1999. Movements of hands and arms in defined motions orchestrate the brilliantly choreographed ballet that is a carrier flight deck in action. (David Peters)*

done at all seems to defy logic, especially since almost everything is done with hand signals and many of the individuals scurrying about the deck are barely out of high school. But it is done, and done well, because each individual involved has been trained as intensely as you will have been trained and knows instinctively where to be and what must be done. And they also know that they must do their job right the first time, every time because mistakes in that environment usually have very serious and distinctly unattractive consequences. Yet the flight operations go on, day and night, day after day, month after month, good weather or bad. And despite

the apparent dangers, we boast a spectacular safety record, and we get better at it all the time."

I tell these young men and women that I used the carrier as the example, but the intensity of operations is similar on flight lines throughout naval aviation. And so is the teamwork. "You see," I say, "we trust, rely on, and, most importantly, support one another. This always holds true, be it that nineteen-year-old aircrewman in the helicopter or the naval flight officer directing sophisticated jammers toward the enemy radars that are attempting to line you up for a shot. That is the way it has always been, that is the way it is today, and that is the way it will be in the future. That is why we are great and grow stronger with each generation."

I pause a moment and ask my audience of four one final question. "So you think you still might want to be a naval aviator? Well," I warn them, "if you are willing to learn, commit, and work your heart out, then come and join us. You will not be choosing an easy path. However, if you succeed, you will become part of an organization where courage, initiative, honor, candor, teamwork, commitment, stamina, integrity, and compassion are descriptive words, but do not and cannot adequately capture the essence of who we are, what we do, and what we stand for."

Top, left: *The landing signal officer watches as an F-14A Tomcat makes a successful landing on the flight deck of* Enterprise *(CVN 65) during carrier qualifications in the Atlantic Ocean. The culmination of every flight by a carrier pilot, the tug of an arresting wire jolting the aircraft to a sudden stop is an exhilarating feeling. (U.S. Navy)*

Top, right: *The wind generated by the forward motion of the ship sends steam from the forward catapults across the deck of* Enterprise *(CVN 65) during flight operations in the Pacific Ocean in September 1985. Clouds of steam, the roar of jet engines, and the pungent smell of jet fuel captivate the senses on board an aircraft carrier. (Department of Defense)*

Above: *An F/A-18 Hornet maneuvers onto the catapult that in a few moments will sling it into the air in a moment of fury. Despite their inherent violence, carrier flight operations are a thing of beauty to watch. (Boeing)*

Above, left: *The pilots of a P-3C Orion of Patrol Squadron 65 rev the engines on the flight line at NAS Point Mugu, California, in March 1997. The aircraft's four Allison T65-A-14 turboprop engines generate nearly 5,000 horsepower apiece, enabling the sizeable aircraft to achieve speeds of nearly 500 mph. (Ted Carlson)*

Above: *Pilots calibrate the weapons system on an F/A-18C Hornet of Strike Fighter Squadron 86 on the flight deck of* George Washington *(CVN 73) operating in the Arabian Sea during 1997. Naval aviation must always be ready when the call comes to engage in combat with an enemy. (U.S. Navy)*

Right: *Their SH-2G Seasprite visible in the background, Lieutenant Commander Mike Branco (left) and Commander Bob Burrus display the confident stride that comes with the successful completion of a mission. (Ted Carlson)*

Opposite, top: *The author, Admiral Leighton W. Smith, at the pinnacle of his career in command of NATO forces in Bosnia. (U.S. Navy)*

Opposite, bottom: *The fulfillment of having survived the perils of combat and flying from an aircraft carrier, the camaraderie of squadron life, and the joy of a reunion with their loved ones that is just moments away—all are reflected on the faces of pilots and radar intercept officers of Fighter Squadron 32 as the Swordsmen return from the Gulf War in March 1991. (National Museum of Naval Aviation)*

Right: *An F/A-18C Hornet of Strike Fighter Squadron 195 strains against an arresting wire after successfully trapping on board* Kitty Hawk *(CV 63) in October 1996. In addition to being capable combat platforms in the air, carrier aircraft must be durable enough to withstand the repeated pounding against the flight deck that is a fact of life in carrier landings. (U.S. Navy)*

As I look at these young faces, their enthusiasm, anticipation, and quest to take themselves out of the mainstream into a way of life that is so different and so exciting that it defies description, I give them one final thought. "If you're lucky, and get to spend as much time as I have in the business of naval aviation, maybe one day forty years from now some young folks like yourselves will ask you if you think you made the right decision in choosing naval aviation. My guess is you'll tell them, as I tell you now, I simply cannot imagine having done anything else with my life."

NAVY FLYER'S CREED

I am a United States Navy flyer.

My countrymen built the best airplane in the world and entrusted it to me. They trained me to fly it. I will use it to the absolute limit of my power.

With my fellow pilots, air crews, and deck crews, my plane and I will do anything necessary to carry out our tremendous responsibilities. I will always remember we are part of an unbeatable combat team—the United States Navy.

When the going is fast and rough, I will not falter. I will be uncompromising in every blow I strike. I will be humble in victory.

I am a United States Navy flyer. I have dedicated myself to my country with its many millions of all races, colors, and creeds. They and their way of life are worthy of my greatest protective effort.

I ask the help of God in making that effort great enough.

A Golden Journey

A Golden
Journey

M. Hill Goodspeed

Pages 20–21: *At roughly 1020 on the morning of 4 June 1942, SBD Dauntless dive-bombers descended upon Japanese carriers in the waters off Midway, releasing their deadly cargoes with precision and transforming the carriers Akagi, Kaga, and Soryu into flaming infernos. It was the beginning of the end of Japanese conquest in the Pacific War. ("Battle of Midway," R.G. Smith)*

Above: *Sailors hold a biplane trainer steady in the waters of Pensacola Bay as a pilot climbs into the cockpit prior to launching on a training flight. The end of the wooden seaplane ramp used for launching aircraft is visible at the extreme left of the photograph. (U.S. Navy)*

In 1898, the Assistant Secretary of the Navy ordered an evaluation of a primitive flying machine under construction by Professor Samuel P. Langley. In so doing, Theodore Roosevelt, who as President of the United States nine years later would send the so-called Great White Fleet around the world in a display of U.S. naval might, marked the Navy's first official interest in aviation.

Langley's Aerodrome never took flight, the honor instead falling to the Wright brothers, who on 17 December 1903 launched the aviation century over the windswept dunes of Kitty Hawk, North Carolina. Their inventive spirits channeled, other visionaries followed in the footsteps of Orville and Wilbur Wright, among them a former motorcycle racer who, in the words of one pioneer airman, "looked as though he had never been on anything faster in his whole life than a tricycle." His unassuming countenance masked technical genius, and on the shores of Lake Keuka in his native Hammondsport, New York, Glenn H. Curtiss set about designing aircraft capable of operating from both land and sea. On 14 November 1910, in the hands of a daring young civilian pilot named Eugene Ely, one of Curtiss's machines successfully took off from a makeshift wooden deck erected atop the cruiser *Birmingham* (CL 2) in Hampton Roads, Virginia. Two months later, on 18 January 1911, Ely successfully guided a Curtiss pusher to a landing on another wooden deck, this one on board the armored cruiser *Pennsylvania* (ACR 4) anchored in San Francisco Bay. A series of ropes weighted

Civilian pilot Eugene Ely pictured moments before landing on the makeshift wooden deck on board Pennsylvania *(ACR 4) anchored in San Francisco Bay, 18 January 1911. Note the wooden tracks running the length of the deck to raise the sandbag-weighted ropes a few inches off the deck. (National Museum of Naval Aviation)*

The Curtiss pusher aircraft in which Lieutenant Theodore G. Ellyson, the Navy's first aviator, learned to fly was a primitive contraption with no enclosed fuselage and the pilot perched at the front with no seatbelt. Like many of the pioneer airmen, Ellyson's life ended in an airplane crash. (National Museum of Naval Aviation)

Above: *Arriving at the recently closed Navy Yard in Pensacola, Florida, in January 1914, the men of the Navy's small air arm found no facilities to support their operations. Erected on the shore of Pensacola Bay, canvas tent hangars protected man and machine alike from Florida's blazing sunshine. Note the makeshift wooden ramps to facilitate the launching and beaching of seaplanes. (U.S. Navy)*

Opposite, top: *The N-9 appeared even before the United States entered World War I, and it remained the Navy's standard primary trainer throughout the Great War and into the 1920s. Pilots found the early versions of the airplane underpowered, particularly when attempting to perform a loop. The single pontoon beneath the fuselage, which became waterlogged over time, did not help when it came to performance. (U.S. Navy)*

Right: *The aviation detachment dispatched to Vera Cruz, Mexico, in 1914 included an AB-3 flying boat (left) and AH-3 "hydro-aeroplane." On 6 May 1914, with Lieutenant (jg) Patrick Bellinger at the controls, the latter airplane was hit by hostile rifle fire during an observation flight. Forbidden to carry firearms aloft, Bellinger later retaliated against the Mexicans by lobbing a big bar of yellow soap into their position, the first "ordnance" launched from a naval aircraft. (U.S. Navy)*

down by sandbags helped bring his aircraft to a stop, achieving the first-ever arrested landing on board a U.S. Navy vessel. Later that year the Navy requisitioned two aircraft from Curtiss, and the first officer, Lieutenant Theodore G. Ellyson, received orders to report for flight training under the tutelage of the New York inventor. A golden journey had begun in earnest.

Their fellow officers thought them crazy to leave the time-tested battleship community and volunteer to fly contraptions that would at worst kill them and at best diminish their careers. However, the adventure and allure of flight beckoned a small number of junior officers, who learned at the hands of Curtiss and the Wrights and passed on flying techniques to those who followed them. In 1914, the Navy established a permanent home for the infant air arm in a recently closed navy yard at Pensacola, Florida, and in January of that year, with aircraft operating from canvas tent hangars erected along the shore of Pensacola Bay, training flights commenced. The panhandle town would come to be known as the "Cradle of Naval Aviation," and to this day all prospective U.S. naval aviators receive a portion of their training there.

The ensuing years marked an age of discovery for naval aviation. In April 1914, operating as an element of American forces assembled in response to the Vera Cruz Insurrection in Mexico, naval aviators flew the first combat missions in the history of American military aviation. In addition, whether catapulting from the decks of ships, experimenting with aerial photography, or soaring high over the white sandy beaches of Pensacola in quest of altitude and endurance records, air-minded officers tested the bounds of flight and sought to integrate aviation more fully into the fleet.

"Now the soldier, the sailor, and the airman are the hero of the hour," wrote Lieutenant Frank Simpson, Jr., from Pensacola the day the United States entered World War I. Indeed, the patriotic fervor that arises every time the nation is called to arms captured another generation of young men in April 1917. With the tales of biplanes jousting over the trenches of Europe having filled the newspapers during the previous months, many men aspired to win their wings as aviators and test their mettle in this new dimension of warfare. In just nineteen months, the naval air arm emerged as a sizeable organization, growing from a handful of personnel and flying machines into a force that numbered more than 2,000 qualified pilots and 33,000 support personnel with 2,337 aircraft, dirigibles, and kite balloons.

Though members of the Navy's air arm were the first U.S. military forces to arrive overseas, going ashore in France on 5 June 1917, naval aviation's combat operations during the Great War were largely unheralded.

Above: *One aspect of the Navy's lighter-than-air experience involved the employment of balloons for observation. During the period 1929–1933, Navy balloonists established six world distance records and a world altitude record. (National Museum of Naval Aviation)*

Above: *During World War I, American aircraft production lagged behind that of its European allies. Hence, naval aviators overseas often found themselves flying foreign-built machines under the tutelage of foreign instructors. The French navy presented this certificate to Joseph Cline following the completion of his training. An enlisted man in the First Aeronautic Detachment that arrived in France in June 1917, Cline received all of his ground and flight instruction in France and received his designation as a naval aviator on 11 November 1918, Armistice Day. (National Museum of Naval Aviation)*

Right: *The officers of NAS North Sydney, Nova Scotia, strike dashing figures in their distinctive aviation green uniforms and gleaming boots. Unlike their successors in World War II, who came from all across the country, the vast majority of fliers who joined the ranks of the Navy in 1917–1918 were from the northeast. Once they received their wings, they served at air stations stretching from Key West to Canada and across the Atlantic in the British Isles, France, and Italy. (National Museum of Naval Aviation)*

Opposite, top: *Fleet operations at Guantanamo Bay, Cuba, in 1919 included operating landplanes from wooden decks erected on battleships. After completing his flight, the pilot would land ashore and his aircraft would be pulled by cart to the beach and loaded on board a boat for transport back to the ship. A time-consuming process that involved a number of sailors, it left little doubt about the need for a platform on which wheeled airplanes could both take off and land. (U.S. Navy)*

A handful of men logged combat missions with the Northern Bombing Group against enemy submarine bases in Belgium, some flew against Austria from bases in Italy, and Lieutenant (jg) David S. Ingalls became the Navy's first fighter ace in the skies over the Western Front. However, most naval aviators spent the war flying antisubmarine patrols from coastal air stations, with sightings of German U-boats quite rare.

Although statistically naval aviation's performance did not equal that of the Army, World War I proved vital to its development. Naval aviators gained invaluable experience under wartime conditions, both in operations

and logistical support of a burgeoning military force. In addition, experience
working with foreign forces stimulated thought regarding the employment
of aircraft in naval operations, particularly with respect to aircraft-carrying
ships, which the British Royal Navy operated during the war.

In the first year of peace, U.S. naval aviation signaled for the entire
world the tremendous promise embodied in the airplane. The successful
flight of the NC-4 flying boat, which in May 1919 achieved the first
crossing of the Atlantic by air, marked the beginning of perhaps the
most important decade in the development of the U.S. Navy's air arm.
In the months preceding the transatlantic flight, ships of the Atlantic
Fleet for the first time departed for winter training in Guantanamo Bay,
Cuba, with a formal aviation detachment, including war surplus Sopwith
Camels for flying off a wooden deck erected on the battleship *Texas*
(BB 35). In July 1919, Congress appropriated funds for the conversion
of the collier *Jupiter* (AC 3) into the U.S. Navy's first aircraft carrier, a
platform that would truly integrate aviation into the fleet. Commissioned
in 1922, she was christened *Langley* (CV 1).

Ashore, the office that controlled naval aviation, which began
with Captain Washington Irving Chambers tucked away in solitude in
the Bureau of Navigation in Washington, D.C., received a more suitable
status. In July 1921, the Navy established the Bureau of Aeronautics,

*Langley (CV 1), the U.S. Navy's first aircraft
carrier, pictured at sea. Converted from the
collier* Jupiter *(AC 3), which ironically had
carried the first naval aviators to France in
1917, the makeshift carrier was too slow to
keep pace with the fleet's battleships and
could operate a limited number of airplanes—
one of her executive officers called her "This
poor comic old ship." Nevertheless,* Langley's
*flight deck served as a veritable laboratory
for carrier aviation, laying the foundation for
the future success of the flattop. (U.S. Navy)*

Top, left: *"The Father of Naval Aviation,"*
Rear Admiral William A. Moffett shepherded
naval aviation through the pivotal decade of
the 1920s, helping to build it into a potent
element of the fleet. A politically astute and
capable administrator, he became the first
Chief of the Bureau of Aeronautics in 1921,
and held the post until his untimely death in
the crash of the rigid dirigible Akron *(ZRS 4)*
in 1933. Admiral John Towers recalled of
Moffett, "I cannot recall any man who loved
a fight and who could think of more ways to
win one." (U.S. Navy)

Above: *Three giants of interwar naval avia-*
tion meet on 8 November 1930. Captain John
H. Towers (left) was the Navy's third aviator
and headed the Bureau of Aeronautics when
the United States entered World War II. As
Commander Aircraft Squadrons, Battle Fleet,
Rear Admiral Joseph Mason Reeves (center)
successfully integrated aviation into fleet
operations. The Navy's first fighter ace, World
War I veteran David S. Ingalls (right) held the
post of Assistant Secretary of the Navy for Air
from 1929–1932. (U.S. Navy)

thus giving aviation a voice in the entrenched bureaucracy. And no better choice could have been made for its first chief. Rear Admiral William A. Moffett was a politically savvy officer who despite early misgivings about flying—he once told a pioneer aviator that any man who flew was either crazy or a damned fool—had embraced air power's importance to the future of naval operations.

Certain obstacles stood in the way of this vision becoming a reality. In 1921 the colorful and outspoken air power advocate, Army Brigadier General William "Billy" Mitchell, led bombing attacks against captured and obsolete battleships off the Virginia coast. The dazzling photographs of exploding vessels captured the nation's attention and seemed to validate Mitchell's claim that air power, under the control of a unified independent air force, had replaced the Navy as the nation's traditional first line of defense. The public bantering between Mitchell and officers of the Army and Navy reached its climax in September 1925. Following bombastic statements by Mitchell in the wake of the crash of the U.S. Navy airship *Shenandoah* (ZR 1) about the conduct of the War and Navy

Departments in regard to aviation, President Calvin Coolidge convened the Morrow Board to establish military and aviation policy in the United States. The board's findings preserved the naval air arm, and Mitchell's subsequent court-martial ended for a time the campaign to incorporate naval aviation into a unified air force.

Though Moffett's acumen in handling political issues in the halls of Congress was important to naval aviation's development, its ultimate success or failure depended on its performance at sea. "The Navy is the first line of offense and naval aviation as an advance guard of this first line must deliver the brunt of the attack," Moffett wrote in 1925. "Naval aviation cannot take the offensive from the shore; it must go to sea on the back of the fleet. . . . The fleet and naval aviation are one and inseparable."

At that time, naval aviation's seagoing force consisted of *Langley*, which following commissioning served only in an experimental role; a handful of seaplane tenders; and scout and observation airplanes deployed on ships of the line. Sea-based naval aviation had yet to demonstrate any offensive prowess that would dispel the traditional tenet of the supremacy

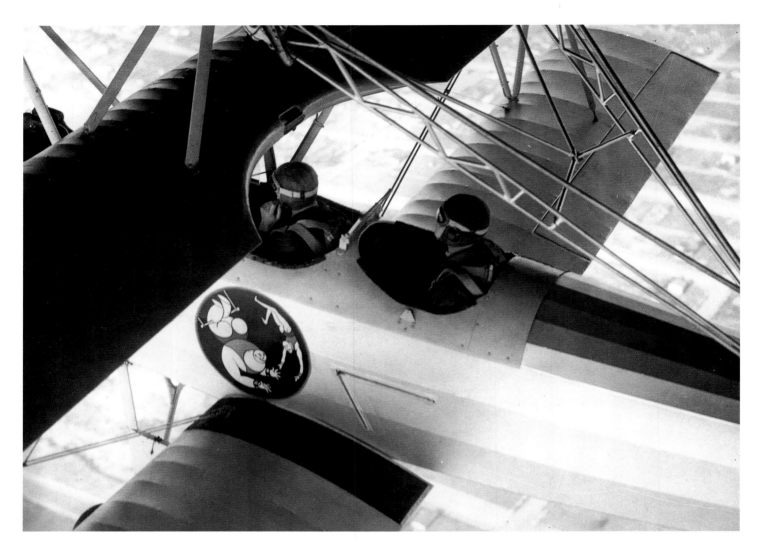

Above: *Landing an airplane on a moving ship was not the only unique endeavor routinely conducted by naval aviators during the interwar years. Pilots assigned to the heavier-than-air units on board the rigid dirigibles Akron (ZRS 4) and Macon (ZRS 5) launched and recovered their aircraft by way of a trapeze lowered from the airship's internal hangar. This N2Y trainer has successfully engaged the trapeze on Macon. The V-shaped crane visible above the pilots' heads secures the aircraft's fuselage. Note the insignia visible beneath the front cockpit, the oversized man representing the dirigible and the smaller one the aircraft. (U.S. Navy)*

Right: *Saratoga (CV 3), the vertical black stripe on her stacks distinguishing her from her sister ship, Lexington (CV 2), recovers aircraft during the 1930s. Deck handlers packed the aircraft onto the forward section of the flight deck in order to clear the landing area. They then maneuvered the aircraft aft and spotted them for the next launch. (National Museum of Naval Aviation)*

Opposite, bottom: *Naval aviation's assumption of a more important role in the U.S. Fleet during the interwar years translated into billing on recruiting posters of the era. Nevertheless, traditionalists remained skeptical of the air zealots' proclamations that the aircraft carrier had supplanted the battleship as the Navy's most potent offensive weapon. (National Museum of Naval Aviation)*

of the battleship. All of this changed with the appointment of Captain Joseph Mason Reeves to the post of Commander Aircraft Squadrons, Battle Fleet. Living up to his nickname, "Bull" Reeves drove his charges hard, demanding that they innovate and push the limits. He ordered the skipper of tiny *Langley* to increase the number of airplanes she operated, and drilled the pilots and deck crews incessantly in an effort to reduce the time it took to launch and recover aircraft. Finally, with *Langley* and later the sister ships *Lexington* (CV 2) and *Saratoga* (CV 3)—monstrous carriers that displaced over 30,000 tons with speeds in excess of 30 knots—Reeves seized upon opportunities to demonstrate the offensive potential of the carrier. During war games, he foreshadowed the Day of Infamy by

launching a dawn attack against Pearl Harbor, and in Fleet Problem Nine in January 1929, separated *Saratoga* and one escort from the main group and launched a surprise strike against the Panama Canal. "We take off at 3:30 a.m. to bomb the canal," an excited Lieutenant Artie Doyle wrote on the eve of the landmark attack. "They haven't a chance to stop us." The success of the strike marked the birth of the concept of the carrier task forces that would roam the Pacific during World War II.

Other elements of aviation developed as well. The patrol planes that had performed so well during World War I continued to form an important element of the air arm. Far-ranging in battle, they dramatically demonstrated their capabilities by staging record distance flights throughout the 1920s and 1930s. And on board the battleships and cruisers of the fleet, catapult-launched biplanes provided the eyes for the ship's great guns. Though marred by three accidents, one of which took the life of Rear Admiral Moffett, the Navy's rigid airship program proved an interesting facet of interwar aviation. Envisioned as long-range scouts, the giants in the sky operated F9C Sparrowhawk fighters in one of the more unique operational evolutions in the history of aviation, launching and recovering them using a trapeze raised and lowered from an internal hangar.

The whine of Stuka dive bombers piercing the air of the Polish countryside on 1 September 1939 signaled the beginning of World War II. Within months the frigid waters of the North Atlantic became the greatest naval battleground in history, and U.S. Navy ships and aircraft engaged in Neutrality Patrol operations to guard the nation's Atlantic shores. Yet,

Above: *Envisioned as cruisers in the sky, with their F9C Sparrowhawk fighters ranging out in search of enemy vessels, the U.S. Navy's rigid dirigibles were short-lived, the service of all but one of them ending in tragic crashes. Macon (ZRS 5), pictured here recovering aircraft, plunged into the Pacific on 12 February 1935, taking four Sparrowhawks with her. (National Museum of Naval Aviation)*

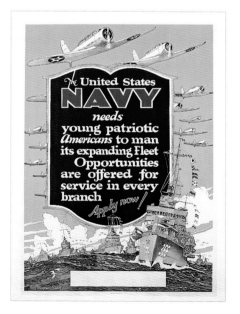

Top: *Its central figure a pilot outfitted in a dress blue uniform with gleaming wings of gold featured prominently on his chest, this wartime recruiting poster and others like it attracted thousands of would-be flyers to the ranks of naval aviation. All told, over 60,000 men earned their wings during the period 1941–1945. (National Museum of Naval Aviation)*

Above: *As this recruiting poster reflects, there was a place for everyone in naval aviation. By 1945, over 430,000 men and women served in the air arm, twenty-six times the number on active duty in 1941. (National Museum of Naval Aviation)*

Right: *Lieutenant (jg) Ray Hawkins of Fighting Squadron 31 flames a Japanese plane for his fourteenth kill. The tenth ranking Navy ace in history, the lanky Texan received three awards of the Navy Cross. He was not yet twenty-one years old. ("14 and Counting," Robert L. Rasmussen)*

much attention was focused west on the broad blue expanse of the Pacific. Throughout the 1930s Imperial Japan sought to expand its influence in the Far East, launching military actions into China and secretly fortifying island bases in the Pacific. That the U.S. and Japan would clash seemed inevitable, though none could envision the manner in which it would begin, with the explosion of Japanese bombs one quiet Sunday morning at Pearl Harbor, Hawaii. The following day, Aviation Cadet Bill Prescott wrote his parents from Pensacola, describing the reactions of his fellow flight students. "The faces of my friends were very changed . . . I realized then what this strenuous training we had undergone was meaning to them now." Naval aviation was off to war.

World War II marked naval aviation's ultimate test, the proving ground for the tactics and doctrine espoused by its proponents. Naturally, the platform upon which the airplane went to sea en masse, the aircraft carrier, figured prominently in combat operations. Four great carrier battles took place between the U.S. Navy and the Imperial Japanese Navy in 1942. The first, occurring in the Coral Sea on 7–8 May, was the first naval engagement in history in which the ships of the opposing forces never came within sight of one another. The battles at Eastern Solomons and Santa Cruz, fought in the waters off Guadalcanal in August and October respectively, represented bitter struggles that, coupled with the vicious air-to-air engagements over the island, broke the back of Japanese naval aviation. Yet, of all the great sea battles, one stands alone as the defining moment of naval aviation's ascendancy.

Outwardly insignificant, a spit of sand and coral west of Hawaii, Midway and its surrounding waters represented a decisive battleground on 3–6 June 1942. In an all-or-nothing gamble, Japanese Combined Fleet commander Admiral Isoroku Yamamoto steamed the lion's share of his forces across the Pacific in an effort to destroy once and for all the U.S. Pacific Fleet's surviving carrier air power. Against all odds, Pacific Fleet commander Admiral Chester W. Nimitz committed all the forces at his disposal to battle, assembling a motley assortment of Navy, Marine

Corps, and Army Air Forces aircraft on Midway. Additionally, he sent three carriers—*Enterprise* (CV 6), *Hornet* (CV 8), and *Yorktown* (CV 5), which had been badly damaged by bombs at Coral Sea— to intercept the invaders. The area at which they assembled was appropriately nick-named "Point Luck."

The Americans benefited from an intelligence coup, namely the breaking of the Japanese naval code, but it was the skill and heroic determination of the aircrews that saved the day. The pilots and gunners pressed home their attacks, and in a stunning blow sank four Japanese flattops in a matter of hours, turning the tide in the Pacific War. Victory did not come without cost, however, particularly among the carrier-based torpedo plane squadrons. Of the forty-one TBD Devastators launched on the morning of 4 June, only six survived the gauntlet of Japanese fighters and antiaircraft fire. One of the surviving aircrewmen was Aviation Radioman Third Class Lloyd Childers. Recovering in a hospital following the battle, he was visited by his brother, who also happened to serve in the same squadron. When he asked about the fates of his fellow gunners in Torpedo Squadron (VT) 3, Childers received the sad news that he was the only one to survive. Half a century later, tears still returned to his eyes as he recounted that moment.

In August 1943, the first of the new *Essex*-class carriers launched strikes against Marcus Island, and over the course of the next two years, the fast carriers spearheaded the offensive across the Pacific. When challenged by Japanese carriers at the Battle of the Philippine Sea in June 1944, F6F Hellcat fighters of the U.S. air groups shot down some 250

Ensign George H. Gay, the sole survivor of the carrier-based element of Torpedo Squadron 8 at the Battle of Midway in June 1942, examines a newspaper recounting the American victory while recuperating in Hawaii following the battle. Covering his head with a seat cushion to avoid capture, he witnessed the destruction of three of the Japanese carriers by Navy dive bombers on 4 June. (U.S. Navy)

African-American sailors on board Intrepid *(CV 11) receive instruction in the operation of a 20mm gun mount as part of their training as ammunition handlers. Though confined largely to service and mess duties during World War II, black sailors served on board aircraft carriers and other vessels in the combat zone and joined their shipmates in defending against enemy attacks. (U.S. Navy)*

attackers in a matter of a few hours, giving the engagement the lasting nickname of the Great Marianas Turkey Shoot. Carrier-launched fighter sweeps neutralized enemy air power, clearing the way for landings at Saipan, Leyte, Okinawa, and numerous other far-flung islands, while bombers and torpedo planes helped render the Japanese navy and merchant marine impotent. And though battered by kamikazes, the Japanese suicide planes that screamed out of the clouds, not one American fleet carrier was sunk by the "divine wind."

Antisubmarine warfare had become a central mission for naval aviation during the Great War, and during World War II it truly came of age in the struggle against Hitler's wolfpacks of prowling U-boats. Whether flying TBM Avenger torpedo bombers off the tiny decks of escort carriers or sub-hunting aircraft like the PBY Catalina or PV Ventura/Harpoon, naval aviators played a role in sending over eighty U-boats to the bottom during the Battle of the Atlantic. Some did so employing advanced technology—the Mk 24 "Fido" homing torpedo, sonobuoys, aerial rockets, and magnetic anomaly detection gear—that represented a monumental leap in the evolution of antisubmarine warfare. The colorful Captain Daniel V. Gallery, in command of the carrier *Guadalcanal* (CVE 60), did things differently. Driving U-505 to the surface during a 4 June 1944 attack off the coast of Africa, his hunter-killer group consisting of *Guadalcanal* and five escorts managed to capture the boat, the first prize at sea seized by the U.S. Navy since 1815. Lighter-than-air craft were also used to great advantage to patrol for enemy submarines. Based in the states and overseas, blimps maintained a silent vigil over convoys traversing the Atlantic, logging some 380,000 flight hours over the course of World War II.

Top: *The Stars and Stripes appropriately fly above the Nazi swastika after the capture of* U-505 *by a hunter-killer group centered on the escort carrier* Guadalcanal *(CVE 60), 6 June 1944. (U.S. Navy)*

Above: *Captain Daniel V. Gallery stands triumphantly on the conning tower of* U-505, *which bears the scars of operating beneath the waves of the Atlantic. Later, he personally campaigned to bring the war prize to Chicago's Museum of Science and Industry, where she can be toured today. (U.S. Naval Institute)*

Left: *One of the famed Goodyear blimps, the G-1 was built in 1929 and procured by the Navy for its lighter-than-air fleet in 1935. During the launch and recovery of the blimp, sailors regulated the ascent or descent of the airship using mooring lines, which are visible hanging beneath the G-1 in this photograph. (National Museum of Naval Aviation)*

Aircrewmen hone their gunnery skills on a firing range at NAS Jacksonville, Florida, in 1945. Nose gunners were an important part of the crew of PB4Y Liberator and Privateer patrol bomber crews. During low-level attacks, their accurate fire was essential in knocking out enemy antiaircraft positions. In addition, as they discovered in the Pacific, Japanese fighters often attacked with head-on runs, putting the nose gunners in a dangerous position where life and death depended on their marksmanship skills. (U.S. Navy)

Navy aircrews did not decorate their aircraft to the extent that was commonplace in the Army Air Forces, but among land-based squadrons it was prevalent. Though most chose scantily clad females, pilots and aircrewmen of this PB4Y-1P Liberator of Photographic Squadron 1 opted to honor the poor maintenance qualities of their aircraft. Based on Guam, this aircraft flew photoreconnaissance missions over Japanese-held positions, the camera silhouettes painted beneath the cockpit signaling the completion of twenty-five hops over enemy territory. (U.S. Navy)

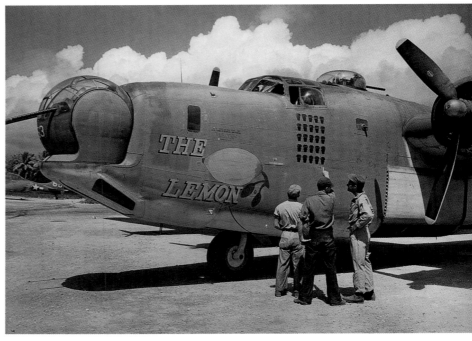

Opposite, top left: *In the closing months of World War II, Navy patrol bombers found lucrative targets in the form of Japanese merchantmen operating near the home islands. Taken during a low-level attack by a PB4Y-2 Privateer on 29 July 1945, this photograph shows a freighter settling by the stern as it is straddled by bombs dropped from the airplane. Navy aircraft sent 1.7 million tons of Japanese merchant shipping to the bottom during World War II. (U.S. Navy)*

Opposite, top right: *Members of the so-called Buzzard Brigade, pilots of Torpedo Squadron 10, pictured on board* Enterprise *(CV 6) in November 1943. Lieutenant Commander William I. Martin, the squadron skipper and pioneer in developing tactics for night operations by carrier aircraft, sits in the middle of the second row. Note the squadron insignia on the banner hanging behind the pilots. (U.S. Navy)*

In 1931, the Army and Navy had reached an agreement preventing the sea service from operating land-based multiengine aircraft, making naval aviation a truly sea-based force of carrier aircraft, floatplanes, and flying boats. But, wartime requirements superceded this prewar arrangement, and Navy and Marine Corps squadrons began operating bombers with names like Liberator and Mitchell that were more familiar to Army Air Forces crews. In the Atlantic, they logged antisubmarine patrols over waters familiar to naval aviators of the First World War. Halfway around the globe, these patrol bombing squadrons operated from captured island bases, launching daring single-plane raids against targets on land and afloat, often at an altitude of just a few hundred feet.

Naval aviation's combat operations during the war also increasingly involved flying at night. The first air-to-air kill under the stars for the

Navy came on 26 November 1943, when the crew of a TBF Avenger off *Enterprise* blasted two snoopers out of the sky near the Gilbert Islands. The following year, VT-10 employed the same type of airplane to attack Truk Island, sinking or beaching thirteen ships in the first nocturnal attack mission from the deck of an aircraft carrier. The most unanticipated use of an aircraft at night proved to be the ad hoc employment of lumbering PBY Catalina flying boats in the attack role. Painted black to mask them in a darkened sky, these radar-equipped airplanes proved highly effective in bombing Japanese shipping and shore installations.

Below: *This painting portrays a PBY Catalina as the aircraft often appeared during World War II, traversing the skies on a lonely vigil in search of the enemy. ("PBY in the Clouds," R.G. Smith)*

Murderer's Row—(front to back) Wasp *(CV 18),* Yorktown *(CV 10),* Hornet *(CV 12),* Hancock *(CV 19), and* Ticonderoga *(CV 14)— pictured at anchor in Ulithi along with other ships of Task Force 58. By 1945, the fast carriers roamed the Pacific with impunity, striking Japanese island strongholds as well as the home islands. (U.S. Navy)*

Opposite, top: F9F Panthers of Fighter Squadron 721 and Composite Squadron 61 pictured high over the ships of Task Force 77 after returning from a strike over Korea in September 1951. The first Navy jet fighter to score an air-to-air kill in Korea, the Panther also chalked up the first Navy shootdown of an enemy jet aircraft. Though it did not receive the same acclaim as the U.S. Air Force's F-86 Sabre in dogfights against enemy MiG-15s, the F9F acquitted itself well in a variety of missions, from photo-reconnaissance to ground attack. (U.S. Navy)

Admiral Arthur W. Radford, Commander in Chief, Pacific and Pacific Fleet, reads a statement during service unification hearings of the House Armed Services Committee on 7 October 1949. A central figure in the fight to preserve a mission for naval aviation in the postwar defense establishment, Radford later served as Chairman of the Joint Chiefs of Staff under President Eisenhower, the first naval aviator to occupy that prestigious post. (AP/Wide World Photos)

Over 70 percent of all attack sorties flown by PBYs during the war came under the cover of darkness.

In 1945 the U.S. Navy had emerged from the ashes of Pearl Harbor into the most powerful fleet ever assembled, and to a large extent it was an air navy. More than in any other conflict, air power played a decisive role in the prosecution of World War II, and sea-based air power proved important to final victory for the United States. U.S. naval aircraft logged 284,073 combat sorties, dropping 102,917 tons of ordnance. Naval airmen destroyed 9,291 aircraft in the air, and sent 564 ships totaling 2,536,664 tons to the bottom. However, one of the last acts of the war portended a volatile future for naval aviation even amidst its greatest triumph. Indeed, the mushroom clouds over Hiroshima and Nagasaki proved symbolic of two monumental struggles, that over naval air power's relevance in the atomic age and a cold war marked by limited conflicts that would call the wings of gold to arms under the most trying of circumstances.

Reminiscent of the interservice controversy surrounding "Billy" Mitchell during the 1920s, a bitter debate over the roles and missions of

the armed forces dominated the immediate postwar years. At issue was their unification under a centralized Department of Defense, the creation of an independent U.S. Air Force, and the contention by those who espoused strategic bombing that the atomic bomb had rendered carrier air power obsolete. The result was a virtual internal war waged on the pages of the popular press and in the halls of Congress. Before it was over, Secretary of Defense Louis Johnson canceled construction of the U.S. Navy's first supercarrier, *United States* (CVA 58), and the Chief of Naval Operations sacrificed his career in supporting the so-called Revolt of the Admirals that ensued. Yet, a congressional report issued in March 1950 vindicated the Navy's viewpoint, saying that strategic bombing was not the essence of air power, but only one vital part. The wisdom of this opinion was revealed just two months later when North Korean troops stormed across the 38th parallel into South Korea.

Naval aviation entered the air war over Korea as a force in transition. Without a supercarrier, aircraft were launched from the decks of World War II-era carriers, and pilots flew not against an enemy fleet at sea, but to project power ashore. The dawning of the jet age introduced a new chapter in air warfare. Flying F9F Panthers and F3D Skyknights—as well as F-86 and F-84 fighters during exchange tours with the U.S. Air Force—Navy and Marine Corps jet pilots were credited with 37.5 of the 52 air-to-air kills recorded by naval aviators during the Korean War. Yet naval aviation continued to rely extensively on propeller-driven aircraft. For infantrymen and Marines on the ground, most notably in the Chosin Reservoir campaign in late 1950, the blue-painted F4U Corsairs and AD Skyraiders roaring in at

Ordnancemen at work on the flight deck of Oriskany (CVA 34) during operations off Korea. The return from a strike meant a respite for pilots and aircrewmen, but not for the men on the flight deck, who quickly set about spotting the aircraft and arming them for the next mission over enemy territory. ("They Also Serve," James Dietz)

Above: *Seven years after flying its first combat mission during World War II, the venerable F4U Corsair proved a vital element of Navy and Marine Corps air operations over the Korean peninsula. The Corsair lived up to its reputation of being a savior for embattled troops on the ground, particularly for the Marines in the Chosin Reservoir campaign of November–December 1951. F4U pilots also scored twelve kills in air-to-air combat over Korea, including one over an enemy MiG-15 by Marine Captain Jesse G. Folmar. (U.S. Navy Combat Art Collection)*

Right: *Nicknamed the "Flying Dump Truck," the AD Skyraider carried the brunt of naval aviation's offensive effort during the Korean War. Capable of carrying up to 8,000 pounds of ordnance, as evidenced by this Attack Squadron 195 aircraft launching from Princeton (CV 37), Navy and Marine Corps Skyraiders logged 64,535 combat flights in Korea. (National Museum of Naval Aviation)*

low altitudes to deliver close air support proved a welcome sight. In addition, Skyraiders participated in an epic attack against the Hwachon Dam, knocking out the locks by using the long-forgotten tactic of dropping aerial torpedoes. Thereafter, the squadron that made the attack assumed a new moniker, the Dambusters, which it carries to this day. Whether jet or prop, naval aviation continued to rule the night, building upon the advances in nocturnal operations begun in World War II by knocking down North Korean snoopers and protecting Air Force B-29s during strategic bombing missions above the 38th parallel.

Flying boats flew long-range patrols throughout the Korean War, but the air-sea rescue duties they had performed so well during World War II

Above: *Following delivery to the fleet in 1946, HO3S helicopters like this one assigned to Helicopter Utility Squadron 1 performed yeoman duty as plane guards on board aircraft carriers, standing by during launch and recovery to pluck pilots from the water in the event a plane went overboard. Pioneering the use of rotary-wing aircraft in combat search and rescue during the Korean War, intrepid HO3S crews logged numerous flights "over the beach," braving enemy fire in their lumbering craft to pull downed airmen from the clutches of the enemy. (National Museum of Naval Aviation)*

Left: *The weather in Korea presented searing heat in the summer and bitter cold winters, the latter necessitating winter flight gear and prompting some pilots in Attack Squadron 195 to sport mustaches and beards. A total of 75 percent of the aviators flying combat missions in Korea by November 1951 were reservists recalled to active duty. (U.S. Navy)*

largely shifted to the helicopter. Popularized in the novel *The Bridges at Toko-Ri*, the intrepid crews of slow and lumbering HO3S helicopters repeatedly braved adverse weather conditions and hostile ground fire to rescue downed airmen over enemy territory.

The men who fought the war represented change as well. Naval aviation lagged behind the surface Navy in the acceptance of African-Americans during World War II. Had it not been for an administrative oversight and his light complexion, the one black man who wore wings of gold during the war, Lieutenant (jg) Oscar Holmes, may not have ever flown as an instructor in a Navy aircraft. However, with President Harry S. Truman's desegregation of the armed forces, black airmen and aviators

Forrestal *(CVA 59), the U.S. Navy's first supercarrier, steams through the Caribbean off Guantanamo Bay, Cuba, during her shakedown cruise.* Forrestal *laid the foundation for the modern force of Nimitz-class carriers that form the backbone of naval aviation today. The signal event of her thirty-eight years of service occurred on 29 July 1967, when a catastrophic fire off the coast of Vietnam killed 134 crewmen and injured sixty-two others. (U.S. Navy)*

Ensign Jesse Brown, the first African-American to complete the Navy's flight training syllabus, flew F4U Corsairs off Leyte *(CV 32) and died after a forced landing in North Korea. (National Museum of Naval Aviation)*

President Harry S. Truman admires the Medal of Honor after placing it around the neck of Lieutenant (jg) Thomas J. Hudner. Hudner, who intentionally crash-landed his airplane in an attempt to rescue squadronmate Ensign Jesse Brown from the burning wreckage of his plane, was one of only two naval aviators to receive the nation's highest award for valor in Korea. The other went to Lieutenant (jg) John Koelsch, a helicopter pilot, for his attempted rescue of a downed Marine pilot and subsequent performance of duty as a prisoner of war. (U.S. Navy)

began serving alongside their white counterparts during the Korean War. On 5 December 1950, the pilot of a F4U Corsair of Fighter Squadron (VF) 32 made a forced landing in the snowy, rugged terrain of North Korea. From above, one of his squadronmates saw him struggling to get out of the cockpit of the burning aircraft, and intentionally made a wheels-up landing near the downed fighter to render assistance. His repeated efforts, along with those of the pilot of a rescue helicopter, failed and Ensign Jesse Brown, the first African-American naval aviator to fly in combat, subsequently died in his plane. His would-be rescuer, Lieutenant (jg) Thomas Hudner, received the Medal of Honor. One African-American sailor, after hearing the story of Jesse Brown, applied for the aviation cadet program. When he retired nearly thirty years later, Frank Petersen wore the stars of a Marine Corps lieutenant general.

All told, naval aviators logged 346,487 flights during the Korean War, dropping some 195,000 tons of ordnance and losing 559 aircraft to enemy ground fire and four to enemy aircraft. They demonstrated that naval air power was indeed relevant in the atomic age. Soon there would be more battlegrounds over which to fight, in the Middle East and again in the waters of the Western Pacific.

Naval aviation experienced a second golden age in the decade following the Korean War. In 1955, the Navy's first supercarrier, *Forrestal* (CVA 59), was placed in commission, providing an added degree of flexibility to carrier aviation that increased with the commissioning of *Enterprise* (CVAN 65), the world's first nuclear-powered flattop, in 1962. It was a period marked by tremendous technological advances in aircraft as well. The front-line fighters of the Korean War could at best achieve speeds of less than 600 mph, but just three short years after the war, the Navy was conducting test flights on the F8U (F-8) Crusader, which became the first operational fighter aircraft in history capable of flying over 1,000 mph in level flight.

Other aircraft designs supported two fundamental elements of sea-based air power's role in national defense—nuclear weapons delivery and antisubmarine warfare. In 1955 the Navy commissioned its first heavy attack squadrons, and the A3D (A-3) Skywarrior and subsequent A-5 Vigilante aircraft joined with the supercarrier to form naval aviation's atomic punch. To combat potential attacks on task forces by Soviet bombers, the Navy procured the F-4 Phantom II, a high-altitude interceptor equipped with Sparrow missiles that could hit targets head-on at extended ranges. However, it was in the traditional realm of hunting enemy submarines in the globe's ocean depths that patrol aviation made its greatest contributions. With the Soviet navy's submarine fleet increasing dramatically, P2V Neptunes and P-3 Orions joined antisubmarine helicopters in providing naval aviation's answer to the enemy's underwater threat. Such was the importance of this mission that selected *Essex*-class carriers were designated antisubmarine carriers and formed the nucleus of task groups that hunted submarines, a modernized version of the escort carrier hunter-killer groups of World War II.

As it built its "blue water" capability, naval aviation found itself on call. Naval aircraft flew top secret intelligence gathering flights along the Soviet border, supported the Marine landing in Lebanon in 1956, patrolled the troubled waters between Taiwan and mainland China, and assisted in photoreconnaissance and blockade operations during the Cuban Missile Crisis in October 1962. And in 1964, U.S. Navy and Marine Corps RF-8A

Flames trailing from the jet intake were an appropriate adornment for this F-8 Crusader of Fighter Squadron 84 approaching the catapult for launch from the carrier Independence *(CVA 62) in 1959. The Crusader was the first operational aircraft in the history of military aviation capable of exceeding 1,000 mph in level flight. (U.S. Navy)*

The mainstay of Navy patrol squadrons since the early 1960s, P-3 Orions possess a range of 4,500 nautical miles and can remain airborne for over fourteen hours. Designed to combat the Soviet submarine menace during the Cold War, the aircraft carries up to eighty-four sonobuoys launched from the circular tubes visible on the undersides of these Patrol Squadron 31 aircraft. (U.S. Navy)

An artistic rendering of a low-level attack by A-4 Skyhawks in Vietnam. Originally designed to deliver tactical nuclear weapons, the Skyhawk bore the brunt of the Navy and Marine Corp's strike missions in Southeast Asia. A total of 257 A-4s were shot down, among them those flown by Medal of Honor recipients Commander James B. Stockdale and Lieutenant Commander Michael Estocin, the most of any carrier-based aircraft. ("A-4 Skyhawk Tribute," Roy Grinnell)

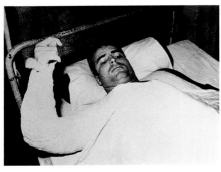

Lieutenant Commander John S. McCain III, badly injured during the ejection from his crippled A-4 Skyhawk and subsequent capture on 26 October 1967, speaks to foreign reporters from a hospital bed in Hanoi. The North Vietnamese employed the prisoners of war as propaganda tools when presenting them to the public. In reality, McCain's injuries were left untreated for many days and his accommodations consisted of a filthy prison cell. (National Museum of Naval Aviation)

Crusader aircraft began flying surveillance missions over Laos, a nation wracked by internal discord. Its neighbor to the east, the divided country of Vietnam, was nominally democratic in the South and Communist in the North. The leader of North Vietnam, Ho Chi Minh, who fought against the Japanese during World War II and later expelled the French from his native land, sought to consolidate his nation under Communist rule. Here his interests and those of the United States clashed, resulting in a gradually escalating crisis that erupted on 5 August 1964 when U.S. Navy carrier aircraft launched air strikes in response to North Vietnamese attacks against U.S. destroyers operating in the Gulf of Tonkin. Enemy antiaircraft gunners shot down two aircraft that day, including the A-1 Skyraider flown by Lieutenant (jg) Richard Sather and the A-4 Skyhawk of Lieutenant (jg) Everett Alvarez. Sather became the first naval aviator killed in action during the Vietnam War, while Alvarez was taken captive, the first prisoner of war of the North Vietnamese. He would not see freedom again until 1973, a span of nearly nine years during which many other naval airmen would lose their lives or share the torturous hardships of captivity.

Vietnam was a most peculiar war, its prosecution governed more by political considerations than those on the battlefield. Nowhere was this more apparent than in the air war over North Vietnam, where periodic bombing halts and restrictive rules of engagement hampered the application of air power and adversely affected the morale of the men who flew into harm's way. Bombing missions over the north commenced in 1965 with the initiation of Operation Rolling Thunder. Following a bombing halt between 1968 and 1972, President Richard Nixon ordered the commencement of Operations Linebacker I and II.

Over the course of the war, twenty carriers made eighty-seven combat deployments to the waters off Vietnam, and sailors soon labeled the constant armada of ships on station there the "Tonkin Gulf Yacht Club." With stocks of Soviet antiaircraft guns and surface-to-air missiles on the ground and MiG aircraft in the air, North Vietnam developed a sophisticated and deadly aerial defense system into which naval aviators flew virtually around the clock. "As the stars diminished into deepening blue, I saw from thirty miles the face of death—SAMs [surface-to-air missiles]," wrote one naval aviator in his diary after returning from a combat mission over North Vietnam in December 1965. "The fear at the moment of the explosions was indescribable. Again, all of a sudden, with stark reality and terror, we were at war."

It proved a costly endeavor, for over the course of the war a total of 711 Navy and Marine Corps aircraft fell to enemy fire. During one cruise, Carrier Air Wing 16, embarked on *Oriskany* (CVA 34), lost thirty-nine

Top, left: *Speaking in the universal language of pilots, Lieutenant (jg) Charles W. Hartman III (left) and Lieutenant Commander Edwin Greathouse describe how Attack Squadron 25 pilots shot down a pair of MiG-17 jets over North Vietnam on 20 June 1965. The kills were unique in that the naval aviators flew propeller-driven A-1 Skyraiders. (U.S. Navy)*

Top, right: *A billowing cloud of black smoke rises above* Enterprise *(CVAN 65) after the exhaust from an aircraft-starting unit ignited a Mk 32 Zuni rocket warhead. The conflagration, which occurred on 14 January 1969, off Hawaii as the "Big E" prepared for a combat cruise to Vietnam, killed twenty-seven men, injured 344 others, and destroyed fifteen airplanes.* Enterprise *was repaired by March, and deployed to the Tonkin Gulf that same month. (National Museum of Naval Aviation)*

Above: *Established and disestablished in Vietnam, Helicopter Attack Squadron (Light) 3 flew "Huey" gunships in support of the riverine patrol boats of the "Brown Water Navy" in the waters of the Mekong Delta. During their five-year existence between 1967 and 1972, the "Seawolves" became one of the most highly decorated squadrons of the Vietnam War. (U.S. Navy)*

Opposite: *A pack of A-7 Corsair II light attack aircraft of Attack Squadrons 146 and 147 create a maze of tails and folded wings on the flight deck of* Constellation *(CV 64) in 1977. Bearing a family resemblance to the F-8 with a gaping jet intake beneath the cockpit, the A-7 began flying combat missions over Vietnam in 1967, eventually supplanting the A-4 on board the large-deck carriers. (U.S. Navy)*

aircraft in combat and ten in operational losses; twenty-seven pilots and aircrewmen did not return home with the ship. Though enemy aircraft proved no threat to the carrier task forces, operational accidents resulted in catastrophic fires on board *Oriskany, Forrestal,* and *Enterprise,* resulting in the deaths of 205 men.

In the face of such adversity, those in the cockpits acquitted themselves well. Naval aviators shot down sixty-one enemy aircraft, including five by Lieutenant Randall H. Cunningham and Lieutenant (jg) William Driscoll, the first aces of the Vietnam War. The diminutive A-4 Skyhawk proved the workhorse of the war, joined by the A-6 Intruder and A-7 Corsair II. The Intruder, an all-weather attack platform, executed many daring, single-plane night raids into North Vietnam, including one flown by Lieutenant Commander Charles Hunter and Lieutenant Lyle Bull on 30 October 1967, in which ten SAMs were fired at the lone airplane. Perhaps the most dramatic air operations of the war involved the rescue of downed airmen by intrepid helicopter crews, who braved heavy enemy fire in slow, lightly protected aircraft to execute rescue attempts deep in enemy territory, both day and night.

Though the air war in the North consumed the majority of carrier assets in Vietnam, other naval aviation elements contributed significantly to the war in the South. Long devoted to antisubmarine and search and rescue duties, Navy helicopters assumed a new role in South Vietnam with the establishment of Helicopter Attack Squadron (Light) (HAL) 3 in 1967. Initially flying UH-1 "Hueys" procured from the Army, the Seawolves supported the Navy's riverine operations, providing close air support for armed patrol boats operating in the Mekong Delta. They joined Light Attack (VAL) Squadron 4, flying fixed-wing OV-10 Broncos, in providing the Navy with a unique strike mission that contrasted sharply with those flown from aircraft carriers. Similarly, the unconventional nature of the war pressed modified OP-2E Neptune maritime patrol planes into service dropping sensors to monitor traffic on the Ho Chi Minh trail. Other patrol aircraft flew from bases in South Vietnam, ranging up and down the coastline executing Operation Market Time, providing surveillance of vessels attempting to supply Viet Cong and North Vietnamese Army forces from the sea.

Commander Eugene B. McDaniel, who was held as a prisoner of war in North Vietnam for nearly six years, is reunited with his family. The central players in an emotionally charged issue throughout the divisive war in Southeast Asia, the POWs were greeted to a hero's welcome upon their return from captivity. (National Museum of Naval Aviation)

An A-6 Intruder pilot straps into the cockpit prior to launching from Saratoga *(CV 60) during operations in the Mediterranean Sea in 1986. Carrier pilots confronted crises in Libya and Lebanon during the 1980s, highlighting the importance of maintaining a strong naval presence in the Med. (U.S. Navy)*

Commander Hank Kleeman (right) and Lieutenant David J. Venlet, F-14 pilots in Fighter Squadron 41 off Nimitz *(CVN 68), describe the combat engagement over the Gulf of Sidra in which they and squadron-mates Lieutenants Lawrence Muczynski and James Anderson shot down two Libyan Su-22 Sukhoi fighters on 19 August 1981. (U.S. Navy)*

Though the cease-fire signed in January 1973 removed the last American combat forces from Vietnam, the North Vietnamese offensive two years later provided the final chapter to a bitter and divisive time in American history. Four U.S. Navy carriers supported Operation Frequent Wind, the evacuation of Saigon, and the haunting final images of the war were of South Vietnamese men, women, and children scrambling to climb aboard Marine helicopters that represented their last chance for freedom.

Like all branches of the U.S. military, the Navy emerged scarred from the decade-long involvement in Vietnam. The tumultuous social upheavals of the era affected the sea service in the form of racial unrest on board carriers at sea and what many viewed as relaxed standards of discipline espoused by Chief of Naval Operations Admiral Elmo Zumwalt to keep pace with changing times. Funding for personnel and hardware dropped dramatically, and a distinct schism existed between the population of a nation tired of war and the military tasked with defending it. However, the world remained fraught with danger, and naval aviation continued to make repeated forays into harm's way.

The forces of naval aviation differed markedly from those that had served in combat over Vietnam. From a personnel standpoint, one noteworthy change was the introduction of women to the ranks of naval aviators and naval flight officers, as Lieutenant (jg) Barbara Allen became the first to earn her wings in February 1974. Tragically, she died in an aircraft accident in 1981 while serving as a flight instructor. In 1990, Commander Rosemary Mariner became the first female commanding officer of an operational squadron in the history of the U.S. military. In addition, in 1993 the Defense Department lifted the restriction on women flying combat missions, and in December 1998 women aviators were among the aircrews that launched off *Enterprise* (CVN 65) to attack targets in Iraq during Operation Desert Fox.

The post-Vietnam era also brought a changing of the guard with respect to ships and aircraft. The last of the World War II-era *Essex*-class carriers were decommissioned, and the nuclear-powered *Nimitz* (CVN 68) and her sister ships began joining the fleet. The F-14 Tomcat, an aircraft

that in many respects symbolized post-Vietnam naval aviation, replaced
the venerable F-4 Phantom II, which had been a workhorse in Southeast
Asia, on carrier decks. Thus, it was appropriate that on 19 August 1981,
a pair of Tomcats assigned to VF-41 off *Nimitz* shot down two Libyan Su-22
Fitter jets that attacked them during exercises in the Gulf of Sidra. The
act defied Libyan strongman Muammar Qaddafi's proclamation of a line
of death in that body of water, and represented the beginning of a decade
in which naval aviation's quick strike capability represented American
interests abroad. Carrier aircraft returned to Libya in 1986, spearheading
a concentrated air strike against military installations in response to a
terrorist attack.

In the eastern Mediterranean, in response to the 23 October 1983
bombing of the headquarters of a Marine peacekeeping contingent in
Beirut, Lebanon, President Ronald Reagan ordered carrier aircraft from
John F. Kennedy (CV 67) to strike targets in Syria, the nation partially
responsible for the attack. That same month, carrier aviation also supported the invasion of the tiny Caribbean island of Grenada, an effort to
rescue some 1,000 Americans trapped amidst a bloody power struggle
over governance of the island.

In addition to these regional crises, the 1980s marked the age of
the so-called "Evil Empire," the term President Reagan coined to describe

*An SH-3A Sea King of Helicopter Antisub-
marine Squadron 6 creates a halo of ripples
as the crew lowers a dipping sonar into
the Pacific Ocean during an antisubmarine
warfare training exercise off California in
1976. Helicopters teamed with destroyers
form a potent weapon against undersea
threats. (U.S. Navy)*

*Still dressed in her flight gear, Strike Fighter
Squadron 37 pilot Lieutenant Carol Watts
describes her mission over Iraq to squadron-
mate Lieutenant Lyndsi Bates on board
Enterprise (CVN 65) during Operation Desert
Fox on 17 December 1998. (U.S. Navy)*

Top, left: Dwight D. Eisenhower *(CVN 69)* *makes her way through the Suez Canal in* *September 1990, having operated in the* *Red Sea in support of Operation Desert* *Shield. On station in the Mediterranean* *Sea when Iraq invaded Kuwait on 2 August* *1990, "Ike" was in position to launch* *aircraft against Iraqi forces within days,* *demonstrating the flexibility of carrier* *aviation. (U.S. Navy)*

Top, right: *Their wings bristling with air-* *to-air missiles, F-14 Tomcats of Fighter* *Squadron 103 sit poised for action on the* *deck of* Saratoga *(CV 60) operating in the* *Arabian Gulf during Operation Desert* *Storm. (U.S. Navy)*

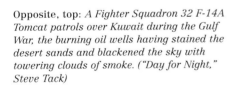

Opposite, top: *A Fighter Squadron 32 F-14A* *Tomcat patrols over Kuwait during the Gulf* *War, the burning oil wells having stained the* *desert sands and blackened the sky with* *towering clouds of smoke. ("Day for Night,"* *Steve Tack)*

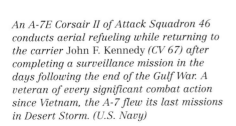

An A-7E Corsair II of Attack Squadron 46 *conducts aerial refueling while returning to* *the carrier John F. Kennedy (CV 67) after* *completing a surveillance mission in the* *days following the end of the Gulf War. A* *veteran of every significant combat action* *since Vietnam, the A-7 flew its last missions* *in Desert Storm. (U.S. Navy)*

the Soviet Union. The growth of the Soviet navy, including a proliferation of nuclear submarines and the introduction of aircraft carriers, prompted the administration to reemphasize a blue water force capable of combating the Soviets in the high seas. Secretary of the Navy John H. Lehman spearheaded the effort to create a 600-ship force, including fifteen carriers. Given the undersea menace, the Navy's antisubmarine capability became increasingly important. P-3 Orion long-range patrol aircraft, carrier-based S-3 Vikings, and SH-3 and SH-60 helicopters based on carriers, cruisers, frigates, and destroyers engaged in nautical games of cat and mouse throughout the decade.

To explain the value of the aircraft carrier, it is often said that when a crisis erupts, the first question a President of the United States asks is, "Where are the carriers?" In August 1990, Iraqi tanks and infantry rolled across the nation's southern border, conquering the tiny nation of Kuwait and threatening Saudi Arabia. Within days *Independence* (CV 62) steamed into the Arabian Gulf and *Dwight D. Eisenhower* (CVN 69) was on station in the Red Sea, their air wings representing the only significant American air power in the region should Sadaam Hussein have ordered his army further south. He didn't, and over the course of the next five months, an American-led coalition assembled the largest collection of military force since World War II. Every element of the Navy and Marine Corps's air component was represented. Six carriers deployed to the theater, their air

Burdened with ammunition and equipment, a combat aircrewman mans an SH-3 Sea King of Helicopter Antisubmarine Squadron 9 on board Theodore Roosevelt *(CVN 69) for an antimine mission over the Arabian Gulf during Operation Desert Storm. (U.S. Navy)*

With battle lamps casting him in a red hue, Captain Marty Chanik, skipper of Enterprise *(CVN 65), monitors flight operations during Operation Desert Fox, a series of air strikes against Iraqi weapons facilities in December 1998. The streak of light visible out the window of the island is from the afterburners of a jet just slung into the air by one of the Big E's steam catapults. (U.S. Navy)*

The flight deck of George Washington *(CVN 73) provides a sea of light as an F-14 Tomcat fighter of Fighter Squadron 103 prepares to launch on a night combat air patrol as part of Operation Southern Watch, enforcing the no-fly zone over Iraq. Positioned at the point of potential crises throughout the world, an aircraft carrier never sleeps while at sea. (U.S. Navy)*

Opposite: An A-6 Intruder of Attack Squadron 95 launches from Abraham Lincoln *(CVN 72) into a golden sky over the Arabian Gulf on 15 July 1991. Though the Intruder has been retired from service, her successors launch and recover from carrier decks each day, their aircrews continuing the tradition that began with Eugene Ely. (U.S. Navy)*

wings augmented by fifty-nine squadrons and detachments based in Saudi Arabia at airfields within range of Kuwait.

On the evening of 16 January 1991, hundreds of coalition aircraft took to the skies, commencing Operation Desert Storm. That day, a pair of F/A-18 Hornets scored the Navy's first air-to-air kills of the war, shooting down two enemy MiG-21s; and squadrons flying the venerable A-6 Intruder and A-7 Corsair II, both of which had flown combat missions over Vietnam, logged strike missions deep into Iraqi territory.

Meanwhile, MH-53E Sea Dragons from helicopter mine countermeasures squadrons helped clear mines from the waters around the Arabian peninsula while carrier-based aircraft, supported by P-3 Orion patrol planes, obliterated the small Iraqi navy. Whether flying through pyrotechnic antiaircraft fire over Baghdad on the war's first night or destroying Iraqi armor to clear the way for ground forces, naval aviation played an important role in the desert victory. "It was an eerie feeling to fly without care over areas which we had attacked," one pilot wrote after the cease-fire.

Unfortunately, the eruption of the Tailhook scandal quickly overshadowed the triumph in Operation Desert Storm. The alleged misconduct by a small group of officers at the 1991 Tailhook Convention reverberated throughout the entire service, forcing the resignation of the Secretary of the Navy and adversely affecting the careers of scores of other officers. This, combined with the force reductions prompted by the end of the Cold War, tested the mettle of the members of the air Navy, who found themselves continually on call around the world. Even after the victory in the Gulf War, Navy and Marine aircraft continued to patrol the "no-fly zone" over southern Iraq, and in 1993, aircrews began manning up to fly over the former Yugoslavia, an area wracked by political unrest. Over the course of the ensuing seven years, names like Bosnia and Kosovo became quite familiar to them. Naval air power executed missions ranging from humanitarian relief for refugees to engaging in a sustained bombing campaign as part of Operation Allied Force in March–June 1999, during which Navy and Marine Corps aircraft logged over 6,500 sorties.

"Under all circumstances, a decisive naval superiority is to be considered a fundamental principle," wrote George Washington in 1780, "and the basis upon which all success must ultimately depend." Though writing specifically within the context of the American Revolution, the words of the father of our country ring true today. For the United States, a maritime nation surrounded on two sides by ocean waters, it is naval forces that secure freedom of the seas and, in the words of the 1998 posture statement "Forward . . . from the Sea: Anytime, Anywhere," serve as "sovereign extensions of our nation." Since the end of World War II the centerpiece of these forces has been naval aviation, embodied in the might of the aircraft carrier, a veritable symbol of American might abroad. Fittingly, one of these mighty ships is named *George Washington*. A far cry from the wooden sailing ships about which the first President wrote, she and her sister ships nevertheless represent the decisive naval superiority of the U.S. Navy. And each time an aircraft roars off the deck of a carrier, it represents the continuation of the golden journey begun in 1910.

Memories & Memorials

Memories & Memorials

Amy Waters Yarsinske

Pages 54–55: *Aligned in perfect ranks, the headstones at Barrancas National Cemetery at NAS Pensacola, Florida, mark the final resting places of heroes. Some made the ultimate sacrifice on a distant battleground, while others served the nation long ago and in the end chose to rest for the ages in hallowed ground among their comrades in arms.* (Al Audelman)

Above: *In the aftermath of the Battle of Leyte Gulf, sailors on board Kalinin Bay (CVE 68) commit their fallen shipmates to the deep on 25 October 1944. As evidenced by the helmets worn by some of the men, out of necessity burials at sea were oftentimes hastily arranged while ships remained in a combat zone.* (U.S. Navy)

The mark of a nation's character is the honor its people pay to their real heroes, and their custodianship of priceless national relics— captured enemy battle flags and cannons," famed Navy test pilot Alford J. Williams, Jr., wrote. "Yes, but that's not all by a long shot; those are combat trophies." His March 1946 column in *U.S. Air Services* magazine went on to call for the Wright Flyer to be preserved and exhibited in the United States as a symbol of American aviation. The airplane was on display in England's Kensington Museum as a result of Orville Wright's rift with the Smithsonian Institution, and Williams passionately argued that it should be brought to Washington, D.C., where it could be enshrined for the edification and inspiration of the nation's children. Now on display at the Smithsonian's Air and Space Museum, the Wright Flyer is one of many tangible representations of aviation's roots.

Naval aviation has similar artifacts of its proud history, such as the NC-4 flying boat displayed at the National Museum of Naval Aviation in Pensacola, Florida, representing the historic transatlantic May 1919 flight. Some other reminders of aviation's past are similarly tangible, like a dilapidated old hangar at the edge of a former airfield or a plaque nestled in a quiet countryside, while others exist only in memory—in the thoughts of an elderly veteran recalling a time of trial long ago, or in the name of a place dedicated to a forgotten hero. Regardless of the form they take, these memories and memorials reflect the dedication and sacrifice of generations of men and women who have proudly served in naval aviation from its inception nearly a century ago.

"A terrible beauty is born," penned poet William Butler Yeats during World War I, a conflict that was grotesquely cruel and hardly the expectation of chivalrous combat so many envisaged, including the men of naval aviation who joined the fray in 1917. World war revisited American naval aviators in 1939, and once again the nation remained neutral, until drawn into the war by the Japanese attack on Pearl Harbor on 7 December 1941. Naval aviation personnel fought courageously in

With the shattered remnants of Battleship Row still visible behind them, personnel receive combat decorations from Admiral Chester W. Nimitz on the deck of Enterprise *(CV 6) at Pearl Harbor in May 1942. Their actions added another chapter to the proud history of the U.S. Navy. (U.S. Navy)*

Members of Fighting Squadron 17 honored a fallen squadronmate by placing a propeller blade from an F4U Corsair at his temporary grave site in the Solomon Islands, noting his kills and the fact that he was a member of the Jolly Rogers. Lieutenant D.H.C. Gutenkunst had just turned twenty-five. (National Museum of Naval Aviation)

For many years a memorial commemorating the defense of Wake Island in December 1941 included a relic of the battle in the form of a cowling and rusted propeller blades from an F4F-3 Wildcat of Marine Fighting Squadron 211. The makeshift signs note that Captain Henry T. Elrod, who died in the fighting, flew the aircraft. His service was later recognized with a posthumous award of the Medal of Honor. (National Museum of Naval Aviation)

Toward the end of the Vietnam War, the personnel of Attack Squadron 43 spearheaded the construction of a memorial in Virginia Beach, Virginia, to honor their comrades held as prisoners of war in Southeast Asia. Formally dedicated on 22 May 1972, the Flame of Hope was intended to only burn briefly, yet today it remains a constant reminder of those whose fate remains a mystery. (U.S. Navy)

all theaters of the war, and in every conflict to follow from Korea, to Vietnam, the Arabian Gulf, and the Balkans. These conflicts, and the service of those who were called to arms, are remembered by memorials spread across the nation and around the world.

Lieutenant Commander Harry Brinkley Bass was a former dive bomber pilot who received a Navy Cross for contributing to the sinking of the Japanese carrier *Shoho* at the Battle of Coral Sea in May 1942. In August 1944, Bass was flying a Grumman F6F-5 Hellcat fighter off *Kasaan Bay* (CVE 69) with Fighting Squadron (VF) 74 as part of Operation Dragoon, the invasion of southern France. Although Bass died in the fierce

Students at the U.S. Navy Pre-Flight School at Del Monte, California, express the youthful exuberance of so many members of the greatest generation called to arms during World War II. Though many experienced the horrors of war, now gray-haired veterans look upon their time in naval aviation as one of the most memorable periods of their lives. (U.S. Navy)

aerial combat that ensued, his memory lived on in the minds and hearts of the French people, who in 1996 dedicated a plaque to him and four of his squadronmates who paid the ultimate price for their country and the liberation of France.

Across the English Channel in the town of Dunkeswell, England, during World War II, the Navy maintained patrol bombing squadrons, many of which flew PB4Y-1 Liberators. In a gesture of thanks for the townspeople's support during the war, members of these squadrons purchased a new organ for the town's St. Nicholas church, replacing the one that had been destroyed in a German bombing. In return, Dunkeswell placed memorial plaques to all the Navy's fallen pilots and aircrew in the church as solemn remembrance for those who gave their lives in the service of the United States Navy and the British people—men like Lieutenants Joseph Patrick Kennedy, Jr., and Wilford J. Willy. At the controls of an explosives-laden

Rear Admiral Calvin T. Durgin receives a briefing from pilots in the ready room on board Tulagi *(CVE 72) following their return from strikes against enemy targets in Southern France during Operation Dragoon in August 1944. Following in the footsteps of their forefathers in World War I, these pilots helped liberate France, losing some of their squadronmates in the process. (U.S. Navy)*

Liberator on 12 August 1944, Kennedy and Willy departed the Fersfield Airdrome on a secret mission to destroy German V-2 rocket installations in occupied France. They were to bail out at 2,000 feet and a remote control apparatus would guide the bomber to the target, but approximately twenty-eight minutes into the flight the aircraft exploded near Beccles, England, killing both aviators. More than fifty years later, on 4 July 1997, the British people dedicated a museum and memorial to the United States Navy's patrol bomber aircrews of so long ago. The dedications took place over three days, culminating in a service at St. Nicholas and the unveiling of a monument on the airfield's edge which reads simply, "Many returned home/Some stayed forever/None will be forgotten."

Closer to home, the very place where naval aviators earn their wings is a living memorial to both the past and the future of naval aviation. Naval Air Station (NAS) Pensacola, Florida's, buildings of red brick and white columns appear almost collegiate, befitting a place called the

Right: *Shrouded in fog as if emerging from the past, seaplane ramps extend out from the seawall at NAS Pensacola, Florida. All naval aviators once learned to fly floatplanes and flying boats, and scores of training flights began and ended on these now long-forgotten ramps. (Al Audelman)*

Below: *An old guard house, its last sentry having long been relieved from his post, stands next to a portion of the brick wall that surrounded the perimeter of the old Navy Yard at Pensacola, Florida. When the first aviators arrived at NAS Pensacola, Florida, the Navy Yard was already nearly ninety years old, having weathered the Civil War and witnessed the transition from sail to steam. (Al Audelman)*

Below, right: *The roar of jet engines from aircraft operating from nearby Forrest Sherman Field now echo off the walls of this antiquated hangar, which guards a waterfront that once bustled with buzzing aircraft. It now stands as a reminder of the Cradle of Naval Aviation's storied past. (Al Audelman)*

"Annapolis of the Air," where the Navy has sent generations of its young men and women to learn to fly. Today, the crisp cadences of marching officer candidates echo off their walls, as did those of the thousands who have preceded them. The waters of Pensacola Bay lap against concrete ramps on which thousands of seaplanes commenced primary training flights. An antiquated looking hangar, a vestige of World War I, maintains a silent vigil over the waterfront that once bustled with noisy aircraft. Samuel Hynes, a decorated Marine Corps pilot in World War II who trained there in 1944, wrote of the air station in his memoirs, published forty-four years later under the title *Flights of Passage*:

And then we came to Pensacola, and there was the Navy's past: old buildings—a round powder-magazine that had served naval vessels a century before, and rows of sedately beautiful old houses where the senior officers lived—old, moss-stained walls, old live oaks hung with Spanish moss. The Naval Station had been there a long time. This, I thought, is what tradition means. The past is all around me; the Civil War was fought from here, the first Navy fliers learned to fly here. The atmosphere of the place made the Navy seem as permanent and as value-filled as a national church, or a parliament. At nineteen I didn't analyze or debate the values of military tradition or elitism; I simply surrendered to the tranquility of the Station.

Hynes went on to remark that his experience in the bosom of the Cradle of Naval Aviation became a cherished memory as the years passed. "Like childhood, it remains in the memory as a good, uncomplicated time."

Across the continent, a desolate island wasteland in San Diego Bay, California, became another key figure in the history of naval aviation. "As near as I can figure out we will camp out on North Island and slide around on the mud flats as best we can. . . . I am supposed to snoop around . . . to find out which particular spot it would be best for we dashing aviators to sink in." These words, written by Lieutenant Frank Simpson, Jr., in October 1917, describe his first impressions of the site on which the Navy chose to establish an air station in San Diego. Though conditions on North

A sweeping, panoramic view of the shoreline at North Island, California, shows seven Curtiss F-Boats at the extreme left, while the remainder of the aircraft are N-9 seaplanes. Though the first naval aviator received part of his training at the site in 1911, Congress did not authorize the Army and Navy to take possession of North Island until 27 July 1917. (Library of Congress)

An entourage of officers inspects the enlisted personnel of Fighting Plane Squadron 2 at NAS San Diego, California. While the Navy constructed permanent structures at the site, members of squadrons assigned to the U.S. Pacific Fleet Air Forces lived in tent cities that despite the heat and dust were preferable to stuffy quarters on board ship. (U.S. Navy)

Above: *An aerial view of North Island, California, taken on 11 August 1933, shows the buildings, hangars, and runway of NAS San Diego in the foreground. The circular mat visible in the left portion of the photograph is Rockwell Field, home to aircraft of the Army Air Corps. The Navy purchased the site in 1937, thus ending the Army's presence on North Island. (U.S. Navy)*

Opposite, top left: *A more modern view of NAS North Island, California, taken in June 1976, shows an expanded area of land, the result of years of dredging San Diego Bay. The town of Coronado is visible in the foreground and modern runways have replaced the old blacktop of the 1930s. (Robert L. Lawson)*

Opposite, top right: *Billowing black smoke rises from Midway following attacks by Japanese aircraft on 4 June 1942. The twisted remains of a hangar are visible in the foreground. Though the Navy presence on Midway ended in the 1990s, civilians visiting there today can still see some of the surviving structures from the period in history when it stood as a lone Pacific outpost in one of history's pivotal battles. (U.S. Navy)*

Island left much to be desired, it seemed a natural choice, if only for the sake of history. Pioneer aviator and airplane manufacturer Glenn Curtiss operated a flying school there in 1911 with Theodore Ellyson among the ranks of his students. Eventually, it was from the dirt landing strip at North Island that the first generation of carrier pilots—the "Top Guns" of the 1920s and 1930s—honed the skills that would change the face of warfare in World War II.

Some of them fought at a place far to the west, a small atoll whose size belies its importance in history. In the skies and waters around Midway, naval aviation won an epic battle that turned the tide of the greatest naval war in history. Today Midway serves as a memorial to the men of June 1942, from the official plaque proclaiming their "incredible victory" to the rusted remains of an antiaircraft gun, still pointing skyward, on one of its beaches. Among those who fought there were the men of Torpedo Squadron (VT) 8 flying from the deck of the carrier *Hornet* (CV 8). Only one of their number survived the squadron's attack against the Japanese fleet, and more than fifty years later, George Gay's ashes were dropped into the same waters over which he flew that fateful day, so that he could rejoin the men he left behind. Midway remains so significant that in 1999, Chief of Naval

Operations Admiral Jay L. Johnson declared that the anniversary of the battle would be celebrated each year.

Memorials conjured from memory rather than stone or brick and mortar also populate naval aviation culture. The Navy named its airfields for prominent pioneer pilots and heroes, thinking of young men such as Lieutenant (jg) Richard C. Saufley, Naval Aviator Number 14, who died while on a record-setting endurance flight off Pensacola on 9 June 1916. An auxiliary field of NAS Pensacola was named in his honor. Then there were men like Captain Kenneth Whiting, Naval Aviator Number 16, for whom Whiting Field at Milton, Florida, was named. Whiting was the first commander of naval aviation units overseas in World War I, first acting commander of the Navy's maiden aircraft carrier, *Langley* (CV 1), and a leader in the development of carrier aviation. Norfolk's Chambers Field was named in memory of Captain Washington Irving Chambers, who spent the lion's share of his career fighting for an aviation presence in the U.S. Navy. When pilots check in and out of the field at NAS Oceana, Virginia, they call out "Soucek" for Vice Admiral Apollo Soucek, the Navy's "test pilot admiral" and Chief of the Bureau of Aeronautics. Waldron Field in Corpus Christi, Texas, was named on 5 March 1943 in honor of Lieutenant Commander

Above, left: *Personnel at Naval Auxiliary Air Station Whiting Field, Florida, all of them far from home, forget the war for just a few hours at a Valentine's Day dance in the station gymnasium. Many men and women in uniform met their future spouses during the war years at similar events, thus making them one of life's cherished memories. (National Museum of Naval Aviation)*

Above, right: *In a scene that became all too familiar during the early years of flight training at NAS Pensacola, Florida, a funeral caisson carries a fallen flier to the train station for transport home to his family. His brother officers, the left sleeves of their dress white uniforms adorned with a black armband, trail behind the casket. (National Museum of Naval Aviation)*

Page 66, top: *F4B-1 fighters of Fighting Squadron 5B pictured with other aircraft on the flight line at NAS Hampton Roads, Virginia, on 7 May 1930. A little more than a decade after its establishment, Hampton Roads (soon to be renamed NAS Norfolk) had become the hub of East Coast naval aviation, even though aircraft based there still operated from a grass strip. (Charles S. Borjes)*

John C. Waldron, killed in action leading VT-8 in an attack at Midway. Van Voorhis Field at NAS Fallon, Nevada, was dedicated to the lasting memory of Commander Bruce A. Van Voorhis who lost his life on a low-level bombing attack on enemy positions in the Solomon Islands, for which he posthumously received the Medal of Honor. The now defunct

Above: *Captain Washington Irving Chambers, a battleship sailor who became one of aviation's greatest proponents. Convinced that an airplane could be launched from a ship, he helped arrange civilian pilot Eugene Ely's launch from* Birmingham *(CL 2) at Hampton Roads, Virginia, on 14 November 1910. Appropriately, in 1938 the Navy named the airfield at nearby NAS Norfolk, Virginia, in his honor. (U.S. Navy)*

Right: *The modern NAS Oceana, Virginia, is currently the largest tactical fighter base in the world, the thunder of the F-14 Tomcats and F/A-18 Hornets based there filling the surrounding skies with the sound of freedom. (National Museum of Naval Aviation)*

naval air station at Sunnyvale, California, was named in honor of Rear Admiral William A. Moffett on 17 May 1933, soon after the admiral's death in the crash of the dirigible *Akron* (ZRS 4). Today, the civilian Moffett Federal Airfield keeps the admiral's name alive.

Gone and largely forgotten are the wartime places in remote corners of the world named for our national heroes. O'Hare Field, no longer active on Abemama, Gilbert Islands, was named during World War II to honor Commander Edward H. "Butch" O'Hare, air group commander, fighter ace, pioneer in night carrier operations, and Medal of Honor recipient, who lost his life during the Gilbert Islands campaign on 26 November 1943. Gone also is Mullinix Field on Bouta, Tarawa, named in December 1943 for Rear Admiral Henry M. Mullinix, a carrier division commander lost in the sinking of *Liscome Bay* (CVE 56) during the same campaign.

While the naming of places and the erection of monuments and plaques preserves the rich fabric of naval aviation's past, memorials come in many forms, some that evoke smiles and sweet memories of times that are no more, and others that prompt solemn reflection. Within the hallowed corridors and back rooms of many a naval air station's commissioned officers club are tucked memorabilia and mementos, photographs and squadron insignias, flight gear, and pieces of aircraft that keep the memory of places, people, and events alive for those who follow their predecessors through the front doors.

When the Navy began downsizing its force structure after the Cold War, extant squadrons and base commanders began aggressive campaigns to increase static displays of aircraft with elaborate paint schemes commemorating squadrons of bygone days. The display of tombstones inscribed for disestablished fighter and attack squadrons in front of the NAS Oceana officers club is legendary, surpassed only by the club's memorabilia-filled corridors and rooms. The same can be said of the Mustin Beach Officers Club in Pensacola, named in honor of Captain Henry Croskey Mustin, Naval Aviator Number 11 and the first commanding officer of the naval air station.

Above: *Alexa von Tempsky Zabriskie welcomes members of Fighting Squadron 10 to her home on Maui in 1943. Military personnel visited "Lex" at her estate during World War II. (National Museum of Naval Aviation)*

Above, right: *Squadrons passing through NAS Cubi Point, Philippine Islands, placed ornate plaques in the Officers Club Bar on board the station, in the process creating a colorful shrine that became famous throughout naval aviation. (National Museum of Naval Aviation)*

Below: *True jewels in the Alexa von Tempsky Zabriskie scrapbook are insignias of wartime squadrons that now live only in memory. Sadly, some of the men who scrawled their names below never returned from Pacific air battles. (Al Audelman)*

Below, right: *Alexa von Tempsky Zabriskie's war years scrapbook contains countless photographs and letters from pilots overseas. Occasionally, an artistic serviceman made one of the pages his canvas, leaving behind a unique reminder of a squadron's visit like this pencil sketch from Torpedo Squadron 12. (Al Audelman)*

The club tavern at NAS Cubi Point, Philippines, grew so near and dear to the hearts of naval aviators that when the base closed in 1992, the entire bar room was transported intact for permanent display at Pensacola's National Museum of Naval Aviation.

Some of the most unique and personal memorials to the flying Navy appeared during World War II when an heiress named Alexa von Tempsky Zabriskie played host to thousands of naval aviators who passed through the naval air stations on Maui, Hawaii, en route to the far-flung combat zones of the Pacific. Whether it be for picnics, card playing, or horseback riding, the doors of Erehwon ("nowhere" spelled backwards), her island estate, were always open for America's men in uniform, and "Lex" became a surrogate mother for an entire generation of warriors. Such was her influence on the war effort that Fleet Admiral Chester W. Nimitz sent her an autographed photograph of the Japanese surrender on board the battleship *Missouri* (BB 63) with the inscription, "You as much as anyone here present helped to make possible this picture."

Alexa von Tempsky Zabriskie's memorial to naval aviators started, however, even before the outbreak of war in the Pacific, as visitors to

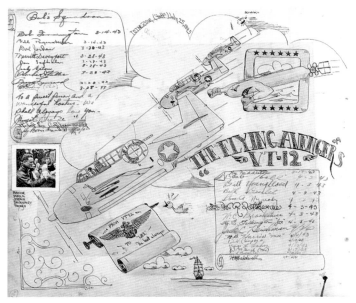

Enterprise *(CV 6), the bustling activity of wartime flight operations on her wooden deck now replaced by the sounds of nearby equipment building the Navy's newest carrier,* Independence *(CVA 62), sits in the Brooklyn Navy Yard in June 1958. The historic carrier was sold for scrap nine days after this photograph was taken. (U.S. Navy)*

Erehwon took to signing their names on the pine-paneled walls of a guest-room in the house. From enlisted crewmen and infantrymen to fighter pilots and a future commandant of the Marine Corps, hundreds of Navy, Marine, and Army personnel affixed their signatures to the wall, leaving behind a veritable World War II honor roll. Although the heiress also kept a scrapbook containing the signatures of all who visited her, some of them complemented by cartoons and colorful squadron insignias, it was the wall that became the stuff of which legends are made. Dismantled plank by plank and rebuilt as a display at the National Museum of Naval Aviation in Pensacola, the wall represents a bygone era for all to see.

While much has been preserved of naval aviation's past, retaining tangible reminders is not always possible. *Enterprise* (CV 6), the most decorated aircraft carrier of World War II, languished at her Bayonne, New Jersey, moorage as a member of the reserve fleet from 17 February 1947 to her redesignation as an antisubmarine carrier on 8 August 1953. Efforts began as early as 1946 to preserve the "Big E" for public exhibit, when the carrier was proposed for donation to the state of New York. Three years later, the San Francisco Museum of Science and Technology made a bid for her, which the Navy declined. When the Navy announced its intention to strike from the record several ships of the mothball fleet in 1956, members of the USS Enterprise Association launched a publicity campaign, endorsed by Fleet Admiral William F. Halsey, to have Congress pass a reso-lution establishing *Enterprise* as a national memorial in Washington, D.C.

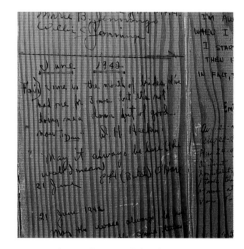

Among those who signed the den wall at Erehwon was Commander Edward H. "Butch" O'Hare, a Medal of Honor recipient and the Navy's first fighter ace of World War II. "May it always be here, the wall I mean," penned the pilot, who was killed in action in November 1943. (Al Audelman)

Above: *A memory not soon forgotten by anyone who ever served on board a U.S. Navy vessel is the unique ceremony that occurs when a ship crosses the equator. In this photograph King Neptune and his Royal Court arrive on board* Midway *(CVE 63) on 14 January 1944, to initiate the unfortunate pollywogs (those who have never crossed the equator) into the domain of shellbacks. The final step in the initiation ceremony, which oftentimes included a haircut from the Royal Barber and eating unpleasant concoctions, was kissing the belly of the Royal Baby, a role traditionally assumed by the most obese member of the crew. (U.S. Navy)*

Top, left: Enterprise *(CV 6), her hull and island masked with a new camouflage paint scheme, slices through the waters of Pearl Harbor, Hawaii, on 2 August 1944. In speaking of World War II, Secretary of the Navy James Forrestal called* Enterprise *"the one vessel that most nearly symbolizes the history of the Navy in this war." (U.S. Navy)*

Top, right: *Almost thirty-eight years to the day after Captain Roy L. Johnson and his crew ceremoniously manned* Forrestal *(CVA 59) and brought her to life on the occasion of her commissioning, Captain Robert L. Johnson, her thirtieth and final commanding officer, saluted the colors for the final time.* Forrestal's *decommissioning ceremony on 30 September 1993 marked the end of her time traversing the world's ocean under the flag of the United States. (U.S. Navy)*

An exuberant crowd gathers beneath cranes and scaffolding at Newport News Shipbuilding and Dry Dock Company to celebrate the christening of Forrestal *(CVA 59), the U.S. Navy's first super-carrier, on 12 December 1954. Always a joyous occasion, the smashing of a bottle of champagne against a ship's bow traditionally culminates the ceremony. (Newport News Shipbuilding)*

However, the financial burden of maintaining the carrier proved too great for her former crewmen, who acknowledged the impossibility of saving their former ship and moved forward with what they could do to preserve parts of *Enterprise* before she was sold for scrap. In return, the Navy named the first nuclear-powered aircraft carrier in her memory and dedicated the elevator tower at the Navy-Marine Corps Memorial Stadium in Annapolis, Maryland, in *Enterprise*'s name.

When *Enterprise* was scrapped in 1958, many felt it was a mistake. But some who had served aboard her, including former TBF Avenger gunner Alvin B. Kernan, felt differently. "Better by far," he wrote, "to leave her to the memory of those who had served on her when she was fully alive, vibrating under full steam at thirty-two knots, the aircraft turning up, guns firing, heeling over so sharply that the hangar deck took on water to avoid the bombs." The effort to save *Enterprise* paved the path for the successful preservation of more than a handful of her famous progeny, such as former active carriers *Intrepid* (CVS 11), *Yorktown* (CVS 10), *Lexington* (AVT 16), and *Hornet* (CVS 12), which now serve as floating museums.

Perhaps the most lasting tributes to the flying Navy's richly imbued history reside in the memories of its pilots, the heroes to the not-so-famous

flyers who set naval aviation apart from its sister services. Vice Admiral Anthony A. Less, former Commander Naval Air Force United States Atlantic Fleet, may never have known the fear and anticipation of piloting the Navy's first generation of aircraft, but he knew all too well the challenges of flying the best fighter aircraft in the modern fleet under the harshest of combat conditions in the skies over Vietnam. Upon his retirement from active duty on 18 March 1994, Vice Admiral Less first asked the question, "What are these gold wings of naval aviation?" His answer provided a fitting memorial to all naval aviators, taken from the cherished memories he held close from the first day he stepped onto the field at Pensacola to the final day of his service to the United States Navy thirty-four years later.

"Perhaps it begins with love for the assignments, the diverse experiences, the places we go. Maybe it's the nostalgia of the early morning fog off Pensacola Bay, or sunrise reflecting off Jacksonville's St. John's River, or the desert wind stirring the evening air at Miramar or North Island, or the hazy sultriness of a summer sunset at Hampton Roads." But more likely, Less said, "it's the pungent odor of jet fuel, the hammer of a steam catapult, the pounding of another plane catching a wire, or the distinctive sound of jet engines in afterburner, straining on the catapult with ocean spray and fresh clean air waiting to lift it toward the sky.

"It was the exhilaration of soloing in a T-34B at Saufley Field," reflected Less, "the immense feeling of accomplishment the first time I felt the jerk on my harness as the tailhook of my T-28 snagged the arresting gear." It was many moments that drove Vice Admiral Less to conclude: "I will always remember that these wings reflect not only the light of this bright noonday sun. They also proudly radiate the talent, the dedication, and the courage of thousands of patriots who served and continue to serve, to keep this great nation of ours free. For the rewarding memories they evoke, the heroic achievements they symbolize, and most of all, for all the dedicated people they represent, these are the wings of which I will forever be proud."

The crew of an F-14 Tomcat mans their plane at NAS Miramar, California, which until it was transferred to the Marine Corps in 1996 was famous throughout the Navy as "Fightertown U.S.A.," home to Pacific Fleet fighter squadrons and the U.S. Navy Fighter Weapons School ("Topgun"). (National Museum of Naval Aviation)

Above: *A T-28C Trojan makes a touch and go landing on the flight deck of the aircraft carrier* Lexington *(CVS 16) during a midshipman flight orientation cruise in the Gulf of Mexico in June 1965. The thrill and satisfaction of making a first carrier landing is a cherished moment in the career of any carrier pilot. (U.S. Navy)*

Vice Admiral Anthony A. Less, Commander, Naval Air Force U.S. Atlantic Fleet, returns the salute of Lieutenant Gregory Glaros of Attack Squadron 35 after presenting him with the Air Medal for combat actions in the Gulf War. In some ways the ceremony marked the passing of the torch in naval aviation, for Less received the same medal for his own combat flights in the skies over Vietnam. (Paul Aiken)

Sea Wings

Sea Wings

Lieutenant Commander Rick Burgess, USN (Ret)

Pages 72–73: *A formation for the ages is led by "Showtime 100," the F-4J Phantom II in which Lieutenant Randall H. Cunningham and Lieutenant (jg) William Driscoll became fighter aces in the skies over Vietnam. Naval aviators scored air-to-air kills in all of the aircraft portrayed. ("A Salute to Navy and Marine Corps Fighter Aces," Roy Grinnell)*

Above: *A Grumman F-14A Tomcat—flown from* Ranger *(CV 61) by Fighter Squadron 2's Lieutenant Dave Chandler and Lieutenant Commander Dan Cain—patrols the skies over the Indian Ocean in 1989. Armed with Phoenix air-to-air missiles, the long-legged Tomcat gave the Navy a credible means to counter the formidable Soviet air-launched antiship missile threat. (Lieutenant Commander. Dave Baranek)*

One evening in July 1917, Lieutenant Frank Simpson, Jr., walked along the sea wall at Naval Air Station Pensacola, Florida. Normally bustling with activity, the buzzing of Liberty engines piercing the air, only the rhythmic lapping of the waves intruded upon the silence. Approaching one of the hangars, Simpson peered through its windows, beholding an array of seaplanes at rest.

I could not but think that with closed eyes, but not asleep, they were meditating upon the things they had seen and felt. Thinking of their days high in the sun with smooth blue water way beneath and cloudless skies above. Or perhaps they thought of the dark days with eddying air, days when they tossed about through dark clouds with the center of [a] squall booming over the horizon. . . . It is not impossible that they meditated upon strange intangible things yet to come. Ominous things of the air that men, dull in such things, would not even know were they close at their elbows.

The sight of an aircraft may not evoke such a poetic reflection in every aviator, yet a certain appreciation and respect exists for the machines upon whose wings they fly high above the earth. And since 1911, scattered among the pages of pilots' log books are the names of scores of airplanes that have helped shape the history of naval aviation.

Though the tailhook is the symbol most unique to naval aviation, the U.S. Navy has operated nearly the full gamut of types of flying

A Curtiss MF wooden-hulled pusher flying boat taxis in the bay at NAS Pensacola, Florida. The 102 MFs built by Curtiss and the Naval Aircraft Factory were used after World War I to train aviators to fly operational seaplanes. (U.S. Navy)

A delta-wing Convair XF2Y-1 Sea Dart seen on a takeoff run in 1953. This jet-powered ski-equipped interceptor was designed to operate from beaches and anchorages in forward areas. One Sea Dart earned the distinction of becoming the first seaplane to break the sound barrier. This radical program was canceled during the mid-1950s; only five Sea Darts were built. (Convair)

machines: land planes, seaplanes, floatplanes, flying boats, amphibians, carrier-based planes, ski-planes, gliders, blimps, airships, helicopters, vertical takeoff and landing aircraft, tiltrotors, and drones. However, the success of carrier-based aircraft and shore-based patrol planes in World War II coupled with the introduction of the versatile helicopter led to the demise of most other naval aircraft types.

While early seaplanes developed a limited antisubmarine warfare (ASW) capability—one that had a significant impact in World War I—naval aircraft did not acquire a potent strike capability until the development of carrier aviation. Although some early land planes were adapted successfully to carrier use, a divergence from conventional design ensued. The resulting carrier aircraft incorporated unique features that, with few exceptions, have endured to this day.

The distinctive tailhook—a necessity for arrested landings on board any carrier, from the wooden flight deck of *Langley* (CV 1) to today's modern supercarriers—remains standard equipment for carrier-based fixed-wing aircraft. Rugged airframes and landing gear became essential to surviving the repeated stress of carrier landings. The limited space on carrier flight decks and hangar decks prompted the development of folding wings, enabling the massing of as many aircraft as possible on board the Navy's floating airfields. Innovative aerodynamic features such as spoilers, variable-pitch wings, variable-height nose struts, and other innovative control surfaces were developed to increase the angle of attack for short takeoffs and decrease speed for carrier approaches.

A Curtiss F8C-4 Helldiver of Fighting Squadron 1B pictured in flight. Like most fighter aircraft of the interwar period, the Helldiver was also equipped for dive-bombing, a tactic which naval aviators honed to perfection in the years leading up to World War II. (U.S. Navy)

Grumman F9F Cougar and McDonnell F2H Banshee fighter jets compete for space with propeller-driven Douglas AD Skyraiders on the flight deck of Oriskany (CVA 34) during a deployment to the Western Pacific just after the Korean War. The early carrier-based jets were short-ranged and carried small payloads, but represented an irreversible wave of the future. (U.S. Navy)

Engines that responded rapidly to throttle commands were highly desirable in the demanding realm of landing an airplane on a moving ship. Aircraft power plants were the main factor in increasing the potency of carrier-based and sea-based aircraft, which improved dramatically during World War II as the reciprocating engine reached the zenith of its design. Jet engines, which powered most naval aircraft designs entering

A Vought F7U-3M Cutlass assigned to Fighter Squadron 83 launches from the deck of Intrepid (CVA 11) in 1954. The unconventional Cutlass was one of the "flash-in-the-pan" jet fighters that came and went quickly during the decade following the Korean War. (U.S. Navy)

powered most naval aircraft designs entering service in the late 1940s and beyond, initially represented a step backward in range and load-carrying capability in return for an increase in speed. As jet engine designs improved, payloads increased, but at the price of heightened fuel consumption. This prompted the adaptation of aerial refueling to carrier aviation during the 1950s, which remains a fact of life as well as a lifesaver for most carrier aviators, even with the relatively fuel-economical turbofan engines that have virtually eclipsed turbojets in carrier aircraft.

For many years it was axiomatic that the extra weight of equipment necessary for shipboard operations condemned carrier-based aircraft to performance inferior to that of contemporary land planes. That began to change during World War II, and by the 1960s the Navy was equipped with fighters and attack aircraft equal to or superior to land planes. Indeed, the U.S. Air Force adopted a few Navy combat aircraft designs—the A-1 Skyraider, F-4 Phantom II, and A-7 Corsair II—because of their favorable characteristics. Adaptation of land planes to carrier use was less successful, with the exception of the North American F-86/FJ Fury.

Above: The *AH-18 (Airplane, Hydro, number 18), shown at NAS Pensacola, Florida, was one of the Curtiss AH-8-class seaplanes that were refinements of the first Navy airplane, the Curtiss A-1 Triad. The early Curtiss AH airplanes also were the first naval aircraft to see combat action. (U.S. Navy)*

Right: *The Curtiss C-2—seen probably at Hammondsport, New York—was the second of a class of aircraft that became known as F-boats. They contributed much to the development of U.S. naval aviation. Later designated AB-2, this aircraft, with Lieutenant Commander H.C. Mustin at the controls, made the Navy's first catapult launch from a ship off North Carolina (ACR 12) in 1915. (U.S. Navy)*

Opposite, bottom: *The Navy's first airship, DN-1, photographed at NAS Pensacola, Florida, in 1917, the year it entered service. Built by the Connecticut Aircraft Company, it was equipped with a boat-shaped gondola and intended to operate much like a seaplane. This unsuccessful dirigible was powered by two 140-horsepower engines, but was so overweight that one engine had to be removed to fly. The DN-1 was scrapped after only three flights. (National Museum of Naval Aviation)*

Eyes of the Fleet

Until the development of carrier aviation, most of the early naval aircraft were seaplanes, including floatplanes and flying boats. They operated from seadromes and ships, either craned over the side or launched by shipboard catapult. Most of these early aircraft, with their limited human and armament payloads, were used for reconnaissance and observation, extending the horizons of the fleet even beyond the radars then beginning to equip battleships.

Seaplanes performed naval aviation's earliest milestone flights, laying the groundwork for its future success. The Navy's first airplane, the Curtiss A-1 Triad, was delivered in July 1911 and used to train the first naval aviators until it was lost in a mishap four months after delivery. A refinement of the A-1, the A-3 (later designated AH-3), suffered the first combat damage to a U.S. Navy aircraft when Mexican bullets found their mark over Tampico in May 1914. The Curtiss AB-2, which developed into the famed F-Boat that saw widespread

service in World War I, was the first U.S. Navy aircraft to be catapulted from a ship.

While some naval aviators flew fighters and bombers with allied air arms, the most important contribution by U.S. Navy aircraft in World War I was in antisubmarine patrol. The Curtiss HS-1/2L and H-16 flying boats proved so effective in preventing German U-boat attacks that in 1918, only three ships were sunk by U-boats in sectors patrolled by Navy aircraft. An improvement of the H-16, the F-5L (later PN-5), became the workhorse of U.S. naval aviation in the decade following World War I, equipping both Atlantic and Pacific scouting squadrons that operated with the U.S. fleet during maneuvers in the 1920s.

The Navy also was intrigued with the potential of lighter-than-air (LTA) aircraft as a long-range, high-endurance reconnaissance platform. The Navy's first airship, the DN-1, made its first flight in April 1917, but the primitive design flew only twice more. Nevertheless, the stage had been set for more than forty years of LTA operations in naval aviation.

Top, left: *Serving in World War I alongside the H-16 was the Curtiss HS-2L flying boat, this example shown at NAS Pensacola, Florida. The HS-2L became the standard single-engine patrol flying boat in the immediate postwar era, serving until 1926. (U.S. Navy)*

Top, right: *A Curtiss H-16 flying boat photographed in August 1918, three months before the end of the Great War. The large H-16's effectiveness in antisubmarine patrols represented a great improvement in capability for U.S. naval aviation. The Navy procured 274 H-16s, some of which served until 1928. (National Museum of Naval Aviation)*

Above: *The twin-engine Curtiss F-5L (later PN-5) was an adaptation of the British improvement of the H-16, with which it essentially was identical. The F-5L was the workhorse of naval aviation in the years following World War I. (San Diego Aerospace Museum)*

Above: Shenandoah *(ZR 1)—the first of the Navy's five rigid airships modeled after German Zeppelins—under assembly in a hangar at NAS Lakehurst, New Jersey. Inflated by helium rather than hydrogen,* Shenandoah *was powered by six 300-horsepower Packard engines and manned by a crew of twenty-three. The airship made fifty-seven flights, including a double crossing of the United States, before it was destroyed in a storm in Ohio in 1925. (Clements)*

Right: *A Curtiss F9C-2 Sparrowhawk fighter approaches the trapeze of* Macon *(ZRS 5) near San Francisco, California. The eight F9C-2s built were small enough to fit through the hangar doors of* Macon *and her sister,* Akron *(ZRS 4). Each airship could carry four F9Cs in its 60- by 75-foot hangar. The Sparrowhawks operated from the airships without landing gear and were launched and retrieved by trapeze. Four F9C-2s were lost in 1935 when* Macon *crashed off the coast of California. (National Museum of Naval Aviation)*

Opposite, top: *The Goodyear ZSG-2 blimp was a postwar modification of the K-series nonrigid airships that served in the anti-submarine role during World War II. A ZSG-2 was fitted with a 527,000-cubic-foot envelope filled with helium. The K-series was the first to have the gondola attached directly to the envelope. The fleet's last blimps were retired in 1962. (Goodyear)*

Navy LTA developed along two tracks, rigid airships and blimps. Five rigid airships based on German Zeppelins were built for the Navy and served in the 1920s and 1930s. However, despite their potential and their ability to inspire the imagination, the rigid airships—which were actually commissioned ships—were doomed by their vulnerability to weather. One was lost prior to delivery; *Shenandoah* (ZR 1) crashed over land during a storm; and *Akron* (ZRS 4) and *Macon* (ZRS 5), both of which could launch and recover F9C-2 Sparrowhawk fighters using trapezes, were lost at sea before they could prove their worth, effectively ending the rigid airship program.

More successful were nonrigid airships, or blimps. In 1937 the Army turned over its blimps to the Navy, which employed 177 blimps of various types during World War II, losing only one to a German submarine. Their deterrent success in the war is reflected in the fact that no convoy escorted by blimps ever lost a ship to enemy submarines. The Navy's last blimps were retired in 1962, and efforts to revive them with new technologies have been met with little encouragement.

The Navy's seaplane fleet included both floatplanes and flying boats. Floatplanes proved their usefulness time and again to their mother

Below, left: Vought O3U Corsairs pictured on the deck of Chicago *(CA 29) at Mare Island Navy Yard, California, in 1931. The aircraft in the foreground are positioned on the ship's catapults, which were swung athwartships for launch. The crane that is visible forward of the stack plucked the aircraft from the water once they returned from their flights. (U.S. Navy)*

Below, right: The Curtiss SOC-1 Seagull scout floatplane entered service in 1935 and served for a decade from battleships and cruisers. The SOC—the last in a long line of Curtiss biplanes to be built for the U.S. Navy—was so successful that it outlasted its intended replacement, the Curtiss SO3C. (U.S. Navy)

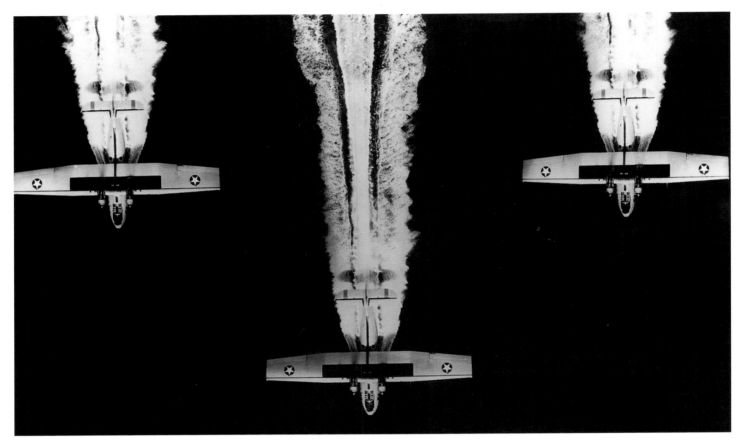

Top, left: *The single-seat Curtiss SC-1 Seahawk was a late entry into World War II and the last floatplane deployed on U.S. Navy surface warships. It was superceded in the late 1940s by the more versatile helicopter. (H.C. Ogles)*

Top, right: *A Vought OS2U-3 Kingfisher scout floatplane assigned to Observation Squadron 5 catapults off the battleship* Texas *(BB 35) in 1944. The Kingfisher fished many downed airmen out of the water, often under hostile fire. During one carrier raid on the Japanese bastion at Truk, an OS2U piloted by Lieutenant (jg) John A. Burns rescued ten fliers under fire and taxied them to a waiting U.S. submarine. (U.S. Navy)*

ships, performing observation, reconnaissance, gunfire spotting, logistics, and rescue missions. The classic floatplane was the Curtiss SOC Seagull, the last biplane to serve in the fleet, which soldiered on so splendidly in World War II that it outlasted the SO3C designed to replace it. The OS2U Kingfisher monoplane also made rescue heroes of many of its crews, including Lieutenant (jg) John Burns, who rescued ten downed fliers from Truk Lagoon in 1944. With men clinging to the wings of his overloaded plane, he taxied them to a waiting submarine. The fleet's last floatplane, the SC Seahawk, boasted the best performance of any design in that class of aircraft, but the end of the war and the advent of the helicopter cut short its career.

The Navy invested heavily in flying boats after their success in World War I and the transatlantic triumph of the NC-4 in 1919.

Squadrons of twin-engine flying boats, supported by a fleet of tenders and organized into fleet air wings, provided long-range reconnaissance for the battle fleet and filled myriad utility roles. The P3M and P2Y, which served in operational roles until 1939, pioneered the operational doctrines that patrol planes would employ in World War II. The PBY Catalina replaced both types in time for the Neutrality Patrols of 1940

Above: *Humorist Will Rogers and pilot Commander George Fairlamb stand in the cockpit of a PD-1 as a ground handling crew secures the flying boat after a 1930 orientation flight. A Douglas-built version of the PN-12, the 25 PD-1s were the first flying boats built in quantity for the Navy on the West Coast since World War I. (U.S. Navy)*

Opposite, center: *Consolidated P2Ys make a formation takeoff run at NAS Pensacola, Florida, in July 1942. Withdrawn from operational use in 1941 and then used to train flying boat crews, the P2Y was the predecessor to the famed PBY Catalina and helped develop the patrol plane doctrine used during World War II. (U.S. Navy)*

Left: *The PM-1 flying boat was the Martin-built version of the PN-12. Many examples of this twin-engine patrol plane eventually were fitted with improvements such as enclosed cockpits. Thirty PM-1s and twenty-five improved, twin-tailed PM-2s were built for naval use in the 1930s. (U.S. Navy)*

Top, left: *Martin won the contract to build the Consolidated XPY-1 flying boat (itself a Naval Aircraft Factory design) as the twin-engine Martin XP2M-1, shown on beaching gear in May 1932. The XP2M-1 was the Navy's first monoplane flying boat. A third engine mounted centerline high on the wing later was fitted but eventually deleted, at which time the XP2M-1 became the XP2M-2. (Martin)*

Top, right: *The Martin P3M-2, a contemporary of the Consolidated P2Y, was not as successful in fleet service as the P2Y and was primarily relegated to training and utility work. Martin's experience with the P3M and earlier flying boats eventually helped the company dominate the patrol seaplane market in late World War II and afterward. (U.S. Navy)*

Bottom, left: *The dual-pilot cockpit of the Consolidated PBY-5A Catalina amphibian reflects the relative simplicity of instrumentation in World War II aircraft. From cockpits such as this Catalina crews tracked the German battleship* Bismarck, *located the Japanese fleet at Midway, and terrorized Japanese shipping during long nights in the South Pacific. (U.S. Navy)*

Bottom, right: *The ubiquitous Consolidated PBY Catalina flying boat, despite its vulnerability, rendered service to the U.S. Navy and Allied air arms during World War II far in excess of its assumed capabilities. The slow Catalina—which enjoyed success in antisubmarine, antishipping, rescue, and reconnaissance roles, among others—was not retired from the Navy until 1957. (U.S. Navy)*

and became the most numerous and successful flying boat of the war. Though excruciatingly slow, its versatility propelled it successfully into antisubmarine, antishipping, and rescue roles. The PBY was the first aircraft to sink U-boats after locating them with magnetic anomaly detection gear, and gained an unlikely reputation as a lethal night-attack aircraft in the South Pacific in its "Black Cat" role. The last Navy PBY was retired in 1957.

The PBM Mariner complemented the PBY and the PB2Y Coronado in World War II and eventually replaced both in fleet service. The PBM also served in the Korean War, where its roles included minehunting. A refinement of the PBM design, the P5M (P-5) Marlin, hunted Soviet submarines in the Cold War and patrolled for infiltrators off Vietnam. However, the SP-5B was the end of the line for flying boats in the U.S. Navy and was retired in 1967. The last Navy amphibian, an HU-16D Albatross, was retired in 1976.

The need for large numbers of patrol bombers as well as the rapid expansion in the number of airfields during World War II led to the dominance of land-based aircraft in patrol aviation. Heavily armed twin-engine PBO Hudson, PV-1 Ventura, and PV-2 Harpoon patrol bombers proved effective in ASW, antishipping, and strike roles. The Navy adopted long-range Army Air Force B-24 Liberators as PB4Y-1s and used them with great success against German U-boats and Japanese island strongholds. An improved version, the PB4Y-2 Privateer, provided splendid

The nose turret and search radome (behind the cockpit) of the Martin PBM-5 Mariner flying boat are shown to good effect as the aircraft receives maintenance attention on the deck of a seaplane tender in World War II. The PBM's performance was superior to that of the PBY Catalina, which it eventually replaced in fleet service. The PBM could carry 2,000 pounds of bombs or depth charges. Production of the Mariner ceased in 1949, but the flying boat served in the Korean War and into the mid-1950s. (U.S. Navy)

A Martin PBM-5 Mariner assigned to Patrol Bombing Squadron 26 is readied for craning aboard the seaplane tender Norton Sound (AV 11) off Okinawa in 1945. Despite the success of seaplane operations with tenders and from shore stations, the demise of the flying boat eventually was mandated by difficulty of maintenance in the face of salt-water corrosion, the hazards of high sea states, and the expansion in the number of airfields worldwide. (William Williams)

service in the strike role and employed the Navy's first radar-guided bomb, the ASN-N-2 Bat, in combat against the Japanese.

After World War II, land-based patrol planes steadily supplanted flying boats. The Privateer saw service over Korea, most famously as a flare ship for night strikes, and patrolled the waters off the Soviet Union. The P4M Mercator entered the fleet in small numbers but was soon diverted to service as an electronic ferret. The P2V (P-2) Neptune became the dominant patrol plane in the late 1940s and 1950s, but after several forays into Korea shooting up watercraft and locomotives, the patrol bomber returned to its customary overwater missions. The Neptune did, however, in its OP-2E and AP-2H versions, later drop ordnance in Vietnam. The radar-guided antiaircraft gun, the surface-to-air missile, and the jet interceptor hindered the antishipping and strike roles of the patrol plane for more than three decades. However, the increasing Soviet submarine threat gave patrol aviation an undeniable raison d'être.

The stealth of Soviet submarines and the increasing sophistication required to hunt them led to the dominance of avionics over armor. A conversion of the Lockheed Electra airliner, the P3V (P-3) Orion, began replacing the P-2 and P-5 in 1962 and became the Navy's sole patrol type in the fleet by the 1970s, serving off Vietnam as well. Several were converted to the electronic reconnaissance role as EP-3s. The computerized P-3C, first deployed in 1970, proved up to the task of tracking the Soviet submarine fleet. Marshal Akhromeyev, chief of the Soviet armed forces, remarked during the late 1980s that whenever he wanted to know where his own submarines were, he would ask his staff where Orions were flying. In 1979, armed with the AGM-84 Harpoon cruise missile, the P-3 began packing a respectable antishipping punch as well. Today, updated P-3Cs can strike targets inland by lobbing AGM-84E Standoff Land Attack missiles, as demonstrated in Kosovo during Operation Allied Force in 1999.

Clockwise from top left:

Ungainly in appearance—its nickname was the "Flying Banana" for obvious reasons— the Piasecki HRP-1 laid the groundwork for the heliborne assault mission that the Marine Corps employed with such success in Korea and Vietnam and continues to develop today. (U.S. Marine Corps)

A Sikorsky HO3S observation helicopter assigned to a detachment of Helicopter Utility Squadron 2 lifts a crewman with its rescue hoist in Korea in September 1951. The HO3S was the Navy's first rescue helicopter to serve in substantial numbers on board carriers, and pioneered the plane guard concept still in use today. (U.S. Navy)

A Kaman SH-2F Seasprite LAMPS (light airborne multipurpose system) Mk I helicopter operates in an antisubmarine exercise with Brooke *(DDG 1) in April 1976. The turbine-powered H-2 replaced the UH-25 as the standard plane guard heli- copter on board carriers before it was selected for the LAMPS program in the early 1970s. The H-2 rescued many aviators downed in North Vietnam, and continued serving the Navy until its retirement in 2001. (Robert L. Lawson)*

A Piasecki UH-25B Retriever assigned to Utility Squadron 1 flies off the starboard side of Constellation *(CVA 64) in 1963. The UH-25 (formerly HUP) replaced the HO3S on board carriers as a utility helicopter, and was the first tandem-rotor helicopter used in substantial numbers by the Navy. (R.A. Carlisle)*

Fleet Angels

Since helicopters supplanted the traditional roles of floatplanes after World War II, rotary-wing aviation has developed in six decades into a force vital to fleet operations. Improvements in these complex machines have been steady, and no well-equipped surface combatant ship today would be found without a helicopter.

The ability of helicopters to hover gave them a natural constituency in rescue, spotting, logistics, and minehunting roles. Sikorsky's HNS, based on the Army YR-4B, was used to train the Navy's first cadre of helicopter pilots. Successive improvements—the HOS, HO3S, and HO5S— brought forth the HRS/HO4S (H-19), the first helicopter with adequate lift capability. The HO3S and HRS saw combat action in Korea as rescue and transport aircraft. The HUS Seahorse/HSS Seabat (H-34) marked a significant improvement over the HRS/HO4S, and gave the fleet its first effective ASW helicopter.

The Bell, Piasecki, Hiller, and Kaman companies also produced a variety of naval helicopters in limited numbers and very limited capabil- ity. Two of the most useful were the Kaman HUK/HOK, with its counter- rotating main rotors, and the tandem-rotored Piasecki HUP. In 1959, what would become the Navy's two longest serving helicopter designs

made their first flights. Kaman's HU2K (H-2) Seasprite and Sikorsky's HSS-2 (H-3) Sea King, the Navy's first turbine-powered helicopters, began hard-working careers as ASW and rescue platforms that took them in harm's way in Vietnam and several conflicts since. The H-2 Seasprite, which enjoyed a second life as the Light Airborne Multipurpose System (LAMPS) Mark I, was phased out of the Naval Reserve in 2001 after forty-two years of service, but continues to serve in several foreign navies.

Three other turbine-powered types that entered service during the 1960s remain mainstays in the Navy and Marine Corps. The UH-1E "Huey" served the Corps in Vietnam and was succeeded by the twin-engine UH-1N, soon to be replaced by the UH-1Y. The Navy also operates Hueys, which were used to great effect in the riverine war in Vietnam.

The pack mule of the helo fleet for more than thirty-five years has been the Boeing H-46 Sea Knight, a twin-rotor transport that in its similar CH/HH/UH-46 versions wrote the book on vertical replenishment. The CH-46 also has been the most numerous Marine Corps helicopter since the late Vietnam War period, but it is scheduled to be replaced by the revolutionary MV-22 Osprey tiltrotor aircraft.

A Sikorsky SH-3A Sea King antisubmarine helicopter approaches the deck of LaSalle (LPD 3) packed with other Sea Kings assigned to Helicopter Antisubmarine Squadron 3. The turbine-powered SH-3A replaced the Sikorsky SH-34 Seabat on board antisubmarine carriers during the early 1960s. The Sea King gave excellent service as a rescue aircraft staged from ships in the Tonkin Gulf during the Vietnam War. (U.S. Navy)

An SH-3A Sea King assigned to Helicopter Antisubmarine Squadron 6 trails its magnetic anomaly detector during an antisubmarine warfare training mission in 1976. The H-3 also was valued for its large capacity as a logistics aircraft, and still serves as a utility aircraft more than four decades after its debut. (Robert L. Lawson)

Above: *A Bell UH-1B "Huey" gunship assigned to Helicopter Attack Squadron (Light) 3 lifts off from the deck of* Harnett County *(LST 821) moored in the Mekong River in Vietnam. The Navy acquired UH-1B/C/M Hueys from the U.S. Army and deployed them in detachments throughout the Mekong Delta to provide rapid-response air support for the "brown-water Navy," a fleet of river patrol boats and other riverine craft used to counter Viet Cong operations. (U.S. Navy)*

Right: *A Boeing Vertol HH-46D Sea Knight logistics helicopter prepares to lift a pallet of cargo from the deck of* Theodore Roosevelt *(CVN 71) operating in the Adriatic Sea in June 1993. The vertical replenishment role personified over more than thirty-five years by the Navy's tandem-rotor H-46 fleet is vital to sustaining carrier battle-group operations at sea. CH-46D, HH-46D, and UH-46D versions, all similar, operate together in paired detachments on board logistic ships of the fleet and the Military Sealift Command. (U.S. Navy)*

Below: *A Sikorsky RH-53D Sea Stallion hovers over the stern of* Voge *(FF 1047). The RH-53D was the first helicopter manufactured as a minesweeping helicopter, and its crews greatly advanced the challenging art of airborne minesweeping pioneered by the Sikorsky RH-3A and CH-53A. (U.S. Navy)*

Bottom, right: *Marines stream down a line suspended beneath the elongated fuselage of a CH-46 Sea Knight helicopter. Modernization programs have kept the venerable "Frogs" in the air long past their retirements, and they will equip Marine medium helicopter squadrons well into the first decade of the twenty-first century. (Rick Mullen)*

For heavy lift, the Sikorsky CH-53 was tailor-made for the Marine Corps, replacing the ungainly CH-37 in combat in Vietnam. The three-engine CH-53E—the largest helicopter produced outside Russia—provides heavy lift for the Corps today. A minehunting variant, the MH-53E, serves the Navy in mine warfare and vertical-onboard-delivery roles.

During the 1980s the Navy procured the SH-60B Seahawk (adapted from the Army's Black Hawk) to replace the SH-2 Seasprite in the LAMPS role; the SH-60F to replace the SH-3 Sea King on board aircraft carriers; and the HH-60H to succeed the HH-1K Huey. The new H-60s—highly successful during Operation Desert Storm in 1991—brought a much-needed airframe modernization to the helicopter community, but now even they are in line for modernization.

The Navy is making great strides in reducing the number of different types of helicopters in the fleet by introducing the MH-60S,

another adaptation of the Army's UH-60 Black Hawk. The versatile MH-60S is slated to replace the UH-3, H-46 series, HH-60H, and HH-1N, and is being evaluated as a replacement for the MH-53E with its ability to employ remote minehunting systems. The SH-60R— a remanufactured version of the current H-60 design—will replace both the SH-60B and the SH-60F in the antisubmarine and antiship-ping roles.

Within two decades the H-60 is expected to be the only helicopter type in the fleet, while rotary-wing aviation stands only to increase its share of the workload of naval aviation.

Fighters, Strikers, and Jammers

During World War I, U.S. naval aviators flew European-built fighters and bombers against their German and Austrian adversaries. Not until the 1920s, with the advent of U.S. carrier aviation, did the U.S. Navy begin to develop and acquire indigenous fighters, dive bombers, and torpedo planes.

Into the 1930s, the Navy relied upon limited production runs of biplanes of ever-increasing capability. This "golden age" featured colorful

A Sikorsky HH-60H Seahawk assigned to Helicopter Combat Support Special Squadron 5 is readied for flight by its reserve crew at NAS Point Mugu, Calif. The HH-60H—designed specifically for combat rescue missions and support of special forces operations—is oper-ated from carriers and by reserve squadrons. The HH-60H operated in support of special operations forces in Iraq during Operation Desert Storm. (U.S. Navy)

A Sikorsky MH-53E Sea Dragon helicopter tows a minesweeping sled during an exercise. The three-engine MH-53E, a development of the Marine Corps's CH-53E, is the largest heli-copter ever operated by the Navy and is flown in minesweeping and vertical-onboard-delivery roles by active-duty and reserve crews. (U.S. Navy)

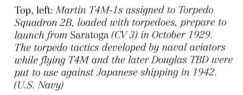

Top, left: *Martin T4M-1s assigned to Torpedo Squadron 2B, loaded with torpedoes, prepare to launch from* Saratoga *(CV 3) in October 1929. The torpedo tactics developed by naval aviators while flying T4M and the later Douglas TBD were put to use against Japanese shipping in 1942. (U.S. Navy)*

Top, right: *A formation of Grumman F3F-1s assigned to Fighting Squadron 4 crosses the California coast in January 1939. Equipped with enclosed cockpit and retractable gear, the F3F was the last biplane fighter built for the Navy. (U.S. Navy)*

Above, left: *Brewster F2A-3s peel off from formation during diving maneuvers near NAS Miami, Florida, in August 1942. The F2A— which was named Buffalo by the Royal Air Force and later assigned that name by the Navy—was the first monoplane fighter built for the Navy. Marine F2As saw combat in the defense of Midway in June 1942, but were overwhelmed by Japanese Zero fighters. (U.S. Navy)*

Above, right: *A Northrop BT-1 assigned to Bombing Squadron 5 photographed in April 1938. The BT featured an all-metal construction as well as retractable landing gear. One BT-1 was diverted to development as the XBT-2—the prototype of the famed Douglas SBD Dauntless of World War II. (U.S. Navy)*

Opposite: *A trio of SB2U-1 Vindicators of Bombing Squadron 3 display the colorful paint scheme worn by aircraft during the years preceding World War II. The two angled lines painted on the tails of the airplanes are references for the landing signal officer, who used them to tell at a glance whether an aircraft was on the proper glide slope for a safe recovery. (National Museum of Naval Aviation)*

aircraft, among them highly maneuverable biplane fighters such as the Curtiss F6C, Boeing F4B, and Grumman F3F. Bombers such as the Martin T4M, Great Lakes BG-1, and Curtiss SBC had limited payloads but paved the way in dive-bombing and torpedo tactics that later aircraft would fashion into glory in World War II.

Late in the 1930s monoplanes began to displace biplanes on board carrier decks. The TBD Devastator torpedo bomber entered service as the Navy's first carrier monoplane, and also proved revolutionary in its all-metal construction. The Brewster F2A fighter and Northrop BT-1 and Vought SB2U Vindicator dive bombers replaced biplanes in their respective specialties, but these aircraft, capable for their day, proved inadequate for the combat that lay ahead. Fortunately for the U.S. Navy, some of the greatest combat aircraft were coming on line when the Japanese attacked Pearl Harbor, Hawaii, in 1941.

One of these was the Douglas SBD Dauntless, a decidedly nonspectacular warplane. Simple, rugged, and possessing graceful lines, its half-ton bomb load was unimpressive and its lack of folding wings eventually crowded the Dauntless from carrier decks. But aided by innovative perforated flaps, it was deadly accurate in a dive and was instrumental in sending more Japanese warships to the bottom of the Pacific than any other aircraft. The SBD was the Navy's foremost offensive aerial weapon for the first year of the war. The Dauntless—with some help from torpedo planes—sank six Japanese carriers by the end of 1942 and was central in making the June 1942 action at Midway one of the greatest naval battles in history. There, SBDs fatally wounded four carriers and sank a cruiser, turning the tide of the war in the Pacific. It proved to be the right plane in the right place at the right time.

The SBD shouldered much of the burden in the Solomons campaign and the early central Pacific drive, and outshone its successor, the SB2C Helldiver, in its last carrier action, the Battle of the Philippine Sea in June 1944. Of the twenty-seven SBDs launched against the Japanese carrier task force, only one was shot down and three ditched because of fuel exhaustion; of the fifty SB2Cs launched, only five returned, most lost to fuel exhaustion. The Dauntless soldiered on until the end of the war, finishing a distinguished combat career with the Marines by showing the Army the effectiveness of close air support in the Philippines.

The TBF (and later TBM) Avenger torpedo bomber recovered from an inauspicious baptism of fire at Midway, where five of six airplanes were shot down, and became a worthy successor to the TBD, perforating many Japanese ships and German submarines, and providing the Navy with its first carrier-based night-attack platform.

Holding the line in aerial combat in the desperate first year of the war was the F4F Wildcat, which prolonged the lives of the carriers that halted the Japanese advance in the Pacific. In the hands of a well-trained pilot, the rugged F4F usually bested the Japanese Zeke, and of the seventeen Medals of Honor awarded to naval aviators for actions in air combat, eight of them went to Wildcat pilots. Later FM-1/2 versions provided cover for the jeep carriers supporting the island-hopping campaign across the Pacific and were pressed into action against the powerful Japanese surface forces in the Battle of Leyte Gulf in October 1944. There, intrepid Wildcat pilots armed only with machine guns made repeated runs against cruisers and battleships, and continued with dummy runs once their ammunition was depleted. Their actions helped

a tiny force of escort carriers and destroyers turn back a superior enemy fleet in the greatest sea battle of the war.

A case can be made that the Wildcat's successor—the Grumman F6F Hellcat—was the most successful naval aircraft of all time. Its arrival in the Pacific theater in 1943 on the decks of *Essex*-class carriers enabled the carrier task forces to achieve complete mastery of the skies. The Hellcat was neither the fastest nor the most maneuverable fighter of the war, and its armament and climb rate proved inferior to other fighter aircraft as well. Its contemporary in Pacific skies, the Chance Vought F4U Corsair, was superior in most respects; indeed, unlike the Hellcat, the Corsair continued to serve in combat after World War II. But the

The great might-have-been: the Grumman F8F-1 Bearcat—the smallest fighter that could be built around the R-2800 engine— was headed to the Western Pacific when World War II came to an end. The F8F was specifi-cally designed to counter the nimble Japanese fighters and no doubt would have exceeded the success of the Hellcat. The Bearcat served on carriers as the Cold War began but was replaced by the early jet fighters just prior to the Korean War. (Ed Baumgarten)

Corsair's initial carrier suitability deficiencies delayed its entry into ser-vice in sufficient numbers and left the carrier war almost completely to the Hellcat until 1945.

The Hellcat—so suited to its role from the start that only two major production versions (F6F-3 and F6F-5) were produced—was instantly popular among its pilots, many of whom had tangled with Japanese fighters in the rugged but less maneuverable F4F. One Hellcat ace is said to have exclaimed, "If it could cook, I'd marry one!"

The Hellcat produced 306 Navy aces; 16 more aces scored some of their kills in an F6F. Many scored multiple kills in a single engagement or in a single day. Commander David McCampbell shot down nine aircraft in a single engagement while flying a Hellcat, a record for which he received the Medal of Honor.

The Great Marianas Turkey Shoot in June 1944 stands as the Hellcat's most glorious moment. F6Fs downed more than 250 Japanese aircraft in thirteen hours and eliminated Japanese carrier aviation as a fighting force. Similar performances at Leyte Gulf, Iwo Jima, Formosa, the Philippines, and Japan drove Japanese aviation from the skies. The Hellcat—aided by increasing numbers of Corsairs—was the main counter to the kamikaze onslaught, and saved many a ship from destruction. The F6F also racked up an impressive record as a radar-equipped night fighter and a rocket-armed antishipping aircraft. The 12,275 F6Fs

An AF-2W Guardian of Antisubmarine Squadron 931 pictured on the flight deck of Bataan (CVL 29). Part of a two-plane hunter-killer team, the AF-2W operated in conjunction with an AF-2S Guardian in the antisubmarine warfare role during the early 1950s. The aircraft's bulbous search radar, operated by the aircrewman in the aft compartment, is visible beneath the fuselage. (National Museum of Naval Aviation)

produced were credited with the destruction of 5,156 Japanese aircraft and 13 German aircraft. Approximately 270 Hellcats were lost in aerial combat—a phenomenal kill ratio of 19 to 1.

The strike capabilities of the F6F and particularly the F4U led to a reduction of specialized dive and torpedo bombers in the last year of the war, and on carrier decks in the late 1940s. The great "what ifs"— the spectacular F8F Bearcat and F7F Tigercat—arrived too late to fight the Japanese. The F8F was replaced before the war in Korea, where the Tigercat saw limited success as a night fighter. And by 1950, the mighty AD Skyraider had replaced both the Helldiver and Avenger as the carrier's heavy hitter.

By the outbreak of war in Korea, three major changes could be seen in the aircraft arrayed on carrier decks. One was the increasing numbers of special-mission aircraft. Avengers, Skyraiders, and AF Guardians proved their versatility with adaptations to the night attack, electronic countermeasures, airborne early warning, and antisubmarine roles. The F4U and the jets that succeeded it provided night fighter and photoreconnaissance services.

Another change was the adoption of the nuclear attack role, the result of the interservice struggles with the U.S. Air Force. Initially, modified P2V Neptunes were pressed into the role of nuclear bombers. These planes could be launched from *Midway*-class carriers, but had to land ashore after completing their missions. The AJ Savage, the first naval aircraft designed specifically for the so-called heavy attack mission, could operate independent of land bases and replaced the P2Vs in the early 1950s. Mechanical difficulties marred the Savage's service, but more jet aircraft were on the way.

The most far-reaching naval aircraft development to impact the Korean War era was the introduction of jet aircraft. The F9F Panther, F2H Banshee, and F3D Skyknight were less agile than their Soviet-built MiG-15 adversaries and shorter-ranged than the F4Us, but the tide toward all-jet air wings was irreversible. The late 1940s and 1950s

Two Grumman F9F-2 Panthers assigned to Fighter Squadron 115 speed past Wasp (CVA 18) in May 1955. The straight-wing Panthers that performed well in Korea were succeeded by more advanced swept-wing fighters, such as the F9F-6 Cougar, within a few years after the Korean armistice. (U.S. Navy)

A North American FJ-3 Fury assigned to Fighter Squadron 51 receives attention on the deck of Bon Homme Richard (CVA 31) in 1957. Second-generation jet fighters such as the Fury were soon succeeded by the supersonic F8U (F-8) Crusader and F4H (F-4) Phantom II. (U.S. Navy)

Above: *A McDonnell F3H-2M Demon assigned to the Jolly Rogers of Fighter Squadron 61 leaves the angled deck of* Saratoga *(CVA 60) in April 1957. The radar-equipped F3H was plagued with engine problems early on but paved the way for the "phabulously" successful F4H (F-4) Phantom II. The Demon was retired in 1965 just as its successor began its MiG-killing career in the skies over Vietnam. (Boeing)*

Right: *A division of Grumman F11F-1 Tigers assigned to Fighter Squadron 21 line up in echelon in 1959, the year the type was withdrawn from front-line use after only two years. The short-ranged Tiger—a development of the F9F-8 Cougar—became familiar to the public as the long-serving aircraft of the Blue Angels flight demonstration squadron. (National Museum of Naval Aviation)*

Opposite, bottom left: *A rocket–armed Douglas A-1H Skyraider assigned to Attack Squadron 52, as seen from the Air Force HU-16 Albatross rescue amphibian it is escorting over Southeast Asia during the mid-1960s. The Skyraider was the Navy's last piston-engine, carrier-based attack aircraft, and proved to be a superb rescue combat air patrol aircraft in Vietnam. (David Wendt)*

Opposite, bottom right: *An EKA-3B Skywarrior of Electronic Warfare Squadron 138 Det 4 prepares to launch from the deck of* Enterprise *(CVAN 65) for a mission over Vietnam in June 1971. The Skywarrior entered service as a carrier-based nuclear weapons delivery platform, but in Vietnam served primarily in tanker/electronic countermeasures (ECM) roles. The fairings bulging from the side and bottom of the fuselage house the aircraft's ECM equipment. (U.S. Navy)*

were a period of dizzying change as a rapid succession of jet fighter designs came and went: the FH Phantom, F9F Panther/Cougar, F2H Banshee, F3D Skyknight, FJ Fury, F7U Cutlass, F3H Demon, F11F Tiger, and F4D Skyray. Carriers sometimes deployed with no two squadrons flying the same aircraft type.

There was much more stability in the attack community, with the AD (later A-1) Skyraider—the most successful Navy aircraft of the Korean War—enduring well into the jet age. The propeller-driven A-1 "Spad" multiplied into a variety of electronic jamming, airborne early warning, and night attack variants. As an attack aircraft its ordnance loads were highly valued by U.S. forces in Vietnam—where it even downed two MiGs—until driven into retirement by increasingly sophisticated air defenses. The A3D (A-3) Skywarrior gave the Navy a credible nuclear-

strike capability, and in later modifications served in aerial refueling, photographic and electronic reconnaissance, and electronic warfare training roles, fading away only after Operation Desert Storm in 1991. The simple A4D (A-4) Skyhawk—nicknamed Heineman's Hot Rod after its legendary designer—entered the fleet in 1956 as the Navy's first tactical jet attack aircraft, and would carry the brunt of the service's air

Above: Douglas F4D-1 Skyrays from a variety of units line the apron at an air station in 1958. The "Ford" was a carrier-based, radar-equipped interceptor that also was used by one unit, All-Weather Fighter Squadron 3, as a land-based, air-defense interceptor. VF(AW)-3 operated from NAS North Island, California, as a unit of the Air Force-controlled Continental Air Defense Command until 1963. (Harry Gann)

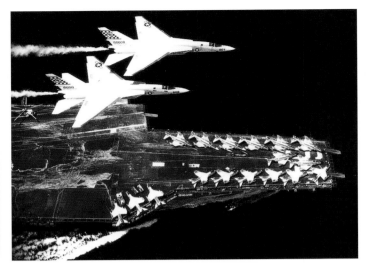

Top, left: *Bomb-laden Douglas A-4E Skyhawk attack aircraft assigned to Attack Squadron 163 wing their way toward targets in North Vietnam in 1966. The Skyhawk carried the lion's share of the Navy's bombing campaign over North Vietnam. A few two-seat TA-4Js remain in Navy service, forty-five years after the Skyhawk's debut. (Wynn Foster)*

Top, right: *Two North American RA-5C Vigilante reconnaissance jets assigned to Reconnaissance Heavy Attack Squadron 11 fly past Constellation (CVA 64) in 1972. The beautiful RA-5C served until 1979, replaced by F-14 Tomcats carrying the Tactical Air Reconnaissance Pod System. (U.S. Navy)*

Above, left: *A McDonnell F-4J Phantom II assigned to Fighter Squadron 96 heads for a target in Vietnam in May 1972. VF-96, squadron of the Navy's only Vietnam aces, shot down ten of the total forty-one North Vietnamese aircraft downed by the Navy. The legendary F-4 was adopted by the Air Force, the first Navy fighter adopted by that service in quantity. (Dave Erickson)*

Above, right: *A Vought F-8J Crusader assigned to Fighter Squadron 194 crosses the ramp of Oriskany (CVA 34) in 1976. The supersonic fighter is credited with the destruction of eighteen North Vietnamese MiG-17 and MiG-21 jet fighters. A contemporary of the missile-armed F-4 Phantom II, the F-8 was labeled "The Last of the Gunfighters." (Pete Clayton)*

strikes against North Vietnam. As an adversary aircraft its service would extend into the twenty-first century. The A3J (A-5) Vigilante enjoyed a short-lived career as a nuclear bomber but excelled as a swift photo-reconnaissance jet (RA-5) over North Vietnam.

The parade of 1950s-era fighters settled on two outstanding types by the beginning of the Vietnam War. The Vought F-8 Crusader—the Navy's first truly supersonic fighter—was for a while the only naval fighter to employ guns. The so-called Last of the Gunfighters proved a master of MiGs over North Vietnam, as well as a fine photoreconnaissance aircraft. The F-4—the "phabulous" Phantom II—was initially forced to attack only with Sidewinder and Sparrow missiles, but it also proved more than a match for its adversaries, and demonstrated its ability as a potent ground-attack aircraft as well. The F-4 defended the fleet until the mid-1980s, when it was succeeded by the F-14 Tomcat.

Though conceived during the Vietnam War, the Tomcat was designed to counter the major threat to U.S. naval forces—Soviet air-launched cruise missiles—with long-range Phoenix missiles. With its ability to track and attack six incoming targets simultaneously, the F-14 humbled the Libyan air force in encounters over the Mediterranean and enabled the Navy's carrier battle groups to sail into waters near the Soviet motherland by providing protection from that nation's long-

range TU-95 Bears and TU-22M Backfires. The Tomcat later took on a strike role and made itself felt by enemies in Iraq, Bosnia, and Serbia.

Teamed with the Tomcat has been the E-2 Hawkeye, which has been flying from carriers since 1965, scanning the skies with its rotodome for enemy intruders. The ever-modernized E-2 replaced the

A Grumman F-14A Tomcat interceptor assigned to the Sundowners of Fighter Squadron 111 climbs vertically over El Centro, California, in May 1979. The Tomcat marked a return of guns to U.S. naval fighters after the fad of "gunlessness" proved deficient over Vietnam. Even so, the F-14 is a missileer without peer.

Top, left: *A Grumman F-14D Super Tomcat assigned to Fighter Squadron 2 fires an AIM-9 Sidewinder missile in 1995. The F-14D was the last production version of the Tomcat. Built as a pure fighter, the F-14's latent air-to-ground bombing capability was realized during the mid-1990s and used to good effect in Iraq and the former Yugoslavia. (Tom Twomey)*

Top, right: *A Grumman S-2G Tracker piston-engine antisubmarine aircraft assigned to Air Antisubmarine Squadron 37 peels off from a formation with a turbine-powered Lockheed S-3A Viking antisubmarine aircraft assigned to Air Antisubmarine Squadron 21, marking the Tracker's retirement from the fleet in 1976. The S-2 tracked Soviet submarines during the Cuban Missile Crisis and saw some action off Vietnam. (U.S. Navy)*

Above: *A Grumman E-2B Hawkeye assigned to Carrier Airborne Early Warning Squadron 116 approaches the flight deck of* Constellation *(CVA 64) in 1974. Introduced into service during the Vietnam War, the Hawkeye proved its ever-increasing usefulness, and today its advanced versions are vital command and control platforms in the increasingly complex electronic battlespace. (Robert L. Lawson)*

Right: *A Grumman C-1A Trader carrier-onboard-delivery aircraft enters the traffic pattern of its mother ship,* Constellation *(CVA 64), in 1974. A development of the S-2 antisubmarine aircraft, the piston-engine C-1 was a workhorse—the most popular aircraft on the carrier—that brought mail, personnel, and spare parts to carriers at sea. (U.S. Navy)*

E-1 Tracer, a derivative of the C-1 Trader carrier-onboard-delivery (COD) aircraft, itself a derivative of the piston-engine S-2 Tracker. The state-of-the-art S-3 Viking assumed the Tracker's antisubmarine role, and a variant of the Viking, the ES-3 Shadow, assumed the electronic reconnaissance duties vacated by the EA-3 Skywarrior. COD variants of the Viking (US-3) and Hawkeye (C-2 Greyhound) carried vital cargo and people to carriers far at sea.

Probably the greatest carrier aircraft of the last half of the twentieth century was another product of the Grumman Iron Works, the A-6 Intruder. The all-weather jet attack aircraft entered combat in 1965 and flew into harm's way in every carrier action—Vietnam, Mayaguez, Grenada,

Lebanon, El Dorado Canyon, Praying Mantis, Desert Storm, Southern Watch—until its retirement in 1997. Its two-man crew, guided by a superb radar, could hit targets with as much as 18,000 pounds of ordnance in virtually any kind of weather.

A derivative of the Intruder, the EA-6B Prowler, entered combat in Vietnam in 1972 and has increased in value and potency ever since. Once armed with antiradiation missiles, it became an electronic attack aircraft, and as demonstrated by Operation Allied Force in 1999, is an indispensable escort for attacking aircraft in the information age.

A derivative of the F-8, the Vought A-7 Corsair II, entered service in 1967 and ably replaced the A-4 as the fleet's standard light attack

Above: *A Vought A-7E Corsair II assigned to Attack Squadron 72 heads for a target in Iraq during Operation Desert Storm in 1991. The long-range A-7, first introduced into combat in Vietnam, eventually replaced the A-4, but was the last of the Navy's light attack aircraft. The A-7 also saw combat in Grenada, Lebanon, Libya, and the Arabian Gulf, and was retired as a front-line aircraft in 1991. (U.S. Navy)*

aircraft, bowing out of service only after it pounded Iraqi forces during Desert Storm in 1991. The A-7 was replaced by the F/A-18 Hornet strike fighter, a jet equally adept as a fighter or attack aircraft that punished Libya in 1986 and struck America's adversaries in virtually every action since. Two Hornets proved the strike fighter concept on the first day of Desert Storm by downing two MiG-21s and then proceeding to bomb their targets.

Right: *A Boeing F/A-18E Super Hornet strike fighter goes through developmental testing in 1998. The Super Hornet—armed with a wide assortment of "smart" weapons—is an advancement of the Hornet design, intended to replace the F-14 and earlier versions of the Hornet in the first part of the twenty-first century. (Boeing)*

Opposite, bottom: *Modern cockpits like this one in a Grumman F-14B Tomcat present an array of instrumentation for the pilot to master. (Ted Carlson)*

As the twenty-first century arrived, the next-generation strike fighter entered full production. The F/A-18E/F Super Hornet—armed with advanced precision weapons—embodies the concept of striking multiple targets with standoff weapons, a generation of difference from the Vietnam-era Alpha strike, which hurled multiple bombers against one target.

Modern U.S. naval aviation is under increased budget pressure to reduce the numbers of different types of aircraft in service. The expense and time required to field increasingly sophisticated aircraft has resulted in excruciatingly long development periods. Through modernization and service-life extension, aircraft types now are serving decades instead of years. Precision weapons expand their striking potential exponentially, allowing a single aircraft to hit multiple targets on a single flight. In addition, improvements in remote control technology are pushing the serious study of unmanned combat aircraft, though for the foreseeable future the traditional call of "Pilots, man your planes" will still be heard throughout naval aviation.

Above: *Two F/A-18C Hornet strike fighters assigned to Strike Fighter Squadron 82 soar skyward armed with Sidewinder, Sparrow, High-Speed Antiradiation, and Harpoon missiles. In two decades the F/A-18—a fighter and a bomber—replaced the A-4, A-7, A-6, and F-4 in many squadrons, and represents the multimission trend that holds fast for the future. (Boeing)*

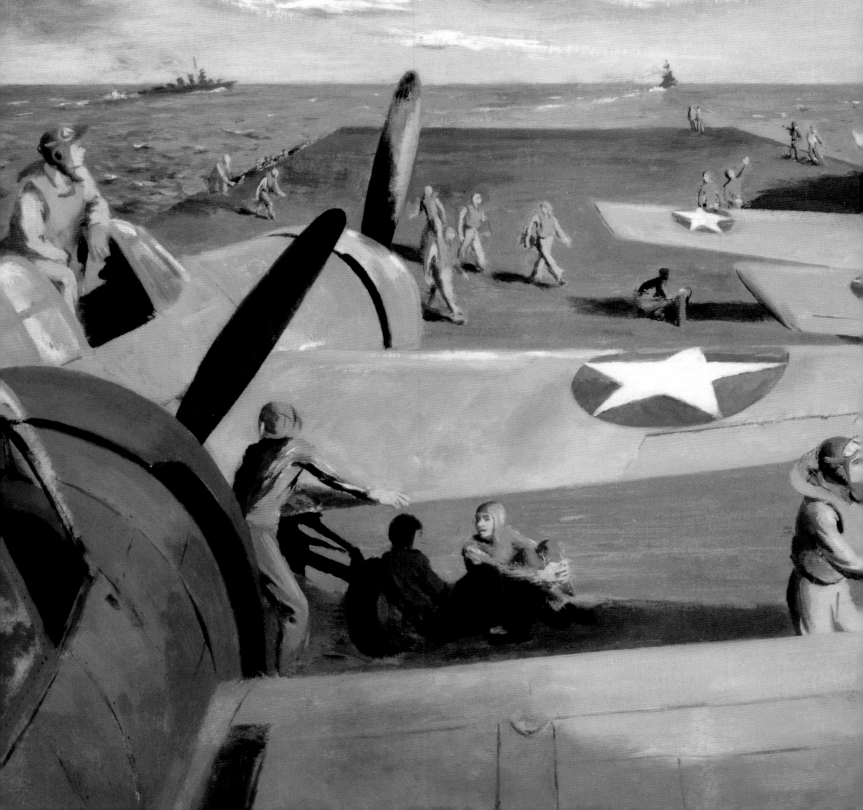

Flattop

Flattop:
The Queen
of Naval Operations

Thomas C. Hone

Pages 108–109: *Pilots and handling crews wait amid a pack of F4F Wildcats for the signal to launch. ("Task Force Hornets," Lawrence Beall Smith, U.S. Navy Combat Art Collection)*

Above: *Her giant bow the face of the modern flattop, the nuclear-powered aircraft carrier* Dwight D. Eisenhower *(CVN 69) plows through the waters of the Atlantic Ocean en route to her next station. The modern carrier serves as a symbol of American might abroad. (U.S. Navy)*

In chess, the queen is the most valuable member of the king's army. She has mobility, striking power, and flexibility. She can lead an attack or serve as the pivot of an aggressive defense. So long as she is in play, the opposing king is in jeopardy. Since 1944, the aircraft carrier has been like the queen in chess—the dominant piece on the maritime chessboard. As her aircraft have grown in sophistication and striking power, she has extended her range inland, challenging land-based aviation and air defenses for control of their skies.

But it hasn't always been so. The aircraft carrier in the U.S. Navy began as an experiment, quickly became a useful complement to the battleship, and then gradually assumed the battleship's role of smashing enemy ships with heavy ordnance. In World War II, fast Navy carrier task forces swept their opponents in the Imperial Japanese Navy from the sea. In the Atlantic, escort carriers were an integral part of an extended, bitter, but ultimately successful antisubmarine campaign. After World War II, however, the fast carrier task forces were almost completely retired because they did not carry nuclear weapons and because it wasn't clear that they could operate high-performance jet aircraft.

The need for conventional air support of ground forces and attacks on enemy lines of communication in the Korean War saved the carriers. So did the ability of carrier attack aircraft to drop nuclear weapons. There was, consequently, a renaissance in carrier construction in the 1950s.

A-4 Skyhawks pass over Yorktown *(CVA 10) during a stormy day at sea. "The Fighting Lady" launched her first strikes against an enemy in August 1943, during a raid against Japanese installations on Marcus Island, and planes from her deck also flew missions over Vietnam. Today, she serves as a floating museum in Charleston, South Carolina. ("USS Yorktown," R.G. Smith)*

A changing of the guard—(left to right) Langley *(CV 1),* Saratoga *(CV 3), and* Lexington *(CV 2) at anchor with other ships of the Pacific Fleet at Limon Bay in the Panama Canal Zone during 1933. The trio of flattops laid the foundation for the elevation of the aircraft carrier to a position as the U.S. Navy's capital ship, supplanting the battleships anchored behind them. National Museum of Naval Aviation)*

The beginning: the collier Jupiter (AC 3) *under conversion to the U.S. Navy's first aircraft carrier,* Langley (CV 1). *The carrier's flight deck was supported above the main deck by trusses; little else in the way of structure enclosed the hangar area. (Naval Historical Center)*

The size of Saratoga (CV 3) *in relation to* Langley (CV 1) *is apparent in this photograph of her bow taken while the ship was in dry dock at Hunter's Point, California, during the late 1920s. Converted battle cruisers,* Saratoga *and her sister* Lexington (CV 2) *possessed sleek lines and a top speed of more than 30 knots. (National Museum of Naval Aviation)*

New, larger ships with angled flight decks and multiple steam catapults took the place of the carriers built during World War II. The older, war-built carriers were modified to carry modern aircraft or converted to anti-submarine carriers, replacing the escort carriers used so extensively in World War II. By the 1970s, when carriers launched both airborne early warning and control aircraft and the high-performance, long-endurance F-14 Tomcat fighter, the conventional and nuclear-powered carriers of the U.S. Navy bore the most powerful mobile tactical air force on earth.

Beginnings

The roots of the carrier concept go back to the early years of U.S. Navy aviation—to discussions among aviators in Pensacola, Florida, before the United States entered World War I. But Navy personnel, including pioneering officers such as Kenneth Whiting and Henry Mustin, gained invaluable experience with actual aircraft-carrying ships in their work with the British Royal Navy during America's participation in the war. Senior officers supported their enthusiasm for the carrier in 1919, and the Secretary of the Navy pressed Congress to authorize the construction of purpose-built carriers. A cost-conscious Congress demurred, however, and the Navy only received funds to convert the collier *Jupiter* (AC 3).

Recommissioned as *Langley* (CV 1)—C for carrier and V for heavier-than-air craft—the ship its crew dubbed "the covered wagon" pioneered the techniques that would revolutionize naval aviation. Even with only a dozen aircraft, *Langley* and her air complement soon justified the cost of her

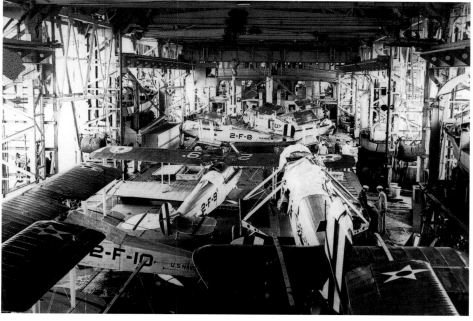

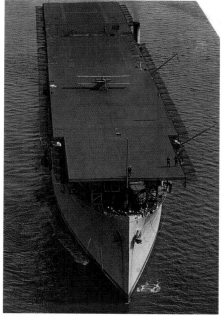

conversion and maintenance. By 1925, the newest American battleships were accurately firing 16-inch shells over 17 miles—beyond the horizon that the ship's spotters could see. At such a great range, aircraft spotted the ship's fire, at the risk of being shot down by enemy fighters. To forestall this, *Langley*'s fighters shielded the battle fleet's spotters and attacked "enemy" spotters in exercises, giving the battleships she supported a tremendous advantage over their opponents.

While *Langley*, her crew, and her air squadrons turned an experiment into operational reality, *Lexington* (CV 2) and *Saratoga* (CV 3), former battle cruisers converted to carriers, appeared. Compared to *Langley*, they were giants—their flight decks were 888 feet long and 105 feet wide, each displaced 36,000 tons, and both could steam at 34 knots. *Lexington* and *Saratoga* had enclosed flight decks—a feature abandoned in subsequent carriers—and both were heavily armed, with eight 8-inch guns for defense against cruiser attack and twelve 5-inch guns for defense against aircraft. For over a decade, *Lexington* and *Saratoga*

Top, left: Aircraft assigned to Fighting Squadron 2 crowd the hangar deck of Langley *(CV 1). The hangar deck also was used as a repair depot for floatplanes assigned to battleships and cruisers.* Langley *was too slow to keep up with the battle fleet, but her utility as a platform for experimentation paved the way for the carriers that swept across the Pacific in World War II. (Naval Historical Center)*

Above: Langley *(CV 1)—shown here with a Vought VE-7 on her flight deck—was forced by treaty tonnage limitations to be retired as a carrier in 1936 and converted to a seaplane tender to make way in the fleet for* Wasp *(CV 7). Japanese aircraft sank* Langley *in 1942 as she transported Army P-40 fighters to reinforce U.S. forces in the Far East. (National Museum of Naval Aviation)*

Lexington *(CV 2) transits the Panama Canal. Converted from a battle cruiser hull, the 888-foot carrier was the Navy's first fleet carrier, capable of launching substantial numbers of aircraft that posed a credible threat to opposing forces. (National Museum of Naval Aviation)*

113

Above: *Grumman F3Fs and Vought SBUs crowd the forward area of the flight deck of* Ranger *(CV 4), steaming behind* Lexington *(CV 2) and* Saratoga *(CV 3) in 1938.* Ranger *was the first ship built from the keel up as an aircraft carrier for the U.S. Navy. She also was the first capable of stowing aircraft in the overhead above her hangar deck. (U.S. Navy)*

Right: *Although aviation ships,* Lexington *(CV 2) (shown here) and* Saratoga *(CV 3) were built with armament that many cruisers would envy—four turrets with two 8-inch guns each, as well as twelve 5-inch guns.* Lexington's *8-inch turrets were removed in April 1942 and replaced with numerous light antiaircraft guns one month before the Battle of the Coral Sea, where she was sunk, the first U.S. carrier lost during World War II. (National Museum of Naval Aviation)*

Opposite, top: *Grumman F2F fighters overfly* Ranger *(CV 4). Because* Ranger *was slow and lacked armor protection, her World War II combat career in the Atlantic was limited, and she was assigned a permanent training role in 1944. ("Grumman F2Fs over* Ranger," *R.G. Smith)*

were the largest, fastest ships in the U.S. Navy, and they became the best known public symbols of carrier aviation before World War II. *Saratoga*, for example, was one of the main characters in the 1932 Metro-Goldwyn-Mayer film "Hell Divers."

Yet they were not regarded as optimal carrier designs. Launched in 1925 and commissioned in 1927, they carried only about twice as many aircraft as *Langley*. Moreover, their conversion to carriers proved very expensive, and together they used up almost half of the carrier tonnage

allowed the United States by the Washington Naval Treaty. Rear Admiral William A. Moffett, the first chief of the Bureau of Aeronautics, privately called them "white elephants" even as he defended them to Congress. Exercises with *Langley* suggested that more smaller carriers would actually better support the fleet. By the late 1930s, however, years of operating *Lexington* and *Saratoga* had shown that their great size had two unforseen benefits. They could operate aircraft even in heavy weather that shut down *Langley*'s flight deck, and they could carry the significantly heavier and more powerful new aircraft.

These advantages were not yet understood when *Ranger* (CV 4), the first ship designed from the keel up as an aircraft carrier, joined the fleet. Pilots wanted her to have a flush deck, free of obstructions. Navy designers could not get rid of the ship's island, but they did give *Ranger* funnels that were rotated to the horizontal over the water during flight operations. They also gave her a large hangar and flight deck (709 by 86 feet) for her size (14,500 tons). *Ranger*'s hangar was actually larger than that of the converted battle cruisers—510 by 56 feet compared to 393 by 68 feet.

Ranger lacked the protective armor and antitorpedo bulkheads of *Lexington* and *Saratoga*, and was therefore very vulnerable to attack. Therefore, during World War II she was not employed in the Pacific

The massive island structure of Saratoga *(CV 3) is accentuated in this view as the carrier squeezes through a lock of the Panama Canal on 24 April 1934. During World War II the Panama Canal made crucial differences in transit times for ships, enabling the later Essex-class carriers to swing into action rapidly after shakedown workups on the East Coast. (National Museum of Naval Aviation)*

Top, left: *Cooks make pies in the galley on board* Lexington *(CV 2). Then, as now, cooking for a crew and air group of a carrier was a job of back-breaking proportions. Though living conditions for a sailor at sea had improved markedly since the days of sail, high-quality food was (and is) a critical morale factor to the ship's crew. (National Museum of Naval Aviation)*

Top, right: *Sailors line up for inspection on the hangar deck of* Langley *(CV 1). Such formalities remain a regular fact of life for U.S. Navy sailors everywhere. (National Museum of Naval Aviation)*

against Japanese carrier forces, although she did launch strikes in North Africa and Norway. For most of the war, *Ranger* served as an aircraft transport, a training platform used to qualify pilots in carrier landings, and an experimental ship. But she was nevertheless the first modern Navy carrier, with characteristics, such as an open hangar deck, that were carried over into her successors. *Ranger* even introduced the cafeteria into shipboard life for enlisted sailors.

Maturity

The next carriers, *Yorktown* (CV 5) and *Enterprise* (CV 6), were both functional and beautiful. Authorized in 1933 to stimulate employment at Depression-era shipyards, both ships were launched in 1936. *Yorktown* was commissioned first, in September 1937, followed by *Enterprise* in

May 1938. These 20,000-ton ships set the pattern for the fleets of fast attack carriers of World War II with their high speed (33 knots), endurance (12,000 nautical miles at 15 knots), protection (4-inch side armor and horizontal armor one deck below the hangar deck), and large air groups (at first four, then five squadrons of eighteen aircraft each). These were the ships for which the Navy's aviators had been waiting.

Yorktown and *Enterprise* were followed in 1940 by the much smaller *Wasp* (CV 7), displacing 14,700 tons. *Wasp* replaced *Langley*, which had much of her flight deck cut away for her conversion to a seaplane tender. Though the size of *Ranger*, *Wasp* had a 20 percent greater steaming range, a larger flight deck and hangar, and flight deck catapults for launching armed bombers. She also stored about 20 percent more aviation gasoline, and her flight deck was 35 percent higher above the water. Like *Ranger*, *Wasp* did not carry torpedo planes, but she had seventy-two aircraft in her air group. *Wasp* also was comparatively slow (28 knots) and unprotected. But she carried the first deck-edge aircraft elevator in any U.S. carrier—a feature that would be carried over into the *Essex* (CV 9) class and every subsequent major carrier design.

Above: *A Vought SB2U Vindicator scout bomber rides the deck-edge elevator of* Wasp *(CV 7).* Wasp *was the first U.S. carrier to feature a deck-edge elevator, an installation featured on every fleet carrier since. The one-of-a-kind* Wasp, *the same size as* Ranger *(CV 4), included many improvements in design. Her combat career was cut short by torpedoes fired by a Japanese submarine during the Guadalcanal campaign. Her loss was desperately felt, leaving the Pacific Fleet with only three fleet carriers, soon to be two with the loss of* Hornet *(CV 8) in the Battle of Santa Cruz in October 1942. (U.S. Navy)*

Right: Lexington *(CV 2) in her death throes during the Battle of the Coral Sea in May 1942, after her air group teamed with* Yorktown's *air group to sink the Japanese carrier* Shoho. Lexington *was the first of only four U.S. fleet carriers lost in World War II, a tribute to the toughness of both their design and crews, and the effectiveness of their escorts and air groups. (National Museum of Naval Aviation)*

Hornet (CV 8), authorized in 1938, was a slightly improved *Yorktown*. Launched in 1940 and commissioned in October 1941, she was rushed into operation in time to carry Army Air Forces bombers on the famous Doolittle raid against Tokyo in April 1942. This was one of the momentous events in a year marked by intense carrier battles. By October 1942, of the three prewar carriers, only *Saratoga*, *Enterprise*, and *Ranger* remained afloat, the remainder having been lost in battle. Yet the Navy's carriers had fought their Japanese opponents to a standstill, which meant that Japan's carrier force would eventually be overwhelmed by the massive carrier armada—centered around *Essex* and her sister ships—then under construction in American shipyards.

Wartime Dominance

In 1940, Congress authorized the Navy to build a fleet that could command both the Atlantic and Pacific oceans. By the end of World War II five years later, three 45,000-ton carriers with armored flight decks were nearing completion; seventeen *Essex*-class fleet carriers, each displacing over 30,000 tons when fully loaded, had been commissioned, and another seven would be completed after the war; eight light carriers (converted light cruisers, designated CVLs) of 11,000 tons each were operating in the fleet; and seventy-seven escort carriers were operational, and an additional seven CVEs would be commissioned after August 1945. Compare these numbers with what Navy planners in the summer of 1940 thought they would have by the summer of 1945: fifteen fleet carriers, including those built before the war, plus five escort carriers. At war's end, the Navy even had two carriers on Lake Michigan, the coal-burning, side-paddle-wheel training carriers *Wolverine* (IX 64) and *Sable* (IX 81).

Several factors contributed to the great success of U.S. carrier task forces in World War II. The tremendous output of American shipyards and aircraft manufacturers allowed new ships and planes to reach the fleet in record numbers, and the Navy's system of very successful schools quickly graduated thousands of highly trained pilots, aircrewmen, mechanics, aircraft ordnancemen, and all the other specialists needed to man them. In addition, wartime refinements to the fledgling science of underway refueling expanded its scope to

Above: *The crew of* Yorktown *(CV 10) in formation for the* Essex-*class carrier's commissioning ceremonies on 15 April 1943. Scenes like this repeated over and over in the second half of World War II fulfilled Japanese Admiral Isoroku Yamamoto's prophecy of doom for his empire following the Japanese attack on Pearl Harbor. (U.S. Navy)*

Wolverine *(IX 64) pictured at Buffalo, New York, in August 1942 after her conversion to a training carrier for duty in Lake Michigan. The ship to her starboard is* Greater Buffalo, *which eventually became the second Great Lake carrier,* Sable *(IX 81). (National Museum of Naval Aviation)*

Opposite, bottom: *The* Sangamon-*class escort carrier* Santee *(CVE 29), seen here escorting a convoy to Casablanca in 1943, was a conversion of an oiler hull.* Santee *transported Army Air Force P-40 fighters to the North African invasion and later joined the jeep carrier groups that supported amphibious assaults in the Pacific. Severely damaged during the Battle of Leyte Gulf in October 1944, she lived to fight another day. (U.S. Navy)*

Above: Wasp *(CV 7) refuels* Buchanan *(DD 484) in August 1942, a month before the carrier's loss to a Japanese submarine. Destroyer escorts were essential to carrier task force operations in World War II, providing valuable antiaircraft and antisubmarine protection, and fishing downed aircrews out of the water. (U.S. Navy)*

Left: *On her way to war,* Ticonderoga *(CV 14) steams with a crowded deck off Hampton Roads, Virginia, in June 1944. The spacious decks of the* Essex-*class fleet carriers were able to carry about ninety aircraft—a decided blessing when swarms of Hellcats and Corsairs were needed to counter the kamikaze threat. (National Museum of Naval Aviation)*

include food and ordnance, which allowed carrier task forces to remain at sea for months at a time. This support, coupled with the high speed of CVs and CVLs, gave the carrier task forces the mobility they needed to take the strategic initiative away from Japanese defenders holding key islands. Thus, American commanders in the Pacific were able to pierce Japan's island defenses in a series of campaigns that stretched from the Gilbert Islands in 1943 to Okinawa, on Japan's doorstep, in 1945.

The centerpiece of U.S. carrier task force success was the *Essex*-class carrier and her ninety-plane air group. The ships were fast, sturdy, and able to absorb the many changes made to their electronic

Opposite: Cowpens *(CVL 25) during workups off the Virginia coast in July 1943. One of* nine Independence-*class light carriers built from* Cleveland-*class cruiser hulls,* Cowpens *and her sister ships ran with the fast carrier task forces and collectively magnified the number of F6F Hellcat fighters and TBF/TBM Avenger torpedo bombers available for action. The SBD dive bomber, which lacked folding wings, was short-lived as an aircraft in light carrier air groups. (U.S. Navy)*

Aircraft Carrier Classes:

CLASS NAME	NUMBER IN CLASS	COMMISSIONED	CLASS NAME	NUMBER IN CLASS	COMMISSIONED
Langley (CV 1)	1	1922	*Independence* (CVL 22)	9	1943
Lexington (CV 2)	2	1927	*Casablanca* (CVE 55)	50	1943–1944
Ranger (CV 4)	1	1934	*Commencement Bay* (CVE 105)	19	1944–1946
Yorktown (CV 5)	3	1937–1938, 1941	*Midway* (CVB 41)	3	1945–1947
Wasp (CV 7)	1	1940	*Saipan* (CVL 48)	2	1946–1947
Long Island (CVE 1)	1	1941	*Forrestal* (CVA 59)	4	1955–1959
Charger (CVE 30)	1	1942	*Kitty Hawk* (CVA 63)	4	1961–1968
Sangamon (CVE 26)	4	1942	*Enterprise* (CVAN 65)	1	1961
Essex (CV 9)	24	1942–1950	*Nimitz* (CVN 68)	10	1975–2008
Bogue (CVE 9)	11	1942–1943			

Opposite, top: Hellcats and Avengers on Monterey *(CVL 26) are readied for strikes against Japanese positions in the Gilbert Islands in late 1943. The* Independence-*class light carriers were a welcome addition of flight decks to the war effort, but their limitations precluded their continued front-line service in favor of fleet carriers in the postwar U.S. Navy. (Robert L. Lawson collection)*

Below: Lieutenant (jg) George H.W. Bush records data in the cockpit of his TBM Avenger torpedo bomber. Future President of the United States Bush flew combat missions from the deck of San Jacinto *(CVL 30). He was shot down near Chichi Jima in 1944 but was fished out of the water by a U.S. submarine. (U.S. Navy)*

Below, right: Camouflaged Hornet *(CV 12) steams off Okinawa in March 1945. The task groups centered on* Hornet *and her sister ships swept the skies clear of Japanese aircraft as they pushed across the Pacific and softened enemy island fortifications that awaited invading Marines. (U.S. Navy)*

equipment and antiaircraft batteries during the war. In March 1943 trials, for example, the fully loaded *Essex* steamed at just over 34 knots at a displacement of 34,300 tons. She had the speed of the old *Lexington*, the durability of *Saratoga*, and the maneuverability of *Enterprise*. By 1944, she and her sister ships also carried a formidable antiaircraft armament that included twelve 5-inch and as many as forty-four 40-millimeter guns, plus dozens of 20-millimeter guns along the gallery deck and around the superstructure.

The light and escort carriers were "mobilization" carriers, designed for wartime use only, and all were conversions of light cruisers. With a displacement near that of *Wasp*, *Independence* (CVL 22) and her eight sisters carried less than half as many planes—only twenty-four fighters and nine torpedo planes. Their hangars measured only 258 feet by 55 feet between their two aircraft elevators, less than one-third the area of *Essex*. But they were useful because they could steam at 31 knots and keep up with the larger carriers.

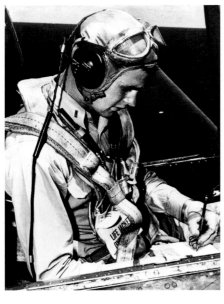

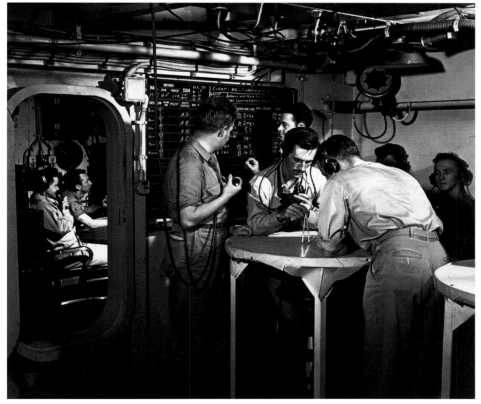

Left: *Personnel on board Nassau (ACV 16) maintain contact with her airborne planes and chart their progress during exercises at sea. These men played for keeps in May 1943 when Nassau launched strikes against Japanese forces on Attu in the Aleutian Islands. Nerve centers like these were increasingly important on Pacific Fleet carriers in 1944–1945 as they coordinated defenses against kamikaze attacks. (U.S. Navy)*

The first escort carrier was *Long Island* (CVE 1), a converted diesel-powered merchantman. She was small, with a flight deck only 418 feet long and a hangar deck only 98 feet long and 54 feet wide. However, it took only three months to turn her into a primitive carrier in 1941, and the Navy desperately needed flattops, so *Long Island* became the prototype for four classes of war mobilization escort carriers.

Above: *The unstoppable juggernaut of U.S. Navy carrier task forces in World War II spelled ruin for the Imperial Japanese Navy and empire. Carrier task forces were able to carry the war to the enemy in the face of furious opposition. The only serious threat to the carriers were the kamikazes, which in the end were soundly defeated. (National Museum of Naval Aviation)*

Sicily (CVE 118) pictured at sea around the time of the outbreak of the Korean War. Operating off the embattled peninsula, she provided her greatest service performing the yeoman duty that her predecessors pioneered during World War II—launching close air support missions against the enemy. (National Museum of Naval Aviation)

There are few atheists in foxholes—and on ships in combat at sea. Catholic mass is celebrated on board Hornet (CV 12). Spacious carrier hangar decks and forecastles accommodated large numbers of sailors for worship services. Carriers in the fleet today also include a small chapel for worship and meditation. (U.S. Navy)

Four ships of the *Sangamon* class were built on large tanker hulls; eleven of the *Bogue* class were like *Long Island* but with much larger hangars and more aircraft; fifty *Casablancas* were mass-produced and powered by reciprocating steam engines; and nineteen ships of the *Commencement Bay* class—eleven of which were built during the war— were the only escort carriers retained by the Navy after World War II. *Charger* (CVE 30), originally intended for the Royal Navy, was operated as a training carrier.

None of the escort carriers operated many aircraft. However, like the versatile Army vehicle they were often compared to, these "jeep" carriers performed a variety of missions, especially one nearly forgotten today but vital at the time—delivering as many as ninety aircraft at a time to their larger, faster cousins.

When the seventy-seven escort carriers commissioned during the war were not serving as aircraft transports, they fulfilled the roles foreseen for them by Navy planners before World War II: conducting antisubmarine patrol and convoy escort, attacking enemy shipping, and training. They also took on a new role by providing close air support for Marine Corps amphibious assaults, which the service had wanted since the mid-1930s. But these essentially unprotected ships also suffered at the hands of the enemy, and six were lost.

Overall, however, war experience demonstrated that a larger carrier was a better carrier. Size brought improved sea-keeping capability, fuel and ammunition storage, spaces for crew and aircraft, defensive protection against bombs and torpedoes, a large and powerful steam plant, and room for increasing amounts of essential electronic gear, particularly

radars and radios. To gain these advantages, in 1942 the Navy proposed building a class of very large, armored-flight-deck carriers capable of holding as many as 128 fighters and bombers. This was the beginning of the *Midway* class.

The *Midways* were 968 feet long with a beam of 136 feet, making them too wide to fit through the Panama Canal. The flight deck was 924 feet long and 113 feet wide; the hangar deck measured 692 by 95 feet. Each had three large elevators—two in the flight deck itself and one at the deck edge, to port, as in Essex. All were fast. At a loaded displacement of 58,600 tons, for example, *Midway* (CVB 41) steamed at 33 knots.

But the design of the three ships of the *Midway* class was based on wartime experience. As a result, they had three weaknesses. First, their initial air groups were so large that it was difficult to easily and quickly

The forward flight deck of Bennington (CV 20) sags from damage inflicted by a typhoon in June 1945. During the 1950s, many of the Essex-class carriers were fitted with smooth, closed-in "hurricane bows" to preclude similar damage. (U.S. Navy)

The flight deck of the ill-fated Franklin (CV 13) seen in the Brooklyn Navy Yard in New York City in 1945. Two 550-pound bombs hit Franklin on 19 March 1945, causing a conflagration among parked aircraft on the flight deck and in the hangar deck that killed 742 of her crew. Franklin steamed to New York City under her own power for repairs but the war ended before she could be returned to active service. (U.S. Navy)

put together aircraft of different types for special missions. Second, the armored flight deck had to be closer to the water than that of the *Essex* class for stability. Third, they were not designed with jet aircraft in mind.

At war's end, the Navy had a huge and very successful carrier fleet. Carriers of one kind or another had been active in the Atlantic, Pacific, Mediterranean Sea, and Indian Ocean. Their aircraft had been at the critical center of the fight against both the Japanese and German navies, and the better ships—especially *Essex* and her sisters—had more than justified the resources put into them. But their great success was about to be marred by several new developments.

The Initial Postwar Years: The Carrier Threatened

The whole face of naval warfare changed after World War II. The development of nuclear weapons seemed to make all naval task forces, both carrier and amphibious, obsolete in one stroke since any force that assembled to mass its firepower would be a prime target for nuclear attack. Early jets lacked afterburners, and therefore required a long runway to get into the air. They might be catapulted off a carrier's deck, but then they had to be recovered back aboard, and their high landing speeds made safe recovery problematic. Also the strategic confrontation with the Soviet Union came to the forefront. The USSR had no surface

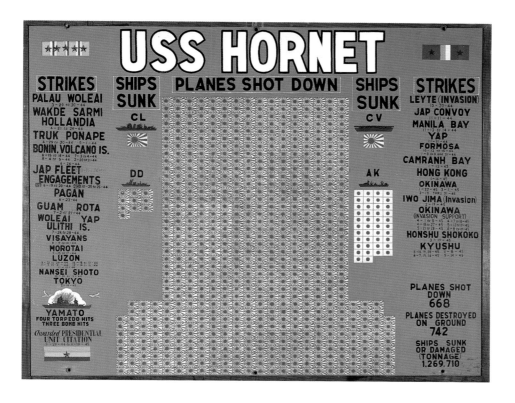

navy to speak of, and aircraft carriers could not effectively attack a nation spread across most of Eurasia. It seemed that the strategic emphasis had shifted from the Navy to the Air Force and the Army.

But what almost drove the carrier from the seas was the advent of early U.S. nuclear bombs—very large devices weighing nearly 12,000 pounds. The Navy responded to the development of such bombs by issuing a requirement for a carrier bomber capable of lifting them. The plane built to meet that requirement was the AJ-1 Savage, ordered in 1946 and first delivered to the fleet in the fall of 1949. The loaded weight of this aircraft was nearly 53,000 pounds—over three times the weight of the TBF/TBM Avenger which flew from the *Essex*-class carriers in World War II and much heavier even than the B-25s that had flown from *Hornet* in the famous Doolittle raid. Initially, *Midway* and her sisters were the only carriers that could launch and recover these large, powerful planes.

Midway *(CVA 41) at sea in 1954. The three* Midway*-class carriers, which incorporated lessons learned from fiery experience in World War II, were built with armored flight decks, heavy armament, and space enough to handle more and larger aircraft. (National Museum of Naval Aviation)*

Twin-engine North American AJ-1 Savage nuclear-strike aircraft assigned to Composite Squadron 6 are readied for launch from Coral Sea *(CVB 43) in 1950. All three* Midway*-class battle carriers were retained in the Atlantic during the Korean War because their nuclear strike capability was required to support NATO in deterring Soviet hegemony in Europe. (National Museum of Naval Aviation)*

An F4U-4 Corsair assigned to Fighter Squadron 24 taxis into takeoff position in front of a pack of other Corsairs and AD Skyraiders on the flight deck of Philippine Sea (CV 47) off Korea. Many of the Essex-class carriers that served in the Korean War were commissioned shortly before or after the end of World War II and replaced combat-scarred veteran sister ships in the fleet. (Roland H. Baker, Jr.)

Ashtabula (AO 51) refuels Essex (CVA 9) in the South China Sea on 20 January 1955. The World War II veteran Essex retains her straight deck, which created more than a few interesting moments during flight operations with the F9F Cougar aircraft arrayed on her deck. Modernized with angle decks, Essex-class carriers served through the Vietnam War, with Lexington (AVT 16) operating as the Navy's training carrier into the early 1990s. (U.S. Navy)

Once the development of the Savage was approved, the Navy began to design a very large carrier around it. Before World War II, carriers had been built as ships; aircraft size and weight influenced, but did not determine, a carrier's design. But in the nuclear age, aircraft began to influence the size of the carriers from which they would operate.

The carrier designed for nuclear war in 1946 was United States, a 79,000-ton behemoth capable of cruising at 33 knots, with an aviation fuel storage capacity for her nuclear bombers twice that of the Essex-class. An expensive investment for striking Soviet targets, a mission that the administration of President Harry S. Truman believed could be more economically executed by Air Force bombers, United States was canceled in April 1949, a week after her keel was laid. This action triggered a bitter and intense conflict between the Air Force and the Navy over nuclear warfare and the control of military aviation. The Navy had to be content with a program to modify some of its Essex-class carriers so that they could participate in a nuclear strike.

By the time the Korean War broke out in 1950, most of the carrier force from World War II had been placed in reserve or scrapped, leaving only three Midway- and five Essex-class ships at the center of the Navy fleet. But the war demonstrated the need for the carrier, and six Essex-class ships were recommisioned. By war's end in 1953, eleven of them, along with five escort carriers and one light carrier, had served in Korean waters. Midway and her sisters did not enter the war, but they did begin carrying nuclear bomb casings (the nuclear cores were kept under Atomic Energy Commission control) in the fall of 1950, when it appeared that the war in Korea might spread into China and even lead to a fight between the U.S. and the USSR in Europe.

Above: *Centered around* Wasp *(CVS 18) in the Mediterranean in 1961, Task Group Bravo displays the antisubmarine warfare might of the hunter-killer groups that evolved from the escort carrier U-boat hunters of World War II. Many* Essex-*class ships, both straight- and angled-deck, served as antisubmarine carriers during the 1950s and 1960s. The increase of nuclear-powered submarines in the Soviet navy diminished the effectiveness and utility of these groups, and their high operating cost led to their phase-out in 1974 in favor of the "CV Concept," in which attack carriers began operating ASW aircraft in the same air wing. (U.S. Navy)*

Left: Antietam *(CVA 36) was the first U.S. carrier to be modified with an angled deck. Installed in 1953, the offset of* Antietam's *angle was not as great as that of angled decks later incorporated on board other* Essex-class *carriers.* Antietam *did not receive most of the modernization received by her sister ships and ended her service in 1963 as the Navy's training carrier in the Gulf of Mexico. (U.S. Navy)*

Unmodified, the *Essex*-class could carry early jet fighters such as the F9F Panther and F2H Banshee, but faster and larger fighters and attack aircraft were entering the equation. Fortunately, the Royal Navy, which had borrowed U.S. Navy carrier aircraft and operating techniques during World War II, returned the favor in the 1950s by developing and sharing the innovations needed to handle the newer, faster jet aircraft. These included the steam catapult, a fixture on U.S. Navy carriers to the present day, the angled deck, and the automatic landing light system to assist pilots in recovering on board the carrier. All were essential for the

Right: Tripoli (LPH 10) was one of seven Iwo Jima-class, purpose-built amphibious assault ships optimized for launching assault helicopters from sea to shore. The ships served off Vietnam and in numerous crises for two more decades. The last of the class, Inchon (MCS 12) now serves as a mine-countermeasure support ship in the Naval Reserve Force. (U.S. Navy)

Above: An HRS-2 assigned to Marine Helicopter Transport Squadron 163 lifts a load of cargo from Sicily (CVE 118) off Korea. Flattops were naturals in the role of amphibious assault ships; their decks could easily be adapted to routine helicopter operations. (National Museum of Naval Aviation)

The advent of Harrier jets and a diverse fleet of transport and attack helicopters have made amphibious assault ships like Saipan (LHA 2) potent supplements to the U.S. Navy's fleet of supercarriers. In the tradition of World War II escort carriers, the ship's aircraft can provide air support for amphibious assaults against a hostile shore. Saipan and her sisters embark a force of more than 1,900 Marines. (U.S. Naval Institute)

operation of increasingly powerful jet aircraft, and the Navy moved in the mid-1950s to equip as many ships of the *Essex*-class as possible with the British innovations. This resulted in fourteen *Essex*-class carriers capable of handling modern jet aircraft and tactical nuclear weapons. Another seven carriers of the *Essex* type became antisubmarine carriers to replace the *Commencement Bay* escort carriers employed in this role after World War II. Three other ships of the *Essex* class were converted into helicopter assault ships, forerunners of the modern amphibious assault ships (LHA and LHD) that support Marine expeditionary forces around the globe.

At this time, tactical nuclear weapons that did not weigh nearly as much as those built during and right after World War II were also being developed. This meant that carriers could now launch more smaller attack aircraft, each of which could carry either a tactical nuclear weapon or several conventional bombs, and that any new carriers would not have to be as large or as expensive as *United States*. More importantly, it meant that any new carriers would not threaten the nuclear deterrent role of the Strategic Air Command.

The First Cold War Supercarriers

Early in 1951, Congress authorized a smaller version of the canceled *United States*. With a design displacement (60,000 tons) that was not quite 25 percent less than that of the *United States*, the new ship— *Forrestal* (CV 59)—had more flight deck area because she was equipped with an angled deck. *Forrestal*'s hangar deck (740 feet by 101 feet), however, was only about three-fourths the area of that designed for *United States*. *Forrestal*'s air group was also smaller, though she carried half again as much fuel for her aircraft. Her mission was as much

conventional as nuclear. Her speed, endurance, complement, and protection were about equal the standards set by *United States*.

Forrestal and her successors were designated attack aircraft carrier (CVA), reflecting their offensive nuclear mission. The size and cost of these ships were dictated by their air wings, the heart of which were the largest heavy attack aircraft to ever operate from a carrier deck. *Forrestal* and her sister ships—*Saratoga* (CVA 60), *Ranger* (CVA 61), and *Independence* (CVA 62)—were followed by four ships of the *Kitty Hawk* class, which featured some flight deck and defensive armament modifications. In addition

FJ-3 Fury fighters assigned to Fighter Squadron 21 fly near their roost, Forrestal *(CVA 59), in 1956. The first of the "super-carriers,"* Forrestal *was the first U.S. carrier built with an angled deck and designed from the beginning to operate jet aircraft.* Forrestal *and her sisters were valued for their extensive flight-deck acreage; ironically, with the advent of the* Nimitz-*class carriers, they came to be referred to as "small-deck" carriers in the 1980s. (National Museum of Naval Aviation)*

to *Kitty Hawk* (CVA 63), the other ships were *Constellation* (CVA 64), *America* (CVA 66), and *John F. Kennedy* (CVA 67).

With the new force of supercarriers under construction, plans were made to modernize the three *Midways*. *Midway* and *Franklin D. Roosevelt* (CVA 42) were withdrawn from service in 1954 and given angled decks, steam catapults, and the landing light equipment. Like the modernized *Essex*-class ships, both had many of their antiaircraft guns removed. *Coral Sea* (CVA 43) was not modernized until 1957.

The possibility of building a nuclear-powered aircraft carrier had been seriously considered inside the Navy since 1946, and the Joint Chiefs of Staff had approved a requirement for such a ship in 1951. A nuclear-powered carrier had two advantages over a conventionally powered one—great endurance and the ability to operate almost constantly at high speed. Unfortunately, nuclear power plants were expensive to install and refuel. Once the basic *Forrestal* design had proven successful, however, Navy engineers began planning to fit existing Westinghouse reactors into it. The result was the new *Enterprise* (CVAN 65).

Her eight reactors generated enough steam (280,000 shaft horsepower) to drive *Enterprise*'s full load displacement of over 80,000 tons at 33 knots. Built with a futuristic island structure and the same flight deck layout as *Kitty Hawk*, *Enterprise* was commissioned in November 1961. But the cost of building her was almost twice that of *Kitty Hawk*, and thoughtful critics of nuclear propulsion wondered whether such a high initial investment was worth it. In August 1964, the Navy set out to prove that it was. *Enterprise*, in company with the nuclear-powered cruisers *Long Beach* (CGN 9) and *Bainbridge* (CGN 7), steamed around the globe—32,600 nautical miles in sixty-four days—without refueling.

The reliability and endurance of these three ships were proof enough for the Navy.

Nevertheless, *Enterprise* remained one-of-a-kind. But the force of which she was a part—built around her, the four *Forrestals* and four *Kitty Hawks*—dominated the ocean chessboard. In the early 1960s, this force was a major part of the nation's nuclear deterrent. However, once nuclear-powered ballistic missile submarines began to come on line, the air wings on these carriers shifted to more conventional strike missions. The new carriers, equipped with modern aircraft, up-to-date radar and other electronic equipment, plus passive defenses against torpedoes, formed the center of mobile, powerful task forces. They would prove their worth in Southeast Asia.

Vietnam and the Contemporary Carrier Force

At the end of World War II, U.S. carrier task forces—which had already destroyed the Japanese fleet—were bombing Japan proper. Their performance showed that carriers had strategic potential as bases for mobile air forces. Twenty years later, carriers again showed that their air groups could play a major role in attacking targets on land, this time in Vietnam. They operated there for almost nine years.

The future of the carrier seemed assured. But what carrier was best—large, nuclear-powered ships or smaller carriers, perhaps with vertical short takeoff and landing (VSTOL) aircraft? As the large force of *Essex*-class ships aged, and the war in Vietnam took the funds that might have been used to modernize them, answering this question became imperative. The desire to deploy as many carriers as possible pushed the Navy and successive

The towering height of a modern supercarrier is evident in this photograph of aviation ordnancemen inspecting and transferring ordnance from the bomb farm to the flight deck on board Kitty Hawk *(CV 63). The ability to quickly arm and launch aircraft from virtually anywhere on the globe is the essence of carrier aviation. (U.S. Navy)*

Above: *Barbara Bush christens* George Washington *(CVN 73) at Newport News Ship-building on 21 July 1990, as her husband, President George H.W. Bush, looks on. In this nuclear age, carrier christening and commissioning events are few and far between, and attract huge crowds of dignitaries and well-wishers who recognize the might that these ships represent. (U.S. Navy)*

Left: *A heavy crane at Newport News Ship-building places the island of* Ronald Reagan *(CVN 76) into position on the flight deck of the Navy's newest nuclear-powered carrier.* Reagan's *island differs from those of her predecessors in the addition of an outboard weapons elevator, new main and aft masts, and updated antennae arrangement. (John Whalen)*

Above: Midway *(CV 41)—seen here in 1989—*
went through two extensive modification
periods during her service and was forward
deployed to Japan for two decades. The first
commissioned and the last decommissioned
of her class, Midway *was retired in 1992 and*
is planned for display as a museum in San
Diego, California. (U.S. Navy)

Above, right: *A view from the island of* Carl
Vinson *(CVN 70) showing flight deck crewmen*
preparing A-6 Intruders, A-7 Corsairs, a C-2
Greyhound, and an EA-6B Prowler for flight
during operations in the Pacific Ocean in
May 1986. All carriers currently in U.S. Navy
service have launched aircraft into combat
from their flight decks, mostly since 1991
against targets in Iraq. (U.S. Navy)

Independence *(CV 62) and* Kitty Hawk
(CV 63) pictured at Naval Station Yokosuka,
Japan, in the early 1990s. Once a base for
Imperial Japanese navy ships that were the
target of U.S. Navy carrier planes, Yokosuka
is home to a forward-deployed carrier, an
important strategic fixture in the Far East.
(U.S. Naval Institute)

presidents toward smaller, less expensive ships. But the need for endurance
and operational experience in Southeast Asia pushed in the opposite direction. Complicating the debate was the growing reach of the land-based,
missile-firing bombers of the Soviet navy. The U.S. Navy's counter to the
bombers was a heavy, missile-armed fighter—the F-14 Tomcat. But only
the largest carriers (*Forrestal* and her successors) could launch and recover
the thirty-ton F-14.

The development of more efficient, large nuclear reactors meant
that the next class of carriers—*Nimitz* (CVN 68) and her sisters—would
have the high endurance of *Enterprise* yet a more reasonable initial
cost. *Nimitz* and her eight sisters have flight decks 1,092 feet long and
over 250 feet wide. Powered by two nuclear reactors providing steam to
four turbines, these carriers, ranging in displacement from over 91,000
tons to over 100,000 tons, are just as fast as the older *Forrestals*. The
hangar deck of *Nimitz* is almost 700 feet long, over 100 feet wide, and
over 26 feet high from deck to overhead. Each of the ship's four elevators can lift over 100,000 pounds. Because the ships of this type are
nuclear-powered, all the fuel they carry—about 3.3 million gallons—is
available for their aircraft or for their gas turbine-powered escorts.

These huge ships at first carried a large composite air wing of F-14
fighters, A-6 Intruder and A-7 Corsair II attack aircraft, E-2C Hawkeye airborne early warning and control planes, electronic warfare and antisubmarine aircraft, and helicopters (for antisubmarine warfare and search and
rescue). However, more multimission aircraft operate from their flight decks
today. Almost 3,000 officers and sailors are in each air wing, and about
another 3,000 staff each ship. These carriers hold over 2,500 tons of ordnance, more than half again as much as the *Forrestals*. This is a more significant figure than it might first appear because modern weapons, such as
the Joint Direct Attack Munition, are far more accurate than weapons used
in the war in Southeast Asia. Put another way, each warhead carried by a
Nimitz-class carrier has the striking power against land targets of tens or

even hundreds of bombs dropped by attack aircraft a generation ago. *Nimitz*-class carriers also have multiple air and surface search radars, satellite dishes, digital links to their aircraft and escorts, computers for planning combat missions, torpedo countermeasures, NATO Sea Sparrow missile launchers, and other defenses against low-flying cruise missiles.

During the Cold War, six of the eight older supercarriers were modernized, entailing the replacement of catapults, modification of tactical data systems, rebuilding of engines, and installation of new radars and air defense weapons. The end of the Cold War, along with the construction of the latest *Nimitz*-class ships, shortened the lives of most of these aging combatants. For example, four of the carriers whose air wings fought in Desert Storm in 1991 have been decommissioned. Thus the *Nimitz*-class carrier is the centerpiece of today's carrier battle group.

Constellation (CV 64) is the second of three oil-fired Kitty Hawk-*class supercarriers whose flight deck arrangement set the standard for all subsequent carriers through the nuclear-powered* Nimitz *class. The ninth* Nimitz-*class carrier,* Ronald Reagan *(CVN 76), is scheduled to replace* Constellation *in 2003. (U.S. Navy)*

The Future of the Carrier in the U.S. Navy

The Navy has considered alternatives to the large, nuclear-powered carrier since the 1960s. Through the Cold War years, the large carrier always came out ahead of smaller alternatives when their operating costs per quantity of ordnance placed on target were compared. That is, the supercarrier was more efficient at attacking targets over her projected lifetime. But the Navy seriously examined a number of alternatives, from ships double the size of *Nimitz* to small waterplane area twin-hull carriers with roughly the same displacement as the *Nimitz*

Carrier Air Wing 1 aircraft pictured in the hangar bay of Theodore Roosevelt *(CVN 71) in March 2001. Packing aircraft into the limited space below the flight deck is akin to assembling a large jigsaw puzzle, though this one involves multimillion-dollar pieces. (U.S. Navy)*

135

Abraham Lincoln *(CVN 72) forms the center of Carrier Battle Group Foxtrot, at sea in July 1991. The obituary of such forward-deployed carrier battle groups has been written many times over many decades by critics, only to be withdrawn each time the President asks during a crisis: "Where is the nearest carrier?" (U.S. Navy)*

The Combat Direction Center on board Kitty Hawk *(CV 63) blends sophisticated radar equipment with primitive record keeping. The sailor logging aircraft information with a grease pencil quickly develops the skill of writing backwards, though computers will render his services obsolete in the future. (U.S. Navy)*

type. There were even studies of a semisubmersible carrier that could resist the blast of a tactical nuclear weapon.

There were three serious alternatives to the existing carrier force. The first depended upon the development of an effective VSTOL attack aircraft—a plane that could lift a heavy bomb load but would not require either the large catapults or the powerful arresting gear units that dictate the size of the *Nimitz*-class ships. Designers have been trying to produce such an aircraft for forty years, and they haven't yet accomplished it. Though the AV-8B Harrier II used by the Marine Corps has proven successful in operating from small, conventionally powered assault ships, it does not possess the capabilities of contemporary jet strike fighters on carrier decks.

The second serious alternative to the existing carrier force would be one built around missile carriers—large tanker-like ships whose long-range weapons would attack land targets and also protect them from air and missile attack. Accompanying such ships would be a carrier one-third the size of a *Nimitz* with airborne early warning and control aircraft and anti-submarine helicopters. This small antisubmarine carrier would resemble the converted *Essex*-class antisubmarine carriers of the 1950s. Such a ship could employ long-range unmanned aerial vehicles for scouting and for battlefield reconnaissance. The Navy has not built these ships for two reasons. First, "smart" missiles are still too expensive to buy in numbers large enough to replace the ordnance carried by aircraft. Second, unmanned aerial vehicles have yet to meet the goals of low cost, operational versatility, and high reliability set for them by the military services.

The third major alternative that has been studied is a mixed force of large and small carriers. In 1972, the Chief of Naval Operations proposed developing what came to be called a "sea control ship" to take the place of the aging *Essex*-class antisubmarine carriers. The idea was to use the large carriers in high threat areas and the sea control ships in places where the danger was less—as convoy escorts, for example, or as "presence" ships to show the flag. In 1974, however, Congress refused to fund the prototype, and the idea was shelved. The small carrier had the same drawbacks that escort carriers had in World War II, sacrificing protection, endurance, bomb and fuel capacity, sustained high speed, and aircraft complement in order to hold down initial construction cost.

The large, nuclear-powered aircraft carrier is still the queen of the naval chessboard. With her air wing, she is versatile, powerful, and mobile. The development of a new generation of "smart" munitions has made her even more effective, and her supporters say that improvements in missiles and unmanned aerial vehicles will just add to her strengths. At the same time, the Navy is committed to reducing the lifetime operating costs of future carriers by reducing the crew of the carrier and the staff of the embarked air wing. Today, Navy carriers are floating air bases, and each ship has to house, feed, and support nearly 6,000 sailors. The key to future carrier design—and carrier survival—will be successful efforts to reduce drastically the number of men and women who make that floating air base the most powerful concentration of mobile tactical firepower known on earth.

Flight Deck

Flight Deck

Lieutenant Commander Rick Burgess, USN (Ret) and Hill Goodspeed

Flight deck personnel scramble away after disengaging an SBD Dauntless from the arresting wires on board Nassau *(ACV 16) in World War II. Once the aircraft is pushed forward, another will slam down onto the deck and begin the cycle again. (U.S. Navy)*

This was a skillet!—a frying pan!—a short-order grill!—not gray but black, smeared with skid marks from one end to the other and glistening with pools of hydraulic fluid and the occasional jet-fuel slick, all of it still hot, sticky, greasy, runny, virulent from God knows what traumas . . . consumed in detonations, explosions, flames, combustion, roars, shrieks, whines, blasts, horrible shudders, fracturing impacts, as little men in screaming red and yellow and purple and green shirts with black Mickey Mouse helmets over their ears skittered about on the surface as if for their very lives . . . , hooking fighter planes onto the catapult shuttles so that they can explode their afterburners and be slung off the deck in a red-mad fury with a kaboom! that pounds through the entire deck—a procedure that seems absolutely controlled, orderly, sublime, however, compared to . . . what is known in the engineering stoicisms of the military as "recovery and arrest." To say that an F-4 was coming back onto this heaving barbecue from out of the sky at a speed of 135 knots . . . that might have been the truth in the training lecture, but it did not begin to get across the idea of what [one] saw from the deck itself, because it created the notion that perhaps the plane was gliding in. On the deck one knew differently! As the aircraft came closer and the carrier heaved on into the waves and the plane's speed did not diminish and the deck did not grow steady—indeed, it pitched up and down five or ten feet per greasy heave—one experienced a neural alarm. . . .This is not an airplane coming toward me . . . and it is not gliding, it is falling, a fifty-thousand pound brick, headed not for a stripe on the deck but for me—and with a horrible smash! it hits the skillet, and with a blur of momentum as big as a freight train's it hurtles toward the far end of the deck—another blinding storm!—another roar as the pilot pushes the throttle up to full military power and another smear of rubber screams out over the skillet—and this is normal!— quite okay!—for a wire stretched across the deck has grabbed the hook on the end of the plane as it hit the deck tail down and the smash was the rest of the fifteen-ton brute slamming onto the deck, as it tripped up, so that it is now straining against the wire at full throttle, in case it hadn't held and the plane had "boltered" off the end of the deck and had to struggle up into the air again. And already the Mickey Mouse helmets are running toward the fiery monster. . . .

—TOM WOLFE, THE RIGHT STUFF

Above: *An F-4 Phantom II assigned to Fighter Squadron 151 departs the "pointy end" of* Midway *(CV 41) for a mission aloft. The two objects protruding from the carrier's forward flight deck are designed to catch the bridle that connected the plane to the catapult. Today, a tow bar attached to the landing gear engages the catapult to launch all current U.S. Navy fixed-wing carrier aircraft. (National Museum of Naval Aviation.)*

Above, left: *Time exposure traces the flight path of an F/A-18 Hornet as it launches from the bow of* Kitty Hawk *(CV 63) during night flight operations in March 2001. The water-cooled, hydraulically lifted jet blast deflector visible in the foreground protects aircraft and crew from the jet's exhaust. (U.S. Navy)*

Pages 138–139: *Crewman instinctively turn their heads as an F4U Corsair assigned to Bombing Fighting Squadron 83 launches from the deck of* Essex *(CV 9) in 1945. A carrier deck fully engaged in flight operations, then and now, is a noisy, fast-moving arena. (U.S. Navy)*

Aviation boatswain's mates align the nose gear of an F/A-18 Hornet with the catapult shuttle on board Independence *(CV 62), steaming in the Taiwan Straits in March 1996. Hundreds of people are required to smoothly operate the flight deck of a modern aircraft carrier. (U.S. Navy)*

An A-6E Intruder assigned to Attack Squadron 115 "traps" on board Midway (CV 41) in the Sea of Japan in August 1984. The tailhook having snagged the arresting wire, the plane will now slam into the deck in what some have called a controlled crash. The trap is the defining event that separates naval aviation from all other flying. (Robert L. Lawson)

Flight deck personnel move an F6F-3 Hellcat assigned to Fighting Squadron 16 on the flight deck of Lexington (CV 16) in December 1943. Tow tractors later were welcome additions to the flight deck, but human muscle power is still a requisite for safe flight-deck operations. (U.S. Navy)

There is nothing quite like flight operations on the deck of an aircraft carrier. It is unlike any airfield in the world, one that keeps pace with the busiest of airports, with an aircraft either landing or taking off every minute. The difference is that this airfield encompasses only four-and-one-half acres of real estate and moves. Of course there are other differences about this unique floating platform, all of which have been developed over time since Eugene Ely's Curtiss pusher rolled down the wooden deck of Birmingham (CL 2) and took flight in November 1910.

The distinguishing feature of an aircraft carrier—the flight deck—was the product of evolution. The crude experimental platforms used by Ely were impractical, as were later platforms built atop gun turrets of battleships. The British Royal Navy was the first to develop practical carrier aviation, commissioning the first operational aircraft carrier. HMS Furious featured a flight deck forward in place of a gun turret and operated wheeled aircraft as well as seaplanes. Later she was modified with an aft flight deck (with no arresting gear), an aircraft elevator, and tracks around the superstructure on which aircraft could be shuttled between decks. HMS Argus, converted from an Italian liner in 1918, was the first flush-deck carrier, complete with a pilothouse that retracted on an elevator during flight operations lest it interfere with takeoffs and landings. HMS Eagle, converted

from a battleship and commissioned in 1920, featured a flush deck and the starboard island superstructure that would characterize most subsequent aircraft carriers. HMS *Hermes*, similar to *Eagle*, was the first carrier built from the keel up.

The basic design of an aircraft carrier had taken shape by the time *Langley* (CV 1) was converted from a collier in 1922 and commissioned as the U.S. Navy's first aircraft carrier. The "Covered Wagon"—as she was called because of her appearance and position operating astern of the fleet's battleships—was not a mighty warship, but she was the ancestor of the greatest warships ever built.

Langley's rectangular deck prototyped the shape of the wooden flight decks of the Navy's carriers through the 1940s. The *Essex*-class carriers that formed the centerpiece of the World War II carrier task forces introduced an American innovation, the deck-edge elevator, that reduced the risks of flight decks being fouled by elevators stuck in a lowered position. Deck-edge elevators became standard on the "supercarriers" of the *Forrestal*-class and their successors.

World War II revealed the weaknesses inherent in the wooden deck. Although light and easy to repair, it proved too vulnerable to explosives, particularly when the Japanese began to unleash the kamikazes in 1944. The British carriers boasted armored decks, which restricted the number of aircraft that could be stored in the hangar deck, but allowed them to withstand direct hits from kamikazes. The three *Midway*-class carriers were the first U.S. Navy carriers to feature armored decks.

The British development that more than any other would define the modern aircraft carrier was the angled deck. The aft two-thirds of the flight deck—the landing area—was aligned offset to port, allowing aircraft that missed the arresting wire to take off again without having to clear a pack of parked aircraft. The angled deck also allowed a carrier to recover

The "greenie board" in the ready room of Fighter Squadron 41 on board Theodore Roosevelt (CVN 71) during Operation Desert Storm in 1991. Such matrices track the proficiency of each squadron pilot in carrier landings, noting the wire he caught on each landing—the "three wire" being the sought-after mark. (U.S. Navy)

Exhausted personnel grab a moment of sleep on the flight deck of Enterprise (CV 6) during a break in flight operations in 1943. During combat, the constant stress and danger of operating a flight deck around the clock takes its toll on the strength of the crew, as sleep becomes a rarity. (U.S. Navy)

aircraft while simultaneously launching aircraft off the forward flight deck. After the *Essex*-class carrier *Antietam* (CV 36) was modified with an angled deck in 1953, it became standard on all subsequent carriers.

Cats

Early aircraft were small and light enough to take off from a carrier aided only by the relative wind generated by the forward motion of the ship. As aircraft weight and payloads increased in greater proportion than the length of the deck, catapults became necessary under certain conditions, especially decks crowded with parked aircraft. The first catapult tests dated to the days of Naval Aviator Number One, Lieutenant Theodore G. Ellyson, prompted by the requirement for seaplanes to launch from ships of the line. It proved relatively simple to adapt them to carrier decks.

Langley was fitted with two catapults—primarily for launching floatplanes—that eventually were removed. The Navy's second carrier, *Lexington* (CV 2), was fitted at first with one mechanical flywheel catapult; the single flywheel catapult on board her sister, *Saratoga* (CV 3), was replaced with two hydraulic ones in 1944. The two *Yorktown*-class ships were equipped with two hydraulic catapults on the bow and a third on the hangar deck, the latter for use in the event of a crowded flight deck. Launching aircraft athwartships, hangar deck catapults were also incorporated into *Wasp* (CV 7), *Hornet* (CV 8), and some ships of the *Essex* class, but rarely used. Hydraulic catapults had become the standard by the 1950s, and they left a lasting impression on any pilot who ever experienced one, especially in the cockpit of an early jet. In the mid-1950s steam catapults capable of launching heavy jet aircraft came on line aboard U.S. flattops, and they remain so today. Electromagnetic catapults are being developed to equip the next generation of aircraft carriers.

Top, left: *Shrouded in a cloud of steam, a yellowshirt directs an F-14 Tomcat onto the starboard catapult on the flight deck of* Abraham Lincoln *(CVN 72). (National Museum of Naval Aviation)*

Above: *An S-3B Viking captured on film just before (above) and after (below) the firing of a waist catapult on board* Carl Vinson *(CVN 70) at the signal of the catapult officer. The culmination of the efforts of dozens of personnel, the decision to launch finally rests with a junior officer, who with the lowering of his arm triggers a process that sends an aircraft from a standstill to flying speed in a matter of seconds. (David Peters)*

Arresting Gear and Barricades

From the beginning of carrier aviation, imaginative methods of landing had to be devised. Some proved comical from the modern perspective, including the practice of equipping early Royal Navy aircraft with leather straps. Upon touchdown, deck crewmen would race to the wings and grab the straps to halt the aircraft. The method proved highly unsatisfactory,

An early arresting gear configuration, designed to snag longitudinal wires that slowed the aircraft enough for personnel to grab the wings, is shown between the landing gear of a Vought VE-7. This design was abandoned in favor of cross-deck arresting gear. (National Museum of Aviation)

Crewmen fold the wings on a T4M torpedo bomber of Torpedo Squadron 1B on the flight deck of Lexington (CV 2) during the late 1920s. Standard procedure in the days of straight-deck carriers was to fold the wings of an aircraft almost immediately after it recovered on board. It was then spotted forward in a pack of aircraft whose size grew as more aircraft successfully trapped. (National Museum of Naval Aviation)

and the Royal Navy developed a system consisting of longitudinal wires to guide the aircraft's landing gear along the deck. Coupled with a flight deck elevated like a ramp, the wires slowed the aircraft enough for deck crewmen to grab thè wings and bring it to a halt. British carriers used this arresting system until 1935.

The commissioning of *Langley* marked the debut of cross-deck arresting gear, an innovation of the U.S. Navy still in use today. At first, both longitudinal and cross-deck arresting gear traversed the flight deck of the Navy's first flattop. Metal "fiddle bridges" supported the ends of the longitudinal wires to a prescribed height above the flight deck, allowing hooks located on the axle of the aircraft's landing gear to catch them on landing. However, these fiddle bridges frequently punctured the tires of the aircraft during recovery.

Langley's cross-deck wires were supported above the flight deck by a number of even more hazardous devices, so-called Ely Elements, known

The arresting gear arrangement of Lexington (CV 2) shows both longitudinal and cross-deck arresting wires. The design of the cross-deck wires does not markedly differ from arresting gear in use on modern aircraft carriers. (National Museum of Naval Aviation)

by carrier crews as "pies" because of their shape. When an aircraft's tailhook snagged the wire, the resultant tension released the pies, which hurled violently in various directions and could injure or kill a deck crewman. Surviving motion pictures taken on board the ship capture these moments of mayhem.

Eventually, the longitudinal gear was removed, but the resulting necessity of a braking system in the cross-deck gear was needed to create drag in order to stop the aircraft. A system of mechanical brakes and weights was only partially successful because it brought the aircraft to an abrupt halt and forced the pilot to desperately apply full power to avoid being dragged back before the tailhook could be disengaged. The gear had no means for compensating for off-center landings, and could as easily drag the aircraft over the side as stop a landing rollout. Hydraulic cross-deck gear became standard, and remains so to this day. A number of arresting wires were rigged across the aft end of the flight deck, giving the aircraft several chances for its hook to snag a wire. The hydraulic systems also allowed tension to be controlled and compensated for off-center landings.

The Navy's modern aircraft carriers are equipped with four arresting wires, compared to the twelve wires that were used on straight-deck carriers of old. The third wire (counting from stern to bow) is the aim

In one of naval aviation history's classic photographs, Lieutenant Commander Forrest Sherman pilots a Boeing F4B-3 to a landing on board Saratoga (CV 3). *Sherman eventually rose to the post of Chief of Naval Operations. (U.S. Navy)*

Flight deck control personnel monitor the parking of aircraft on board John C. Stennis (CVN 74) *in March 1998, using a model of the carrier's flight deck. Moving aircraft about a tightly congested flight deck requires a high degree of skill, discipline, and experience, as well as planning. (U.S. Navy)*

Above: *The barricade is rigged on the flight
deck of* America *(CVA 66) in 1970. Air
department personnel regularly train to
swiftly rig the nylon barricade to safely
recover disabled aircraft. (U.S. Navy)*

Above, right: *An F9F-5 Panther assigned to
Fighter Squadron 72 is brought to a stop by a
barricade rigged on the flight deck of* Tarawa
*(CVA 40) in August 1953. The barricade is
designed to stop an aircraft while causing
only minimal damage and keeps an expensive
piece of equipment from going over the side.
(U.S. Navy)*

point for a landing pilot, and makes for the safest landing because it
provides the optimum clearance between the hook and the flight deck as
the aircraft passes over the extreme aft end of the flight deck, or "ramp."
Arresting wires today include a detachable cross-deck pendant that bears
the impact of the tailhook. These pendants are discarded and replaced
normally after 100 "traps." A failure of a cross-deck pendant can mean
the loss of an aircraft and crew. An additional danger is the possibility
of deck crewmembers losing legs as a pendant snaps under the strain of
the tailhook.

Another part of a carrier's arresting gear is the barricade. The
net-like barricades were designed for straight-deck carriers and used
routinely. Unfolded to prevent recovering aircraft—whether landing too
long, or unimpeded by a failure of its landing gear or the cross-deck
pendants—from plowing into the pack of aircraft parked forward on the
deck, the barricades were lowered to allow aircraft to taxi forward into
the pack.

On today's angled-deck carriers, barricades are not routinely necessary, but occasionally must be rigged to save an aircraft that suffers from

a landing gear malfunction or other emergency. The purpose of the barricade now is more oriented toward saving the aircraft's crew and their expensive aircraft than toward protecting the aircraft parked on the bow. Carrier air departments routinely practice rigging the barricade, with the goal of having it ready within two minutes.

A landing signal officer flees the LSO platform aboard Cabot *(CVL 28) in an attempt to escape an oncoming F6F Hellcat during World War II. Every crew member on the flight deck of an aircraft carrier is a potential target of an out-of-control aircraft, which makes it one of the most dangerous places on earth. (U.S. Navy)*

Paddles and Shirts

When it comes to the business of carrier aviation, the pilot and airplane are only part of the successful equation, for scattered around the flight deck are scores of men and women who orchestrate this most demanding of evolutions. As tradition has it, one day during flight operations on board *Langley* an aircraft was having difficulty coming aboard. Observing the happenings on deck, Commander Kenneth Whiting grabbed the white hats from the heads of two sailors and waved them in the air to guide the errant aviator to a successful landing. This was the birth of the landing signal officer (LSO).

149

LANDING AN AIRCRAFT *on a moving ship is a daunting proposition even when everything proceeds as it should. However, when something goes wrong, catastrophic and sometimes deadly results can occur in a matter of seconds. On 21 October 1961, Lieutenant (jg) John T. Kryway made a hard landing on the flight deck of* Franklin D. Roosevelt *(CVA 42). The impact caused the right wheel of his F8U-1 Crusader to break away, and the magnesium landing gear strut quickly ignited due to friction with the flight deck. To make matters worse, the tailhook separated from the fuselage upon snagging an arresting wire, allowing the flaming aircraft to barrel down the flight deck.*

This amazing sequence of photographs was taken in a matter of seconds. With the airplane nearing the end of the deck, Kryway reached over his head for the handles that triggered his ejection seat. As his doomed aircraft took a fiery plunge into the Atlantic, he was propelled away from the aircraft, his parachute deploying before he hit the water. The pilot survived with only minor injuries, and within moments was plucked from the rough seas by a rescue helicopter.

In earlier times, Kryway would have had no recourse but to ride the aircraft over the side. Thanks to ejection seat technology and his own reflexes, he survived the harrowing ordeal. (U.S. Navy)

LSOs still have the ultimate say on whether a plane lands or not, but it was only into the 1950s that they physically waved aircraft aboard. Perched on a platform on the aft section of the flight deck, they held paddles akin to tennis rackets, waving their arms back and forth and leaning to and fro in a set of prescribed signals—too high, too low, too fast, too slow. A sharp motion across his chest—the much sought-after "cut" signal—indicated that a pilot could cut his engine for he was in the groove for a safe recovery.

The advent of jet aircraft with high landing speeds proved the end of the traditional task of LSOs signaling aircraft, for technology had outpaced the speed of human reaction. The Fresnel lens system, a series of lights visible from the air that signals the pilot whether he is on the correct glide slope for a safe recovery, now accomplishes the corrective functions once exclusively the domain of "Paddles." However, each air wing and squadron has a designated LSO, who can be found on the platform during carrier operations. All designated naval aviators, modern LSOs maintain

Above: *The Fresnel lens, an arrangement of colored lights on the port deck-edge of the carrier that automatically signals attitude and course corrections to an approaching aircraft, has replaced the paddles used by LSOs. Pilots "call the ball" over the radio when they have the light in the middle in sight. (U.S. Navy)*

Above: *Landing signal officers communicate with pilots coming aboard* Theodore Roosevelt *(CVN 71) in February 1987. The LSO platform of modern aircraft carriers is often crowded because of the expertise required to guide aboard widely varying types of aircraft. Given the importance of hearing every minute variation in an approaching plane's engine and seeing the smallest variation in bearing or altitude, the LSOs are the only personnel allowed on the flight deck without protective headgear. (U.S. Navy)*

Above, right: *Lieutenant Eric Rasmussen (left) and Lieutenant Commander Steve Brennan watch an F/A-18 Hornet make a successful trap on the flight deck of* America *(CV 66) in 1991. Visible on the monitor on the equipment behind them is the view from the flight deck camera that captures all recoveries on film. (Robert L. Rasmussen)*

Right: *A boatswain's mate briefs greenshirts, photographers, and aircraft mechanics on board an escort carrier off the coast of San Diego, California, during World War II. Safe and smooth carrier flight operations require strong, experienced leadership and closely choreographed coordination. (U.S. Navy)*

contact with their fellow fliers via radio, offering guidance based upon what they see and hear. And clasped in one of their hands is a device known as the "pickle," which consists of a trigger that when released signals the pilot to abort a recovery and to go around again for another try.

To step onto a flight deck in the midst of flight operations is to be immersed in another world. A legion of humanity, each bedecked in different colors symbolizing their duties and masked by goggles and helmets, maneuver amidst the whine and roar of bellowing man-made beasts and steam wafting almost mystically over the deck with each firing of the catapult. Each color symbolizes a different function and represents the carefully prescribed order so necessary in the dangerous environment of a carrier flight deck. With rubber hoses slung over their shoulders, those in purple pump thousands of pounds of jet fuel into thirsty aircraft. Those in blue spot airplanes around the crowded flight deck and operate the

The "Air Boss" heads an assembly of air department personnel arrayed in front of the island on the flight deck of Coral Sea (CV 43) in July 1989, displaying the rainbow of colorful jerseys worn by flight deck personnel. (U.S. Navy)

Left: Ghostly figures amidst the steam of the catapult, an aviation boatswain's mate (second from left) on board Carl Vinson (CVN 70) directs an aircraft to the catapult track while another (right) displays a dialed readout of gross takeoff weight for verification by the aircraft's pilot. Launching an aircraft requires the closely coordinated teamwork of many individuals. (David Peters)

Opposite, bottom: Safety checkers give the "thumbs up" to the catapult officer (right) for the launch of an F/A-18 Hornet assigned to Strike Fighter Squadron 87 from the flight deck of George Washington (CVN 73). Full-time attention to safety is an uncompromising requirement of carrier flight operations. (U.S. Navy)

155

Afterburners blaze against a blast deflector as an RA-5C Vigilante assigned to Reconnaissance Heavy Attack Squadron 6 prepares to launch from the deck of Nimitz (CVAN 68) during the early 1970s. The blinding flashes of after-burners add to the chaos of night operations on a carrier flight deck. (National Museum of Naval Aviation)

Aviation ordnancemen carry an AIM-7 Sparrow air-to-air missile to a waiting F/A-18 Hornet on the flight deck of Carl Vinson (CVN 70) in March 1999 during Operation Southern Watch. Safely handling ordnance on the hazardous flight-deck requires absolute attention to procedures to avoid fires like those that devastated three carriers during the Vietnam War. (U.S. Navy)

aircraft elevators, while the red shirts handle weapons, loading bombs and sophisticated guided missiles onto airplanes heading into harm's way. Among the duties of the green shirts are crouching beneath roaring jets and hooking them up to the catapults that will send them from a standstill to flying speed in seconds, and sprinting out onto the flight deck after each landing in order to ensure the proper functioning of the arresting gear. Plane captains dressed in brown strap pilots into their aircraft and

Above: *An aviation boatswain's mate attaches a catapult bridle to an EKA-3B Skywarrior being readied for launch from the flight deck of* John F. Kennedy *(CVA 67) in June 1972. Men and women tasked with this job must work in close quarters with aircraft engines and moving control surfaces, as well as hot catapult tracks and jet blast deflectors. (U.S. Navy)*

Far left: *Airman Gerald Gaffney, a member of the Aviation Fuels Division on board* John F. Kennedy *(CV 67), hauls a fuel hose to a waiting aircraft during Operation Desert Shield in December 1990. "Grapes," a nickname derived from the purple shirts they wear, are responsible for the safe refueling of aircraft on the hazardous flight deck. (U.S. Navy)*

Left: *Aircraft handlers stand ready with tie-down chains to secure aircraft to pad-eyes on the deck of* Kitty Hawk *(CV 63) in 1987. Chains keep aircraft from rolling on a pitching carrier deck. (U.S. Navy)*

bid them good luck before launch, while no aircraft moves around or leaves the deck until a figure in yellow, using prescribed hand signals, tells the pilot to do so. Those in white ensure quality control and safety, and just like your neighborhood doctor in his white lab coat, the seagoing medical personnel on the flight deck wear white jerseys, standing by for the worst. And overseeing it all, perched in the highest tower atop the carrier's island superstructure, is the Air Boss.

Epitome of Teamwork

A carrier flight deck is many things to many people given one's perspective. For the carrier pilots flying at altitude, it is a postage stamp, and the realization that they must plant a 50,000-pound machine on it, especially at night, is a daunting one no matter how many times they have done it. For those working on deck, it is an atmosphere that permeates all senses—the searing heat of jet blast, the ever-present aroma of burning fuel, the violent roar of engines at full power as aircraft thunder off the catapult, and the constant movement of people and machines in a relatively tiny space. It is all these things, but for those fortunate enough to witness flight operations at sea firsthand, the most striking realization is the fact that it is a demonstration of teamwork and professionalism that makes the most difficult of endeavors look routine.

Left: *A catapult officer on board* America *(CV 66) signals the crew of an F-14A Tomcat assigned to Fighter Squadron 102 during Operation Desert Storm. Hand signals take the place of voice communications for most personnel on the noisy flight deck. (U.S. Navy)*

Above: *The "air boss" and his deputy, the "mini boss," direct flight operations from the tower of* Carl Vinson *(CVN 70), an area known as Primary Flight Control or "Pri-Fly." The safe and efficient conduct of all operations on a carrier's flight deck weighs heavily on the shoulders of the air boss. (David Peters)*

Opposite: *Cast in a golden hue, an aircraft director uses flashlights to signal a pilot on the flight deck of* John F. Kennedy *(CV 67) in October 1999. Use of light on a carrier deck is carefully controlled for safety purposes to enhance night vision. (U.S. Navy)*

A master chief aviation boatswain's mate briefs his subordinates prior to the commencement of flight operations on board George Washington *(CVN 73) in the Gulf of Mexico in March 1999. The sweat and toil of personnel like these, a blend of seasoned experience with young men and women barely out of high school, are factors that make successful flight deck operations. (U.S. Navy)*

A Breed Apart

A Breed Apart

Barrett Tillman

Pages 160–161: *The sting of a pair of Strike Fighter Squadron 192 F/A-18 Hornets is visible beneath their wings during a training flight in February 1990. Eleven months after this picture was taken, the "Golden Dragons" found themselves playing for real over the sands of Iraq. (Tom Surbridge)*

Above: *The pilot's eye view from the front of an A-7 Corsair II reflected in his face shield, Commander John Leenhouts leads his wingmen during a training flight. He retired from the Navy as a captain in 2000, holding the distinction of having logged more carriers arrested landings than anyone—1,645. (National Museum of Naval Aviation)*

For almost nine decades, they have arrived at Naval Air Station Pensacola, Florida, converging on the "Cradle of Naval Aviation" to take the first steps toward a dream. Though the natural technological evolution of aviation has replaced open cockpit biplanes with thundering jet engines and whirling helicopter rotors, the impetus for young men and women to aspire to serve their nation in naval aviation remains the same. Each possesses a thirst for adventure and sense of duty, as well as the desire to wear the wings of gold, signifying membership in an elite group within military flying. Not all of them make it, for the rigorous physical, mental, and psychological demands placed on the aspirant are designed to weed out those found

Above: *A newly commissioned ensign completes the rite of passage that has transformed him into a naval officer, receiving his first salute from his Marine drill instructor after completing Officer Candidate School at NAS Pensacola, Florida. The DI finishes commissioning day a richer man than he began it, for tradition holds that a newly commissioned officer must bestow a silver dollar on the one who renders him his first salute. (U.S. Navy)*

Below: *Their rigorous training completed, a group of newly commissioned ensigns receive their wings of gold from Captain William F. Halsey at NAS Pensacola, Florida, during the late 1930s. (National Museum of Naval Aviation)*

Returning from a combat mission, an SB2C-1C Helldiver of Bombing Squadron 1 passes astern of Yorktown (CV 10), its extended tailhook indicating that it will soon enter the pattern for recovery on board the ship. From this perspective, with the flight deck a relatively small area surrounded by miles of ocean, it is no wonder that naval aviators liken a carrier landing to planting an airplane on a postage stamp. (U.S. Navy)

wanting. It has to be that way, for naval aviators, flight officers, and aircrewmen are a breed apart.

In the early days, while their fellow fliers plied their trade from landing fields, only naval aviators routinely operated aircraft from water. And, from Eugene Ely's Curtiss Pusher of 1910 to the twenty-first century's F/A-18E/F Super Hornet, landing an aircraft on a moving ship has been the most demanding task that humans have routinely conducted. It is far safer now than it was half a century ago, but it is still extremely difficult. Not everyone can do it. Perhaps that's why the very name is different—other air arms produce pilots while the U.S. Navy produces aviators. Naval aviation is in the realm of precision; it always has been and always will be.

The first generation of naval aviators was drawn to flying for a variety of reasons. Unfortunately, few of them recorded their motivation for posterity, but some logical deductions can be made. Certainly they were risk takers, both physically and professionally. U.S. naval aviation began when the flying machine was barely seven years old and very much an unproven concept. Consequently, the airplane's naval use remained conjectural at best.

Unquestionably the one trait that characterized early aviators was an independent spirit. Apart from the novelty and excitement of flying, it was obvious that airmen necessarily would operate alone or in very small

Aviation's earliest days involved a certain degree of showmanship, and given the accident rate, the general public viewed those who climbed into a cockpit as a little bit crazy. An unofficial part of the curriculum for prospective naval aviators at NAS Pensacola, Florida, during World War I was to climb out onto the wing of an N-9 trainer without the benefit of a parachute. (National Museum of Naval Aviation)

Bedecked in the leather flight gear and scarves traditionally associated with aviators during the years between the World Wars, pilots of Fighting Squadron 5 gather around the squadron skipper for a briefing on the flight deck of Lexington *(CV 2). (National Museum of Naval Aviation)*

numbers. It was wholly different from the entire history of naval warfare, as ships by their nature require dozens or hundreds of men working toward a common goal. The aviator, literally above it all, was largely on his own between takeoff and landing. That sense of independence appealed to innovative young men seeking responsibility beyond their years and seniority.

Many of naval aviation's future leaders risked their professional lives by applying for flight training. Before World War I, submarines were barely acknowledged as viable weapons, let alone airplanes. Ships of the line had constituted sea power for centuries, and the fundamental concepts remained little changed by advances in ship construction, propulsion, or ordnance. By taking warfare into the third dimension, airmen posed a tacit

Top: *Members of the first aviation detachment to participate in winter fleet maneuvers in Guantanamo Bay, Cuba, in 1913. Among the missions flown was testing the ability of an aircraft to detect a submerged submarine from the air. The commander of the submarines during these exercises was a young officer named Lieutenant Chester W. Nimitz, while the pilot on many of the flights was Lieutenant Jack Towers. Thirty-one years later, Vice Admiral Towers served as deputy Commander in Chief of the U.S. Pacific Fleet under Admiral Nimitz. (National Museum of Naval Aviation)*

Above: *Lieutenant Marc A. Mitscher pictured during his tour as commanding officer of NAS Miami, Florida, during World War I. The aggressive commander of Task Force 58, he led the fast carriers to victory in the Pacific during World War II. (National Museum of Naval Aviation)*

Right: *John Henry "Jack" Towers pictured at the controls of a Curtiss pusher during his flight training under the tutelage of Glenn Curtiss at Hammondsport, New York, in 1911. Towers held a certain stature among his fellow fliers in that he was the Navy's second aviator. He eventually wore four stars and became the first naval aviator ever ordered to command the U.S. Pacific Fleet. (National Museum of Naval Aviation)*

challenge to the status quo—never a good risk in any bureaucracy, especially a naval one.

However, a crop of eager young officers emerged during the Great War and its immediate aftermath. Brash to the point of irreverence—they derided the battleship navy as the Gun Club—they possessed the zeal of true believers. Yet, they were a contradictory lot that included visionaries and thinkers like John Towers, popular leaders like Marc Mitscher, organizers like Arthur Radford, and instinctive fighters like Jocko Clark. As a group, they tended to be tough-minded, goal-oriented, and bright. A sample of pioneer aviators reveals that most graduated in the upper half of their classes at the Naval Academy in Annapolis, Maryland. Among the early leaders, Ernest King graduated fourth of 67 in 1901, Ralph Davison ranked third of 177 in the Class of 1916, and Forrest

Sherman was second among 199 in 1918. But academic success was not the only indicator of tactical competence, for Mitscher was 108th of 131 in the Class of 1910 and William F. Halsey finished forty-third among his sixty-two classmates in 1904.

Above all, what the early aviators possessed was that intangible spark common to all true believers, an abiding faith in their message and in themselves. Such were their convictions that they adopted a symbol of their uniqueness, one worn over their hearts to signify the fact that they were men of the air—the famous Navy wings of gold, which many have sought and only a select few have earned. The centerpiece of these wings is a shield, an instrument of battle from time immemorial that evokes the warrior ethos. Naval aviation is a profession of arms, and thus many of its greatest contributions to our nation have been set against the backdrop of war.

While the vast majority of the men who won their wings during naval aviation's first five years were career officers, the war in Europe unleashed a patriotic fervor that filled the ranks with individuals from other walks of life. In the skies over places like Pensacola, Florida, and Hampton Roads, Virginia, these men demonstrated the same adventurous spirit as their predecessors. Unique among them were the men of the First Yale Unit, wealthy Ivy Leaguers who even before the formal declaration of war purchased their own seaplane and conducted flight training on Long Island, New York, and in Palm Beach, Florida. Inducted into the Naval Reserve Flying Corps, they formed the nucleus of naval airmen who fought

Top: *Lieutenant Commander Arthur W. Radford reads in his cabin on board* Saratoga *(CV 3) during his time in command of Fighting Squadron 1B, the famed High Hats. Like other officers who as admirals led the U.S. Navy to victory in World War II, Radford received his first command experience at the helm of a fleet squadron. (National Museum of Naval Aviation)*

Above: *William F. "Bull" Halsey, pictured as commanding officer of NAS Pensacola, Florida, in 1936. Representing the "Johnny-come-lately" class of aviators, Halsey received his wings at the age of fifty-two. His colorful personality and fighting spirit made him one of the more popular fleet commanders of World War II, particularly during the first six months of the war and in the dark days of the Guadalcanal campaign. (National Museum of Naval Aviation)*

Left, top to bottom: *The wings of gold signify inclusion in the unique fraternity of naval aviation. Differing little from the original design that appeared in 1917, the pilot's wings are the oldest in naval aviation. The designation of Naval Flight Officer (NFO) replaced that of Naval Aviation Observer in 1965, but not until 1968 did the NFO wings begin to appear on uniforms. The wings of gold awarded to enlisted aircrew were adopted in 1958, replacing silver ones of a different design first issued during World War II. (Al Audelman)*

Above: *Lieutenant Artemus Gates (left) and Lieutenant (jg) Robert Lovett served as members of the First Yale Unit during World War I. Assigned to fly with a French pursuit squadron, Gates was shot down in aerial combat in October 1918 and held as a prisoner of war by the Germans. Lovett served as a key figure in the formation of the Northern Bombing Group, which flew missions against German submarine bases in Belgium. Gates later held the post of Assistant Secretary of the Navy for Air and Undersecretary of the Navy during World War II and Lovett was appointed Secretary of Defense by President Harry S. Truman in 1951. (National Museum of Naval Aviation)*

the Great War. Their ranks included men like Curtiss Read, one of four brothers who volunteered to fly for the Navy, and the first wearer of the wings of gold to fall in France. "Have orders for the front any day," he penned in his diary shortly before his death. "[It] would be a climax if I should have the privilege of making the greatest sacrifice."

Two decades later, on the eve of World War II, the U.S. Navy possessed most of the knowledge and many of the tools necessary to prosecute a war at sea, but the battleship was still the centerpiece of the fleet. In the fall of 1939 only six carriers operated in the Atlantic and Pacific Fleets, and the aircraft on those flight decks included obsolescent biplanes. However, extremely competent professionals flew them. Both commissioned and noncommissioned officers flew Navy and Marine aircraft, and they were highly proficient at their trade.

With his own battle line rusting in the mud of Pearl Harbor, Hawaii, in the wake of the 7 December attack, new Pacific Fleet commander Admiral Chester W. Nimitz turned to submarines and aircraft carriers to prosecute the war against the Imperial Japanese Navy. The subsequent engagements of Coral Sea, Midway, and Guadalcanal conclusively proved the ascendancy of the aircraft carrier as an essential weapon of the Pacific war. The combat leadership of relatively junior officers was crucial in carrier air groups—men like Wade McClusky and Dick Best of *Enterprise* (CV 6); Wally Short, Joe Taylor and Max Leslie of *Yorktown* (CV 5); and Paul Ramsey, Weldon Hamilton, and Bob Dixon of *Lexington* (CV 2). All were "trade school" products of Annapolis who welded their squadrons into capable, efficient organizations dedicated to sinking the enemy.

Above: *Ensign Curtiss Read, designated Naval Aviator Number 83 in August 1917, died in February 1918 when the French Donnet-Denhaut seaplane he was flying plunged into the waters off NAS Dunkirk, France. (National Museum of Naval Aviation)*

Above, left: *While the pilot of an SBD Dauntless dive bomber of Bombing Squadron 6 makes some final notes on his navigation board, his gunner climbs into the rear cockpit before launch from* Enterprise *(CV 6). The Dauntless was the most important carrier aircraft during the first year of the war, playing a key role in the four great carrier battles of 1942. (U.S. Navy)*

Left: *Aircrewmen relax in a ready room on board* Ticonderoga *(CV 14) the night before an air strike against Manila on 4 November 1944. sharing the camaraderie of squadron life.The dawn will bring another flight over enemy territory, and the chance thar some of them will not return. (U.S. Navy)*

Opposite, top: *Bundled against the elements, an enlisted aircrewman stands at the ready behind a Lewis machine gun in this posed photograph taken in December 1918. Weighing some twenty pounds and capable of firing 500 rounds per minute, the Lewis gun was the standard Allied aerial machine gun during World War I. The circular pan visible atop the gun contained the ammunition, and expended shell casings were ejected into the bag hanging below it. (U.S. Navy)*

Page 170: *Aviation cadets at one of the preflight schools established at colleges and universities throughout the United States scale ropes during physical training. The first step toward wings of gold, preflight school transformed civilians into military men, instilling the discipline required in the cockpit. (U.S. Navy)*

While American industry began turning out millions of tons of combatant vessels and thousands of airplanes, the Naval Air Training Command produced individuals to man them. Tens of thousands of young men were screened for aviation duty, and those who hoped to win their wings endured rigorous specialized training. At Preflight School, they left behind their civilian ways as they were indoctrinated into the ways of the military. Classroom instruction in such subjects as navigation and radio code, coupled with daily marching and running the obstacle course, hardened them both physically and mentally. Those who survived entered the actual flying phase of their training, learning the basics in open-cockpit biplanes, and gradually advancing into flying formation and guiding an aircraft through unforgiving skies using only the instruments in the cockpit. Operational training in fighters, dive bombers, torpedo planes, patrol bombers, blimps, or transport aircraft ensued, and for those would-be tailhookers, there remained the rite of passage in the form of their first carrier landings on the training carriers *Wolverine* (IX 64) and *Sable* (IX 81) in Lake Michigan.

Others joined the ranks of naval aviation's most unheralded fliers: the combat aircrewmen. These enlisted and noncommissioned "airdales" served as radiomen, gunners, observers, and flight engineers. Whether in carrier aircraft, patrol planes, floatplanes, or transports, the "white hats" and chiefs were an integral part of the naval aviation team almost from the start. The aircrewmen were the "backwards dancers" of tactical air power, riding into battle facing aft, prepared to defend their pilots from enemy interceptors. One who embodied the devotion and courage of combat air-crewmen was Aviation Radioman Second Class Mike Brazier, who flew in a Torpedo Squadron 3 TBD Devastator during the Battle of Midway. His plane riddled by fire from Japanese Zero fighters, Brazier put up a valiant fight until severely wounded. En route back to the carrier *Yorktown*, he somehow managed to change the coils in the airplane's radio receiver, enabling his pilot, Chief Aviation Pilot Bill Esders, to guide the aircraft to

Top, left: Boston Red Sox slugger Ted Williams pictured after joining the ranks of naval aviation. The famed ballplayer eventually received his wings and a commission in the Marine Corps. Though he did not see action during World War II, he flew combat missions in Korea as a recalled reservist. (AP/Wide World Photos)

Above: *In a daily ritual that occurred at training bases throughout the United States during World War II, students at NAS Pensacola, Florida, check the flight schedule for the day, hoping not to draw an instructor with a reputation for being particularly tough on his students. Those whose turn it was to fly drew their parachutes from the shelf to the left of the chalkboard. (National Museum of Naval Aviation)*

Below: *A flight student awaits the final comments of his instructor about a recently completed training hop. An "up" meant he passed and could move on to the next flight in the syllabus. A "down" meant failure and the need to repeat the flight in order to master a particular procedure or maneuver. (U.S. Naval Institute)*

Top, left: *Lieutenant Edward H. "Butch" O'Hare achieved lasting fame as the first naval aviator to receive the Medal of Honor during World War II after shooting down five enemy bombers and damaging a sixth as he single-handedly defended* Lexington *(CV 2) during an air attack in February 1942. Also a pioneer in night carrier operations, he was killed in action near the Gilbert Islands during the first successful night intercept by U.S. Navy carrier aircraft on 26 November 1943. (Robert L. Lawson collection)*

Top, right: *An enlisted aircrewman loads his twin .30-caliber machine gun with a belt of ammunition in the rear cockpit of an SBD Dauntless dive bomber of Composite Squadron 22. Sitting partially exposed in their cockpits and dueling with enemy fighters that on most occasions attacked from the rear, gunners lived hazardous lives. (Boeing)*

Above: *The camera captures a ball-turret gunner in a TBM-3 Avenger of Torpedo Squadron 83, his hand at the ready on the pistol grip that will trigger his machine guns. (U.S. Navy)*

a ditching point closer to American ships. Once in the water, Esders pulled Brazier from the cockpit. He had been hit nine times, two of them 20mm explosive projectiles that blew the flesh from the lower part of both legs. He died in his pilot's arms.

Carrier aviation came of age during World War II, and thousands of young men entered the realm of precision, the arena of carrier landings that provided constant challenges. It was particularly demanding on pilots assigned to light and escort carriers with narrower flight decks than those of the larger fleet carriers. Most challenging of all was night flying, advocated by daring, progressive officers such as Captain Daniel Gallery and Commanders William I. Martin and Turner F. Caldwell. Their pioneering work in proving carriers as nocturnal platforms for both offense and defense set a standard that the world's other navies could not match. However, the conventional wisdom was reportedly expressed by a sailor on board *Independence* (CVL 22) watching Caldwell's night carrier air group during flight operations. "Man was never meant to fly, no how," observed the white hat. "And if he was meant to fly, he was never meant to fly off no boat. But if he was meant to fly off a boat, he dang sure wasn't meant to do it at night!"

Night operations cost the Navy and Marine Corps some of their finest pilots. Commander Edward H. O'Hare, recognized as the U.S. Navy's first fighter ace of World War II, was an early advocate of using carrier-based "bat teams" to intercept enemy bombers. He died proving his concept off the Gilbert Islands in November 1943, leading a mixed division of F6F Hellcat fighters and a radar-equipped TBF Avenger. However, with experience came mastery of the complex endeavor, and eventually full-time night flying squadrons operated with safety records comparable to their daytime counterparts. The expansion of night flying had a particular effect in the Atlantic, where escort carrier hunter-killer groups hounded German U-boats around the clock, eventually helping to reduce Allied convoy losses to near zero.

172

Aside from precision flying to "get aboard the boat," carrier aviators also had to be accomplished navigators and instrument pilots. These skills were simply to get them to the target, where precision gunnery and ordnance delivery defined their purpose in life, namely to destroy enemy ships and aircraft.

Though dive-bombing probably originated with the British Royal Air Force in World War I, certainly the U.S. Navy and Marine Corps prior to World War II perfected it. It was by far the best way to hit a difficult moving target such as an agile warship making 30 knots or more in open water. Horizontal bombing accomplished very little against shipping throughout the war, but dive-bombing single-handedly won the epic Battle of Midway. The stellar performance by Lieutenant Richard H. Best, skipper of *Enterprise*'s Bombing Squadron 6 embodied the proficiency of naval aviators in this trade. Previously a fighter pilot, he foresaw the Pacific war and decided he could make more of a contribution in scout bombers. On 4 June 1942 he flew two strikes, leading his squadron in sinking the Japanese carriers *Akagi* and *Hiryu*. Two launches, two bombs, two hits, two landings, and his career was over. Best was medically retired with tuberculosis following the battle.

Perhaps the best description of dive-bombing comes from Commander Harold Buell, one of the most experienced SBD Dauntless and SB2C Helldiver pilots in the fleet. Using sniper terminology, Buell said that he "fired" rather than dropped his bomb, much as a precision rifleman aims and shoots at a specific mark. Buell was present at every carrier battle from

A pair of F6F-5N Hellcat fighters of Night Fighting Squadron 41 leave a Japanese destroyer in flames in the waters off China after a 12 January 1945 attack. The radar pod distinctive on night fighter versions of the famed Hellcat is visible on the starboard wing of the aircraft in the foreground. ("F6F-5N, Coral Sea, 1945," R.G. Smith, National Museum of Naval Aviation)

His face hidden by his goggles and oxygen mask, a night fighter pilot sits in the cockpit of an F6F-3N Hellcat. A specialty of the Japanese in the Pacific War was night attack, which prompted the U.S. Navy to develop a skilled cadre of pilots capable of combating nocturnal intruders. (Clay Jansson)

173

Lieutenant Roland P. Gift downs a dose of medicinal brandy in the ready room on board Monterey *(CVL 26) following a harrowing flight during the Battle of the Philippine Sea on 20 June 1944. For the pilots returning at night low on fuel, finding a flight deck on which to land created as much excitement as dropping ordnance on the enemy. Note that the chalkboard in the ready room still contains the mission's objectives, underlined emphatically. (U.S. Navy)*

the Battle of Coral Sea in May 1942 to the Battle of the Philippine Sea in June 1944, and fired his bombs at more than a dozen Japanese ships.

In its own way, aerial torpedo delivery required precision as well. The endeavor was complicated by the poor quality of the Mark XIII torpedoes delivered to the fleet, and dozens of carrier aircrews perished trying to put defective ordnance into Japanese hulls. However, remedies were found and by the latter part of 1943 the U.S. Navy's torpedo squadrons were capable of putting enemy ships on the bottom. In the fleet engagement off Saipan in June 1944, during which carrier aircraft attacked the Japanese fleet at great range and had to return to their ships at night, Lieutenant George Brown of *Belleau Wood* (CVL 24) led three Avengers against *Hiyo* and destroyed her, the only carrier sunk entirely by aerial torpedoes in the war. Brown, the aggressive aviator, flew his aircraft the entire length of *Hiyo*'s flight deck after dropping his fish in an attempt to draw fire away from his squadronmates. Joining up in his battered airplane for the return trip home, Brown's injuries prevented him from maintaining formation. He never returned from the so-called Mission Beyond Darkness.

Naval aviators also excelled in the esoteric art of aerial gunnery. Of all the world's air arms, only the U.S. Navy and Marines, plus the tiny but extremely proficient Finnish Air Force, routinely practiced high-angle gunnery. The U.S. Army Air Forces, the British Royal Air Force, and the German Luftwaffe concentrated on the traditional pursuit curve that typically gave the fighter pilot a 30-degree deflection shot at his quarry. Naval

aviators learned 90-degree shooting both from the horizontal and vertical positions, and destroyed Japanese air power in the process. Hellcats alone were credited with downing as many Japanese aircraft as the combined fighters of the Army Air Forces. Deadly gunnery combined with innovative tactics such as Commander John Thach's defensive-offensive weave was virtually unbeatable, and was practiced well into the jet age. Commander David McCampbell, air group commander on board *Essex* (CV 9), turned in the virtuoso performance. In ninety minutes over Leyte Gulf on 24 October 1944, he was credited with nine confirmed and two probable kills, using barely 200 rounds per target. Upon landing he was out of ammunition and had only two gallons of gasoline remaining. Years later, he commented, "I practiced until I couldn't get any better. On my last training hop I shot the [target sleeve] tow cable in two."

Above: *A depiction of Marine Captain Joe Foss flaming another enemy aircraft during a heated air battle over Guadalcanal. The colorful leatherneck pilot received the Medal of Honor for his actions with the so-called Cactus Air Force, scoring twenty-six kills. ("Victory over Guadalcanal," Ted Wilbur)*

Opposite, top: *TBF Avengers launch torpedoes during a training flight near Hawaii. Flying low and slow—the Mark XIII torpedo could not be released at speeds over 100 mph or altitudes greater than 120 feet—torpedo planes proved susceptible to enemy fighters and antiaircraft fire. (National Museum of Naval Aviation)*

175

McCampbell and O'Hare were the only two Navy fighter pilots who received the Medal of Honor in World War II. Ten Marine fighter pilots also received the nation's highest award, nine in the Solomons campaign of 1942–1943. It was clearly disproportionate, as only two dive bomber pilots and two patrol plane commanders were similarly recognized.

Wide-ranging sea battles and the island-hopping campaigns that took the Allies to the very doorstep of the Japanese home islands were the hallmarks of the Pacific war and showcased the versatility and capabilities of naval aviation. However, when next called to arms over the Korean peninsula, the men in the cockpits found themselves in a different kind of war.

In an ironic way, carrier aviation may have been partly saved by the Korean War. When North Korean tanks rolled south in June 1950, *Valley Forge* (CV 45) was on hand to help oppose the overt communist aggression. She was one of only fifteen carriers of all types still in commission, compared to some 100 just five years previously. For the next three years, U.S. carriers provided badly needed close air support and interdiction missions in support of often hard-pressed allied troops ashore. At one point, with only the area around Pusan, South Korea, remaining in friendly

Top: *Members of Carrier Air Group 15 pose for a group photograph in front of the personal aircraft of their leader, the Navy's top ace Commander David S. McCampbell. The squadron scoreboard notes their mark of 310 kills. (National Museum of Naval Aviation)*

Above, center: *Naval aviation's foremost fighter tactician of World War II, Lieutenant Commander John S. Thach developed the famed Thach Weave for combating the faster and more maneuverable Japanese Zero. The recipient of two awards of the Navy Cross, Thach shot down six planes in becoming a fighter ace, including four at the Battle of Midway. (U.S. Navy)*

Above: *The fiscal constraints brought on by the Great Depression prompted David McCampbell to be released from active duty following his graduation from the Naval Academy in 1933. He eventually returned to service and during 1944 became the Navy's leading fighter ace with thirty-four kills while leading Carrier Air Group 15 from the deck of* Essex *(CV 9). He received the Medal of Honor for actions in two aerial engagements, shooting down seven planes on 19 June 1944 and nine more on 24 October 1944. (U.S. Naval Institute)*

hands, all Air Force squadrons withdrew to Japan, and the resulting long-distance flights limited their time over Korea. Navy and Marine Corps carrier squadrons remained the only on-scene air power until the amphibious landing at Inchon in September 1950 reversed the Communist tide. Some 400 naval aviators lost their lives in Korea—the first of repeated "hot spots" in the Cold War—and hundreds more served with distinction.

Lieutenant Commander William T. Amen scored the Navy's first "MiG kill" on 9 November 1950. Among the others who shot down the

His F4U-4 Corsair's giant propeller slicing the air as its engine runs up to full power, a Fighter Squadron 63 pilot prepares to launch from Philippine Sea *(CV 47) for a mission over Korea during 1951. (Roland H. Baker, Jr.)*

Opposite, bottom: *Fighting Squadron 17 pilot Lieutenant Andy Jaeger pumps his fists with exuberance after describing an air battle to ground personnel on Bougainville, in February 1944. His squadron, the Jolly Rogers, flew F4U Corsairs from shore bases because technical maladies prevented them from operating safely from carrier decks. During the heated air battles over the Solomon Islands in 1943–1944, they shot down 152 Japanese aircraft. (U.S. Navy)*

Left: *Navy AD Skyraiders lay waste to North Korean tanks. With the first generation jet aircraft unable to carry heavy ordnance loads, propeller-driven aircraft like the Skyraider and F4U Corsair provided the bulk of naval aviation's offensive firepower against ground targets. ("Douglas AD-4 Skyraider," R.G. Smith)*

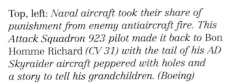

Top, left: *Naval aircraft took their share of punishment from enemy antiaircraft fire. This Attack Squadron 923 pilot made it back to* Bon Homme Richard *(CV 31) with the tail of his AD Skyraider aircraft peppered with holes and a story to tell his grandchildren. (Boeing)*

Top, right: *A percentage of Navy and Marine Corps pilots during the Korean War served on exchange duty with U.S. Air Force squadrons, including Major John H. Glenn, who logged missions flying the F-86 Sabre. In the war's waning days, the Marine pilot shot down three enemy MiG-15s in just nine days, earning the sobriquet "MiG Mad Marine." (Clay Jansson)*

Above: *Pictured here as a rear admiral, James Bond Stockdale was already an esteemed Navy fighter pilot at the beginning of the Vietnam War, having become the first man to log 1,000 flight hours in the F-8 Crusader. However, it was in the prison camps of North Vietnam that he achieved his greatest legacy, receiving the Medal of Honor for his leadership and determined resistance in the face of unimaginable torture. (National Museum of Naval Aviation)*

Right: *An F9F Panther of Fighter Squadron 191 pictured on the deck of* Princeton *(CV 37). Visible under the wing are 5-inch high-velocity aircraft rockets for use against targets of opportunity on the ground. With few opportunities to engage enemy MiG-15 jets, Navy fighter pilots flew numerous air-to-ground missions. (National Museum of Naval Aviation)*

Soviet-built jets in "MiG Alley" were future astronauts Lieutenant Wally Schirra and Marine Major John Glenn. However, what tested the mettle of naval aviators most was the intense ground fire thrown at them during each mission, which from July 1951 to July 1953 knocked down 384 Navy and Marine aircraft. One squadron skipper, Commander Paul Gray, was shot down on five separate occasions. Helicopter pilots also created a legacy of valor in Korea. Among them was Lieutenant (jg) John Koelsch, who on 3 July 1951 volunteered to attempt a pick-up of a downed Marine pilot despite gathering darkness and deteriorating weather that precluded fighter escort. In the face of intense ground fire, Koelsch and his crewman, Airman Third Class George Neal, made repeated attempts to hoist Captain James V. Wilkins aboard before a direct hit sent the helicopter down in flames. Despite the fact that Wilkins's legs were burned in the crash, the trio avoided capture for nine days. Koelsch subsequently died in a prisoner of war camp and posthumously received a Medal of Honor. The man he attempted to rescue called his actions "the greatest display of guts I've ever seen."

Only ten years of relative peace followed Korea. Naval aviation's torturous experience in Southeast Asia began in 1964, and ended when Marine helicopters assisted in the evacuation of Saigon in 1975. A microcosm of naval aviation's experience in Vietnam is the career of Commander James B. Stockdale, who flew combat air patrol over U.S. destroyers during the Tonkin Gulf incident in August 1964, and led the first naval

air strikes against North Vietnam that same month. Shot down in September 1965, he was captured, joining what eventually numbered some 150 Navy and Marine airmen held under miserable conditions that included extortion and torture. Among the leaders in the "Hanoi Hilton," he at one juncture attempted to kill himself during one torture session as a symbol of defiance, an action for which he received the Medal of Honor. All told, Stockdale spent some seven and one half years in captivity.

Other heroes could be found in cockpits of all varieties. Lieutenant (jg) Clyde Lassen embodied the heroic crews of search and rescue helicopters, piloting his UH-2 Seasprite deep into North Vietnam one June evening in 1968. He emerged later having dodged surface-to-air missiles and small arms fire, as well as a collision with a tree, and landed aboard a destroyer with precious little fuel sloshing in his tanks. Most importantly, he had two extra passengers on board in the form of the grateful F-4 Phantom crew he had been sent to rescue. Pilots of A-4 Skyhawk jets suffered losses disproportionate to the diminutive size of their aircraft, with a

Contrails stream off the wing tips of an F-8D Crusader of Fighter Squadron 111 as it roars through the humid air over South Vietnam. Their aircraft distinguished by the shark mouth paint scheme on the nose, the Sundowners completed nine deployments to the Western Pacific during 1965–1975, flying both the F-8 and the F-4 Phantom II. (U.S. Navy)

total of 257 falling to enemy fire. Among those lost was Commander Michael Estocin, the only carrier-based naval aviator to receive the Medal of Honor for action in air combat over Vietnam. One A-4 pilot who survived was Commander Wynn Foster, who despite taking a round in the cockpit that severed much of his right arm, managed to get his aircraft over the Tonkin Gulf and eject. He remained on active duty, and when promoted to the rank of captain received the moniker Captain Hook.

Carrier-based fighter pilots had a field day against North Vietnamese MiG aircraft. Through 1968, when air-to-air combat all but ended, tailhook

Commander Wynn Foster, recovered from having his arm blown off by antiaircraft fire during a 1966 combat mission over North Vietnam, returned to active duty in Southeast Asia on the staff of Commander Carrier Division One. Here he speaks with Commander James Busey, skipper of Attack Squadron 163, Foster's command when he was shot down. (Wynn Foster)

aircrews had managed a 2:1 victory ratio over the yellow-starred fighters, while the Air Force barely broke even. The Navy owed much of its success to the pilots of the F-8 Crusader, an aircraft called the "Last of the Gunfighters," for it still mounted 20mm cannon. Thus, Crusader jocks continually honed their dogfighting skills, which proved extremely valuable even in the fast-paced world of jet combat. However, the ratio paled against that achieved in World War II and Korea. Clearly something was wrong, and the Navy assigned an officer to evaluate the service's air-to-air weapons systems.

When Captain Frank Ault completed his exhaustive study, one recommendation was the establishment of a formal course of instruction in air-to-air tactics, the beginning of the Navy Fighter Weapons School at Naval Air Station Miramar, California. With a core of hard-charging F-8

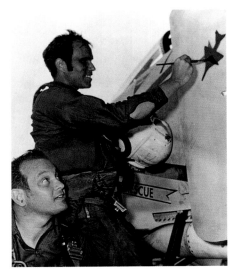

Above: *Commander Sam Flynn decorates the side of his F-4J Phantom II with the silhouette of a MiG-21 fighter as his radar intercept officer, Lieutenant William H. John, looks on. The Fighter Squadron 31 crew, flying from* Saratoga *(CVA 60), bagged the enemy aircraft on 21 June 1972. (National Museum of Naval Aviation)*

Right: *Lieutenant Randy Cunningham describes the 10 May 1972 air battle in which he and radar intercept officer Lieutenant (jg) William Driscoll shot down three enemy MiGs over North Vietnam. Exiting the battle they were hit by a surface-to-air missile and were forced to eject off the coast of North Vietnam, where they were rescued by helicopter. (U.S. Navy)*

pilots, Top Gun set about producing dedicated air-to-air instructors within each fleet fighter squadron, especially in the previously air defense-oriented F-4 Phantom II community. Crusaders, with the worst safety record in naval aviation, also had by far the best kill-loss ratio, and the aggressive methods of their pilots were widely disseminated. Testament of the program's success was the fact that during Operations Linebacker I and II in 1972, Navy fighter pilots knocked down twenty-four MiGs, achieving a kill ratio of 6:1. Flying a Phantom II, Lieutenant Randall Cunningham and Lieutenant (jg) William Driscoll shot down five of the enemy, including three in one day during an epic dogfight on 10 May 1972, to become the first American fighter aces of the war.

While America absorbed the unnecessary lessons of its loss in Southeast Asia, the world did not wait. In the troubled Middle East, Libya, and Grenada, naval aviation flew into harm's way. Yet, not until 1991 would the specter of Vietnam be laid to rest in the desert sands of the Middle East. On the first day of the Gulf War against Iraq, Lieutenant Commander Mark Fox and Lieutenant Nick Mongillo, a pair of pilots assigned to Strike Fighter Squadron 81 operating from *Saratoga* (CV 60), set the tone for naval aviation's participation in Operation Desert Storm by splashing two enemy MiG-21s. Over the course of the next forty-three days, whether in the cockpit striking targets on the ground or surviving grueling captivity as prisoners of war, naval airmen helped achieve victory in the desert.

The world remains an unstable place as evidenced by the fact that nearly a decade after the end of the Gulf War, naval aircraft still help patrol the skies over Iraq, and remain vigilant in the Western Pacific. The men and women who fly them represent the tip of the spear, a special breed of warrior.

Lieutenant Commander Mark Fox draws a crowd on the flight deck of Saratoga *(CV 60) as he uses a chart to relate a mission over Iraq during Operation Desert Storm. Fox and his wingman, Lieutenant Nick Mongillo, shot down a pair of MiG-21 fighters on 17 January 1991, the Navy's only MiG kills during the Gulf War. (U.S. Navy)*

Opposite, bottom: An F/A-18 Hornet intercepts a Soviet Bear-D bomber that flew too close to a carrier battle group in a game of cat and mouse played out many times during the Cold War. (National Museum of Naval Aviation)

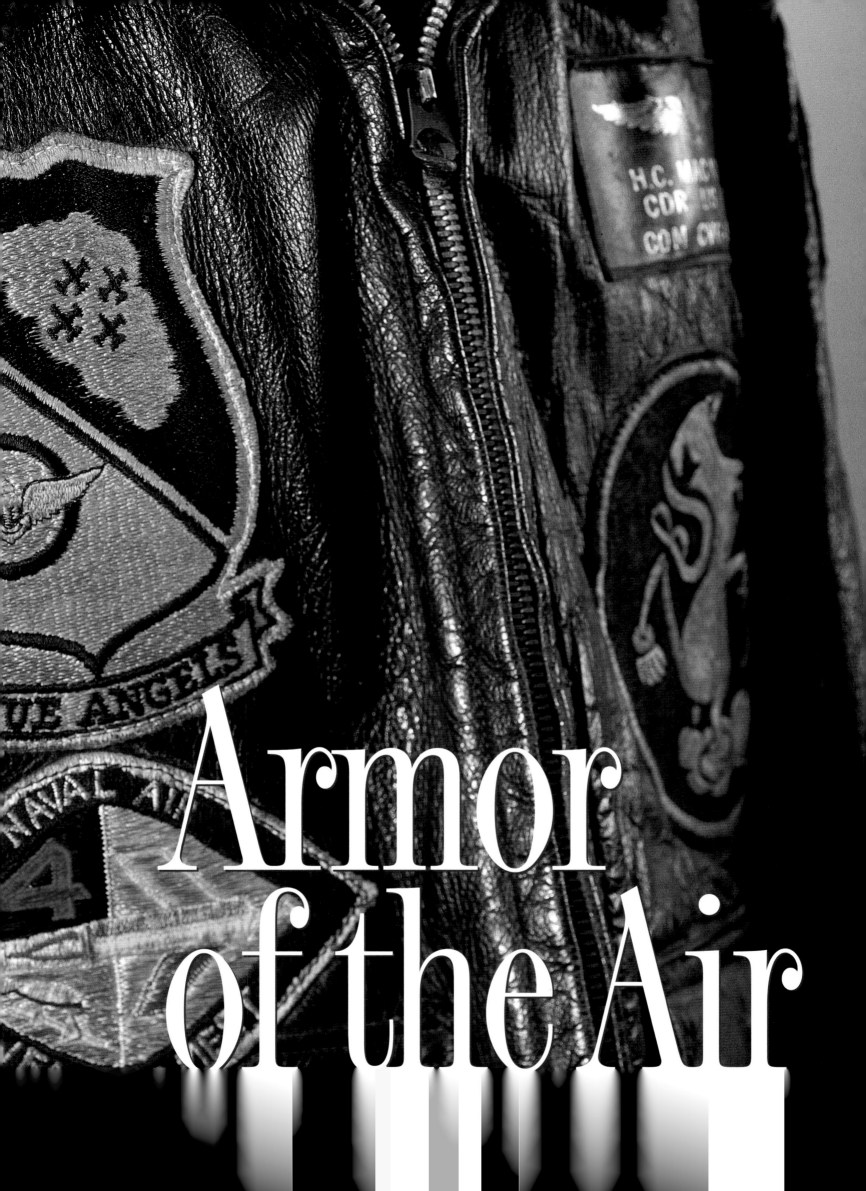

Armor
of the Air

Armor of the Air

Lieutenant Commander David Parsons, USN (Ret)

Pages 184–185: *The weathered leather flight jacket of Captain Harding MacKnight provides a veritable resumé of his Navy career, the patches commemorating ships and squadrons that he called home during his years in uniform. (Al Audleman)*

Above: *A reflection of the era, Eugene Ely wore somewhat formal attire beneath his leather flight jacket when he landed a Curtiss pusher on board the armored cruiser* Pennsylvania *(ACR 4), the first shipboard landing of an aircraft. A football helmet protected him in the open-cockpit aircraft, while bicycle inner tubes served as a makeshift life jacket. (U.S. Navy)*

The photograph says much about the primitive nature of aviation. Eugene Ely stands on a temporary wooden deck on board the armored cruiser USS *Pennsylvania* (ACR 4) having completed the first-ever landing of an aircraft on board a ship. From the vantage point of the present, he looks almost comical, outfitted in a leather jacket, football helmet, and several bicycle inner tubes for flotation in the event he missed the mark and found himself splashing into San Francisco Bay. Since that January day in 1911, aviation has progressed exponentially, and so too have the uniforms and equipment worn by the men and women in the cockpit.

The first naval officers who learned to fly under the tutelage of Glenn Curtiss and the Wright brothers wore no formal uniforms, instead donning civilian clothes as they climbed into the early pusher aircraft. When the infant air arm established an aviation camp at a site across the Severn River from the U.S. Naval Academy in Annapolis, Maryland, its attendees' appearance contrasted with the spit-and-polish atmosphere at the school for future officers. To this end, the Naval Academy commandant insisted that aviators report for duty in the uniform of the day. Wearing the white uniform with choker collar proved problematic when working around the exposed engines and grease of the first catapult installed on the Annapolis waterfront, but such was the misunderstanding of aviation in the traditional Navy. Within a few years aviators designed a working uniform unique to them. While most naval uniforms of the day were white or blue, the airmen took to wearing what became known as aviation greens, featuring the same choker collar on the traditional white and blue uniforms as well as shoulder boards signifying

World War I officers model the types of uniforms worn in naval aviation's early years. The dress blues outfitted all naval officers, but the aviation greens, worn with brown shoes and sometimes puttees, were unique to the men of the air. (National Museum of Naval Aviation)

Though aviation greens do not hang in the closets of many aviators anymore, they are still approved uniforms. This jacket, which dates from the 1940s, sports ornate bullion wings, which were commonplace on aviation green uniforms until after World War II. (Al Audleman)

rank. Later, aviation greens were modified to include an open collar and sleeve insignia similar to dress blues.

Aviators also took to wearing brown shoes. Regardless of the uniform of the day, aviators prized their brown shoes. They have been de rigueur since the earliest days of naval aviation except for a brief period in the late 1970s when they were banned in favor of uniform black shoes for all naval personnel. In response, on board many carriers at sea aviation personnel staged mock funerals for their distinctive footwear, launching them into the sea using the aircraft catapults. A resounding cry of protest from airmen eventually prompted Secretary of the Navy John Lehman to announce—to a standing ovation—their return at the 1986 Tailhook

Top, left: *Ensign Wayne Duffett pictured in the aviation green working uniform worn by aviators of the World War I era, his bullion wings a less than accurate representation of the wings of gold. Duffett flew with the Italian navy during World War I, receiving the Navy Cross for his combat service. (National Museum of Naval Aviation)*

Top, right: *Lieutenant William M. Corry displays the primitive flight gear worn by pioneer aviators at NAS Pensacola, Florida, prior to World War I. Note the seat belt dangling beneath him, an innovation resulting from a 1913 flight in which Ensign William Billingsley was thrown from a similar aircraft and fell to his death. The helmet and goggles, like almost all flight gear in this era, were procured commercially (U.S. Navy)*

Above: *Ensign J.C. Herron displays the quintessential garb of the World War I aviator— the full-length leather flight jacket, helmet, and goggles—veritable symbols of the dashing knights of the air. Note the insignia painted on the hull of his HS flying boat. The training squadrons at NAS Pensacola, Florida, were among the first in naval aviation to adopt insignias, beginning a practice that continues today. (National Museum of Naval Aviation)*

Spalding Aviation Equipment

Spalding
Military Aviators' Uniforms

No. 4. Army cloth olive drab suit, consisting of coat, army regulation style, and riding breeches. . . . . Complete, **$25.00**

Canvas suit, khaki color coat and riding breeches. Regulation style. . . . . . Complete, **$15.00**

Made to Measure on Special Order.

No. 3. Consists of knee length leather overcoat; tan, with belt and three very large pockets. Now worn by aviators of the European belligerent nations. . . . . Each, **$50.00**

Light leather (jacket) with the fleece on it, to fit the above coat as a lining. . . . Each, **$15.00**

No. 4

No. 3

Spalding Aviation Suits
Overall Style

Special "Navy" Suit

No. 5. Made of imported gaberdine, cravatted, absolutely waterproof; overall style in riding breeches effect, or long trousers. Not carried in stock, but tailor-made to order. . . . . . Suit, **$25.00**

Special "Mechanics'" Suit

No. 6. Made of brown canvas, khaki, or moleskin. Regular one-piece overall suits. Brown canvas only carried in stock.
Suit, **$3.00**

All prices subject to change without notice

No. 5

No. 6

Spalding Aviation Equipment

Spalding Aviation Equipment

convention, and aviators did not wait for the offical naval message before once again sporting their beloved brown leather shoes. But in 1996, the Navy Uniform Board released the restriction on brown shoes, allowing them to be worn outside the aviation community. Despite this, brown shoes still symbolize aviation so strongly that to this day naval aviation personnel are called "brown shoes" and all others are known as "black shoes."

In addition to adopting a unique uniform, naval aviators soon discovered that the nature of their work, in which they literally hung out in the slipstream while flying at altitude, necessitated protective gear. To this end, the leather flight jacket soon appeared, and with the exception of the wings of gold, there is no more enduring symbol of naval aviation. With no such item in the Navy supply system, airmen initially obtained most of the early flight jackets, as well as flight helmets, from commercial sources, including sporting goods manufacturers like Spalding. Since individuals had to outfit themselves, period photographs reveal an array of clothing as aviation struggled to make a place for itself in the battleship navy.

Spalding Brothers found a lucrative market in the fledgling aviation industry, both civilian and military. The sporting goods manufacturer marketed flight suits, helmets, and goggles at prices that for today's population are hard to believe. (Dave Parsons Collection)

Above: *Flight clothing during the first two decades of naval aviation came in a variety of forms, with aviators outfitting themselves with what best suited their individual needs. Lieutenant Elmer F. Stone (left) and Lieutenant Commander Holden C. Richardson, both assigned to NC flying boats for the attempted flight across the Atlantic in 1919, certainly required the warmest clothing they could find given the route the flight took to Europe. (U.S. Navy)*

Opposite, bottom: *In April 1917, the same month the United States entered World War I, the Secretary of the Navy established standard flight clothing for the Naval Flying Service. Thus, wartime aviators found themselves well equipped with protective garments that were essential in the harsh environment of an open-air cockpit at altitude. (National Museum of Naval Aviation)*

Page 190, top: *The pilots of Fighting Squadron 5S, pictured on the flight deck of Lexington (CV 2), display the array of flight gear worn by naval aviators during the 1920s. Leather jackets of varied lengths and styles are reflected in the ranks, as is the appearance of a functional flight suit. Also note the inflatable life jackets worn by the men, a forerunner of the famed "Mae West." (National Museum of Naval Aviation)*

Pilots of Marine Fighting Squadron 10 pictured at NAS San Diego, California, with the Schiff Trophy they captured during 1931–1932. The differing styles of flight jackets worn by the aviators all include the squadron insignia painted over the left breast, which by this time was fast becoming a standard feature on flight jackets. (National Museum of Naval Aviation)

Commander W.G. Chield (right) shakes the hand of Lieutenant Al Williams at NAS Anacostia in Washington, D.C., on 26 August 1931. Chield wears a variation of the aviation green uniform with his rank on the sleeve and a tie instead of the original choker collar. (Naval Historical Center)

The snow on the ground indicates the low temperatures in Great Lakes, Illinois, but this airman need not worry. Outfitted in a heavy winter flying suit complemented by gloves and insulated boots, he is ready to ward off the cold amongst the clouds. (National Museum of Naval Aviation)

Technological advances eventually led to fuselage designs that afforded considerable protection for the pilot, but cockpits remained open to the elements and airmen continued to rely on leather jackets to provide a barrier to the wind and ward off the cold. As U.S. naval aviation entered the golden age of the interwar years, aircraft designs began to feature enclosed cockpits with sliding canopies. Leather jackets evolved from purely functional lengths (thigh and even calf length) for near freezing temperatures at altitude to waist-length styles that could be worn away from the aircraft. This resulted in the jacket becoming a symbol of membership in the elite and daring fraternity of flyers, both civilian and military, that during that time captured the public's interest with a seemingly endless series of record-setting flights.

Aviators quickly adopted the practice of adorning their flight jackets with the insignias of their squadrons, mostly in the form of patches, though some were painted directly on the leather. Dating from World War I, the practice of squadrons adopting unique insignias as veritable coats of arms

created esprit de corps, and the tradition continues to this day. For example, the pilots of Fighting Plane Squadron 1 chose a top hat for their insignia. Confident in their abilities in the air, the choice was evidently an outward demonstration of the slang term high-hat, which means to treat someone in a condescending or supercilious manner. Today, the Navy's oldest continuously serving squadron, Fighter Squadron (VF) 14, maintains the same insignia and is known throughout naval aviation as the Tophatters. The insignia of the Fighting Squadron 5B Red Rippers, featuring the distinctive boar's head design also found on the Gordon's Gin bottle, has proven so popular that it has endured a succession of squadron deactivations only to be picked up by another squadron that preferred it over their own design. This practice has survived to this day, as demonstrated by VF-103, which in 1995 opted to drop their traditional Club Leaf insignia and adopt the Jolly Rogers insignia. The famed skull and crossbones, which first appeared during World War II, was on the verge of disappearing from

Top: *Feisty skipper Lieutenant Commander Gerald F. Bogan, pictured here with top hat on his knee, is credited with originating one of the most enduring squadron insignias in naval aviation history. Fighting Squadron 1 was known as the High Hats during the 1920s and 1930s. (National Museum of Naval Aviation)*

Above, left: *As this photograph reveals, the original high hat insignia has endured into the jet age, and now belongs to Fighter Squadron 14, which holds the distinction of being the oldest continuously serving squadron in naval aviation. No longer called the High Hats, the squadron now carries the nickname Tophatters. (U.S. Navy)*

Above: *Certainly the most prized possession of any aviator joining his first squadron is his leather flight jacket emblazoned with his squadron's insignia. Lieutenant (jg) Haley wore this one while serving with the High Hats during the 1930s. (Al Audleman)*

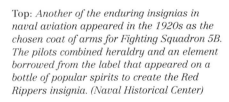

Top: *Another of the enduring insignias in naval aviation appeared in the 1920s as the chosen coat of arms for Fighting Squadron 5B. The pilots combined heraldry and an element borrowed from the label that appeared on a bottle of popular spirits to create the Red Rippers insignia. (Naval Historical Center)*

Colorful patches have appeared in all shapes and sizes and commemorated a variety of squadrons and events during the colorful history of naval aviation. (Clockwise from left) Completion of a six-month deployment is reason enough for the crew of an aircraft carrier to produce a patch signifying that accomplishment. One of the most cherished milestones of any carrier pilot's career is recording 100 landings on a particular flattop, thereby earning the right to be called a centurion. Surviving 200 combat missions over North Vietnam was a badge of honor for one F-4 Phantom II pilot. A rare original leather patch, this one of Torpedo Squadron 12 shows that the squadron was ready to come out swinging against the Japanese. Astronaut Neil Armstrong wore the patch of Fighter Squadron 51, the Screaming Eagles, during his service in Korea. (Al Audleman)

naval aviation following the deactivation of VF-84. Squadrons take their insignia and heritage quite seriously, mirroring the devotion of fans to sports teams.

Bureau of Aeronautics records are indistinct on the formal adoption of the G-1 leather flight jacket, but some records reveal its appearance in the supply system by 1931. Nevertheless, the issuing of the G-1 represented the adoption of a flight jacket unique to naval aviation, one

instantly recognizable because of a distinct fur collar. Merging functionality with fashion, the jacket was a standard-issue item for personnel on flight status by the beginning of World War II, and became a symbol of naval aviation itself.

The leather flight jacket came into its own during World War II, particularly when it came to decoration. The Army Air Forces went further in this regard with the widespread painting of their A-2 flight jackets, particularly in the European theater of operations, where the lighter weight A-2

The two most prominent flight jacket designs that outfitted naval aviators during World War II are visible in this photograph of student pilots. The men to the instructor's left wear the famous G-1, while those on his right are outfitted with the M-445 shearling jacket. Of the two, only the G-1 has stood the test of time and is worn today. (Dave Parsons collection)

A pilot and his gunner examine battle damage on their SBD-3 Dauntless after returning from a combat flight during the Battle of Midway in June 1942. Both men wear G-1 flight jackets beneath their Mae West life vests, revealing that even in the relatively warm climate of the Pacific, flying at altitude required extra protection against the cold. The pilot's light-weight summer cotton flying helmet and Willson MkII goggles were prevalent during the war years. (Dave Parsons collection)

Above: *The equipment worn by this wartime Navy fighter pilot includes a Mae West life vest with a dye marker to enable a search plane to spot him from the air in the event he has to bail out over water. A cord for the radio earphones in his helmet hangs down over his shoulder and an oxygen mask dangles from a string around his neck. For personal protection he carries a .38-caliber pistol, its bullets draped across his chest. (National Museum of Naval Aviation)*

Top, right: *Navy pilots censor their squadron's outgoing mail in their quarters at a base in the Aleutian Islands, circa 1943. The two officers wear aviation green covers, and given the location of their duty station it is no surprise that the man on the right sports a G-1 and heavy flying boots. (National Archives)*

Right: *The message on the ready room bulkhead is the only explanation needed for the serious looks on the faces of these carrier pilots as they receive final instructions before launching as part of the first raid by carrier planes against the Japanese capital in February 1945. Most of these pilots wear flight jackets underneath their flight suits for added warmth. (National Museum of Naval Aviation)*

Bottom, left: *Commander Joseph C. Clifton, the colorful skipper of Fighting Squadron 12, passes out congratulatory cigars on board* Saratoga *(CV 3) following a successful strike against Rabaul on 3 November 1943. The well-worn squadron insignia on his khaki flight suit reveals the intensity of wartime flight operations. (U.S. Navy)*

Bottom, right: *Walt Disney studios lent the artistic talent of its illustrators to the military services during World War II, resulting in many squadron and unit insignias having cartoon characters as their central figures. Among them were the torpedo squadron insignias visible on the flight jackets of these aviators on board* Essex *(CV 9). (U.S. Navy)*

was not worn in the heavy bombers that required heavy insulated and heated flight clothing. Due to atmospheric cooling at altitude, the Navy's G-1 went into combat at Midway, as evidenced by photographs of SBD Dauntless dive bomber crews that flew with canopies open. However, the more temperate climates of the Pacific, where naval aviation focused most of its attention, limited the G-1's use as a functional item. And in sharp contrast to the Army Air Forces, which allowed extravagant decoration of

flight jackets that mirrored the nose art on their aircraft, the practice was never adopted to a wide extent in the Navy. Typically, naval aviators adorned their jackets with their squadron insignia, which took the form of either an embroidered patch or painted facsimile. Occasionally, they painted their names on the jacket as well.

In the postwar years the G-1 flight jacket survived the challenge of advanced designs that prompted the abolishment of the A-2 by the U.S. Air Force. Textile research developed a series of flight jackets featuring fabric that blocked the wind and retained body heat. When conflict erupted in Korea, the service had refined its intermediate jacket into the definitive B-15 flight jacket in sage green or navy blue. Naval aviators, however, continued flying their missions in the venerable G-1 leather flight jacket, especially during the harsh winter months on the Korean peninsula.

As jets supplanted propeller-driven aircraft in virtually all tactical roles by 1960, the ejection seat became standard equipment, and the G-1 flight jacket came to be worn only outside of the cockpit because it interfered with the constricting harness that attached the pilot to the seat. However, it remained very functional for aircrews assigned to patrol aircraft and helicopters in which the operating environment necessitated a flight jacket to stay warm and aircrew were not encumbered by the protective restraints of an ejection seat. In addition, the widespread availability of embroidered patches resulted in a rich variety of colorful insignia that appeared throughout naval aviation. These patches not only identified squadrons in which an individual had served, but also commemorated particular aircraft flown and

Jet age pilots like these members of Fighter Squadron 31 continued wearing their G-1 flight jackets in the cockpit, particularly in the harsh winter air over Korea. All wear H-1 flight helmets, the first Navy-issue hard helmet for fighter aircraft. (National Museum of Naval Aviation)

Actor Robert Taylor wears heavy winter flight gear in this wartime photograph taken during the actor's stint as a flight instructor. Other Hollywood stars, among them Bert Morris and Tyrone Power, earned their wings as naval aviators during World War II. (Robert L. Lawson collection)

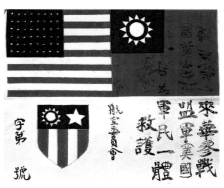

Top: *Helicopter pilots like Lieutenant Bill Stuyvesant continued wearing their G-1s aloft long after the advent of ejection seats prompted jet pilots to abandon them as flight gear in the cockpit. (National Museum of Naval Aviation)*

Top, right: *Pilots of Marine Attack Squadron 211 pictured in front of one of their A4D Skyhawks at Marine Corps Air Station Iwakuni, Japan, in 1959. Given the bulky survival vests worn by some of the men, it is no surprise that there was simply not enough room for pilots to wear the time-honored G-1 in the cockpits of tactical jets. (Naval Historical Center)*

Above: *A World War II "blood chit" employed in the China-Burma-India theater of operations. Most often sewn inside the backs of flight jackets, these items were literally IOUs for survival in the event an airman was shot down, announcing to the native population that the bearer was an Allied pilot and required their assistance. They have been used in every major conflict since World War II. (Al Audleman)*

associated milestones such as 1,000 flight hours in a certain airplane. The centurion patch, marking 100 arrested landings on board a particular carrier, was especially coveted. Interestingly, the U.S. Air Force evolved their B-15 to the MA-1 nylon sage-green jacket, but standardized how patches could be worn, a far cry from the scantily clad females and bomb silhouettes that appeared on the backs of the the venerable A-2. The Navy now took the lead when it came to flight jacket decoration, the backs of flight jackets becoming a visual biography of an aviator's career.

There were unwritten but generally accepted rules governing the wearing of patches, most significantly that individuals must have earned those worn. Options included American flags on sleeves. Virtually all aviators settled on wearing the patch of their current squadron on the right breast and the aircraft they flew on the right shoulder. The name tag appeared on the left breast, while an optional milestone patch, like one denoting service at the Navy Fighter Weapons School (Topgun), could be worn on the left shoulder. Flight suits typically had this minimum layout and most squadron commanding officers dictated a standard flight suit appearance. The flight jacket remained an individual's choice in most commands, although the Marine Corps has typically mandated that the flight jacket mimic the flight suit, thereby relegating the freelance adornment to the green helmet bag.

Wearing of flight jackets and flight suits has always been a point of pride for naval aviators—and a source of contention with uniform policies and those in positions to enforce them. Occasionally, some nonaviators in charge of naval districts were loath to relax rules concerning the wearing of flight jackets. Flight jackets were considered part of a "working uniform" allowed on the flight line and in squadron spaces, but they were not considered appropriate or allowed by regulations elsewhere on base, and off base they were specifically forbidden for wear with uniforms. Base

Left: *Lieutenant Commander Richard Poor, skipper of Bombing Squadron 10 on board Enterprise (CV 6), chose to decorate his Mae West with the insignia of his squadron. Many pilots and gunners personalized their flight equipment, either with sketches of the aircraft they flew or a listing of the battles in which they participated. (National Museum of Naval Aviation)*

Above: *An AD Skyraider pilot displays the piece of shrapnel and section of his aircraft's cockpit canopy that it damaged during a combat mission over Korea. He wears an H-4 protective helmet, and the left shoulder of his G-1 flight jacket is adorned with the Task Force 77 insignia issued to those serving in the waters off Korea. (Dave Parsons Collection)*

commanders had no choice but to follow the policy despite its unpopularity. This led to friction at master jet bases, where in some cases gate guards inspected every automobile in hopes of catching some aviator attempting to wear a flight jacket onto the base. One of the paradoxes is that despite the immense popularity of the flight jacket and the lengths to which aviators went to in order to wear them, the jackets were generally no longer functional in the aircraft based at the naval air stations where the "gate wars" took place. Aviators were proud of the leather flight jackets and preferred to wear them not only over their flight suits, but with their khaki and winter blue working uniforms as well, despite availability of other uniform jackets. The flight jacket had become a treasured badge of accomplishment and status and aviators pushed the rules beyond the limit to display their flight status and affiliation. In the late 1990s Chief of Naval Operations Admiral Jay Johnson finally yielded to popular demand and allowed the flight jacket to be worn as part of the uniform.

Meanwhile, the G-1 was in jeopardy of being banished forever from the backs of U.S. naval aviators. Although not the target of any particular vendetta or probe, nor the threat of improved technology in the form of better fabric, by 1980 it was no longer standard issue. A routine audit—sparked by suspicions that the Department of Defense was procuring material in excess of requirements due to largesse of congressional favoritism toward manufacturers in their home states—revealed stockpiles of boots and other equipment far in excess of need. While it did not find excess flight jackets languishing in a warehouse, the audit revealed an unusual situation: the number of flight jackets issued by the supply system was exponentially greater than the number of aviators. Since the flight jacket was simply another item with a part number, it could be requisitioned by any command. What had happened over the years was that the popularity of the flight jacket had made it the quintessential bartering

The CWU-series Nomex flight jackets are currently worn alongside the G-1, though today's regulations prevent the level of decoration seen on the jacket of Commander Dan Cain. A centurion on board two carriers and veteran of over 4,000 flight hours in the F-14 Tomcat, he flew as a radar intercept officer in seven fighter squadrons. (Commander Dan Cain)

Above: *The "Three Sea Hawks," a 1920s era Navy stunt team whose members included (left to right) Lieutenant (jg) William Davis, Lieutenant Daniel Tomlinson, and Lieutenant (jg) Aaron P. Storrs, wear the standard flight helmets of the era. Two of the men wear neckties, which was the uniform of the day in cockpits during naval aviation's golden age. (National Museum of Naval Aviation)*

Right: *One type of flight helmet worn by World War I-era naval aviators was the Spalding hard-shell style, borrowed from the sport of football. Note the different styles of goggles worn by the aviators. (National Museum of Naval Aviation)*

Opposite, top: *Open cockpits like the one in this F3B-1 fighter afforded little protection against the slipstream in flight, though the small windscreen helped somewhat. The men who flew in this era were certainly a hardy lot. (National Museum of Naval Aviation)*

Machinist Floyd Bennett, famed pilot of the first aircraft to fly over the North Pole, pictured during the 1920s. The absence of earpieces on his leather flight helmet reflects the lack of cockpit radios during the era. Note the fur-lined goggles for extra warmth. (U.S. Navy)

medium. This was evidenced by the situation during the formative years of Topgun, which was desperate for parts for its cast-off Air Force T-38 trainers. On one occasion an officer loaded a C-130 cargo plane with a box of leather flight jackets for a trip to a nearby Air Force base. The C-130 returned with the needed parts and an empty box. And flight jackets weren't just used for barter, for many a surface sailor somehow managed to acquire one to wear on the bridge of a cruiser or destroyer at sea.

The resulting investigation brought a halt to procurement of the G-1 leather flight jacket that had been in continuous use virtually unchanged since its appearance in the early 1930s. By 1979, the remaining stocks at Naval Air Station Pensacola, Florida, where the vast majority of jackets were issued as aviators began their training, diminished rapidly. The U.S. Air Force–developed sage green CWU-36 intermediate flight jacket was substituted in place of the leather flight jacket, and it appeared that the G-1 would go by the wayside along with the brown leather shoes traditionally associated with naval aviation. Yet, they have returned and it is a proud day for all aspiring aviators when they receive their shiny new G-1 flight jackets from the supply clerk at NAS Pensacola, the symbol of their having joined an elite fraternity.

In addition to necessitating the wearing of flight jackets, the open frame construction of the early aircraft designs, to say nothing of the frequent calamities in the dangerous business of flying, prompted the need for head protection. The early flight helmets were derived from those used in football and automobile racing, the only ones that seemed remotely suitable for the purpose. The outbreak of World War I prompted the development of more specialized designs. Still, aviation physiology was a crude science at best and even the cutting-edge protection at the time amounted only to leather or cloth helmets and goggles worn more to fend off effects of wind and cold air than protect someone in the event of a crash. The cockpit designs generally enclosed the pilot to the shoulder level, exposing him to the effects of the slipstream and the elements. In

addition, in the case of fighter aircraft, the pilot typically was subjected to oil particles and gun exhaust, though in the 1920s and 1930s, aircraft began to feature windscreens for protection.

By the beginning of World War II, many aircraft designs featured fully enclosed cockpits, affording aircrew a quantum leap in protection. This was mandated by the never-ending quest for speed that greater

Below: Lieutenant R.S. Klingler describes a kill to fellow pilots on board Hancock *(CV 19) after a mission over Kagoshima in April 1945. He wears a late-war flight suit in contrast to the khaki ones worn by his squadron-mates. Note the .38-caliber pistol and survival knife worn by the other pilots, life insurance in the event they are shot down. (U.S. Navy)*

Famed photographer Edward Steichen captured Fighting Squadron 16 skipper Lieutenant Commander Paul D. Buie briefing his pilots for upcoming strikes against the Gilbert Islands in November 1943. Some of the pilots wear white helmets with personalized decorations, reflecting the inherent flamboyance associated with fighter pilots. (National Archives)

Above: *An F4F Wildcat pilot pictured in the cockpit of his fighter in August 1941 during war games in South Carolina. The parachute straps are visible on his shoulders, and he wears an early oxygen mask for high-altitude flight. (National Air and Space Museum)*

Right: *With all of his equipment in place, Lieutenant Harry Harrison exudes a fearsome demeanor. Taken on board* Yorktown *(CV 10) in 1943, the photograph reveals the rapid advance of the oxygen mask in relation to the image above. (Robert L. Lawson collection)*

Below: *Aviators observe flight operations from deck level in the catwalk surrounding the flight deck of* Nassau *(ACV 16), circa 1942. Note the letters "U.S.N." visible on the upturned collar of the G-1 worn by the pilot in the foreground, a distinguishing characteristic of jackets issued during World War II and Korea. He also wears innovative goggles that may be fitted with lenses of varied color and tint depending on flying conditions. (National Museum of Naval Aviation)*

understanding of aerodynamic flow yielded. It is arguable whether the enclosed cockpit was a result of concern for the pilot or simply a practical reality of aerodynamic design with crew comfort being a side benefit. Regardless, technological leaps in all areas brought oxygen masks for high-altitude flight and radios for in-flight communication. Heating remained problematic in many designs, and as supercharged engines which allowed for flight at higher altitudes arrived on the scene, so too did the challenge of developing corresponding protective clothing to ward off the extreme cold at altitude. The resulting changes included leather or cloth helmets modified to house ear cups for radio speakers.

The modern style hard case helmet arrived on the scene in the late 1940s with the advent of jet aircraft. Again, they shared many common features with helmets beginning to appear in professional football and automobile racing. The original designs were ungainly and heavy

Above: *The H-3 helmet featured ridged reinforcements. Gold was the standard issue color, but personalization was not uncommon. Adorned with a fierce-looking dragon, this one logged combat missions over Korea on the head of Fighter Squadron 151 pilot Lieutenant (jg) Al Bedford during 1953. (Al Audleman)*

Left: *Fighter Squadron 11 pilots pictured wearing Mk-2 life vests, which were worn in cockpits from the late 1940s through the Vietnam War. A signal light is visible on the front of the vest, and the pockets contain a compass, smoke flares, shark repellent, dye markers, and a hunting knife. (National Museum of Naval Aviation)*

Below: *The advent of increasingly faster aircraft capable of routinely eclipsing the sound barrier prompted the introduction of high-pressure suits like this Mk4 worn by Fighter Squadron 142 skipper Commander George Whisler. The squadron flew the F-8 Crusader, the first operational fighter in history to exceed 1,000 mph. (Commander George Whisler)*

by today's standards, but they did afford better protection and sound attenuation for the ear cups. Flight helmet design continually improved as technology advanced rapidly in all aviation sciences. The helmet lost its distinctive ridges and began shedding weight ounce by ounce; under G forces several ounces can became several pounds of debilitating weight on an aviator's head. Lightweight, form-fitting helmets with "poured" liners shaped to the aviator's head became a major breakthrough in the 1970s, with many individuals shelling out several hundred dollars to commercial providers when the Navy could not keep up with the commercial market. The Navy introduced its own form-fitting helmets by the early 1980s and continues to seek designs that fit the aviator's head snugly for comfort and noise attenuation, coupling minimum weight with maximum protection. In addition, night vision goggles adapted to today's flight helmets allow for more effective performance of missions on even the blackest of nights.

Similarly, survival equipment worn by today's aircrew is the result of decades of progress. Initially, aside from the parachute, aviators had little to rely on for survival. During the interwar period, a practical inflatable life preserver, nicknamed the "Mae West" because of its busty appearance

Top and above: *The development of flight helmets during a half century of naval aviation history is evident when comparing a leather helmet with attached neck protection worn by Navy test pilot Al Williams during the 1920s and Lieutenant Randy Cunningham's flight helmet worn when he became the first ace of the Vietnam War. (Robert K. Ander, top; Al Audleman, above)*

Top, right: *Ensign Robert E. Bennett pictured next to his torpedo-laden AD Skyraider on the flight deck of* Princeton *(CV 37) on 1 May 1951. He wears standard Korean War-era flight gear, though the mission on which he is about to launch is anything but normal—a torpedo attack against the Hwachon Dam. (Commander Robert E. Bennett)*

Modern night vision goggles like these worn by Commander Chuck Antonio allow pilots to fly with increased proficiency in dark and stormy conditions. (U.S. Navy)

after inflation, and a deployable personal life raft appeared. These two items greatly increased the chances of survival for aviators forced to abandon their aircraft over water, and undoubtedly saved countless numbers of men in World War II as they ventured forth over the vast expanses of the Pacific Ocean.

During the war a flight suit or coverall design became available in summer and winter designs, giving aviators an alternative to wearing a

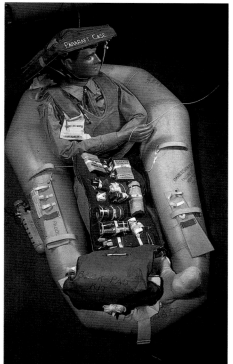

working uniform. It is interesting to note that up to this time the working uniform consisted of a shirt and tie, which gave birth to a lasting tradition in naval aviation. When a student returned from his first solo flight, his instructor clipped the student's tie with scissors, thus signaling to everyone his achievement of that particular milestone.

Advances in treated materials in the 1970s brought Nomex fire-retardant material, and by 1980, the models still in use today began to replace the older model flight suits. G-suits, which reduce the flow of blood away from the head and keep the pilot from blacking out during high-G maneuvers, arrived later in World War II and quickly became standard equipment on tactical aircraft. The advent of the aforemen-

Above, left: *Fighter pilots at NAS Jacksonville, Florida, practice inflating rubber rafts in a swimming pool in August 1944. Given the fact that their operations routinely involve long-distance flights over water, naval aviators receive extensive training in water survival. (U.S. Navy)*

Above: *World War II life rafts carried on board naval aircraft contained equipment and provisions designed to meet almost any emergency situation. Many airmen survived on the open water for days thanks to rafts like this one. (U.S. Navy)*

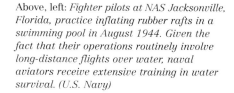

No World War II-era aviator could forget striding out to his aircraft with the bulky seat-pack parachute slamming against his posterior. Some remembered it for another reason, namely the fact that the parachute saved their lives. (Dave Parsons collection)

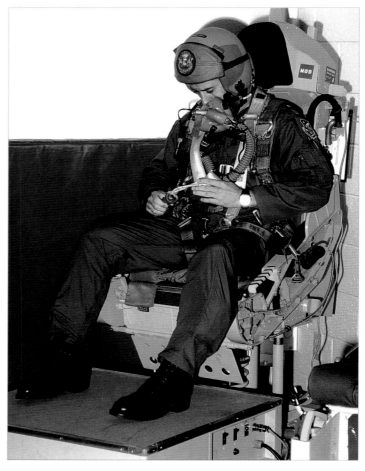

tioned ejection seat necessitated a specialized torso harness to attach the occupant to the seat and parachute, as well as an integrated life vest. By the late 1950s, the vest featured pouches for additional survival equipment such as flares, dye markers, water, a flashlight and other necessities. The torso harness itself not only safely attached the wearer to the ejection seat, but featured a D-ring for attachment to a helicopter hoist for rescue purposes.

Above: *Lieutenant Commander Kelly McBride of Fighter Squadron 114 arms himself with a M-9 9mm pistol on board* Abraham Lincoln *(CVN 72) prior to launching on a patrol over Iraq on 5 August 1991. Survival vests worn by modern aircrews contain up to ten pounds of signaling gear and provisions in addition to inflatable flotation devices. (U.S. Navy)*

Top, right: *Under the watchful eyes of rescue swimmers, a student aviator practices swimming from beneath a billowing parachute during training at NAS Pensacola, Florida. Repeated practice of proper procedures lays the foundation for survival in the event the real thing occurs in the fleet. (Al Audleman)*

Middle, right: *The "Helo Dunker," a cylindrical device that is dropped into a pool, teaches pilots and aircrewmen how to escape from the cabin of a helicopter that has crashed into the sea. (Al Audleman)*

Right: *Astronaut John L. Swigert experiences the feeling of plunging into the water in the "Dilbert Dunker," a device known throughout naval aviation. Once submerged, the cockpit rolls inverted and the student trainee must unstrap his seat belt and swim to the surface. (U.S. Navy)*

Even the modern age of survival equipment, has seen continual advances. Ejection seat design eventually permitted an integrated seat pack housing a raft and survival gear. By the 1980s, aviators had added protection afforded by sea-water-activated release of the Koch parachute fittings to prevent the possibility of being dragged by the parachute upon a water

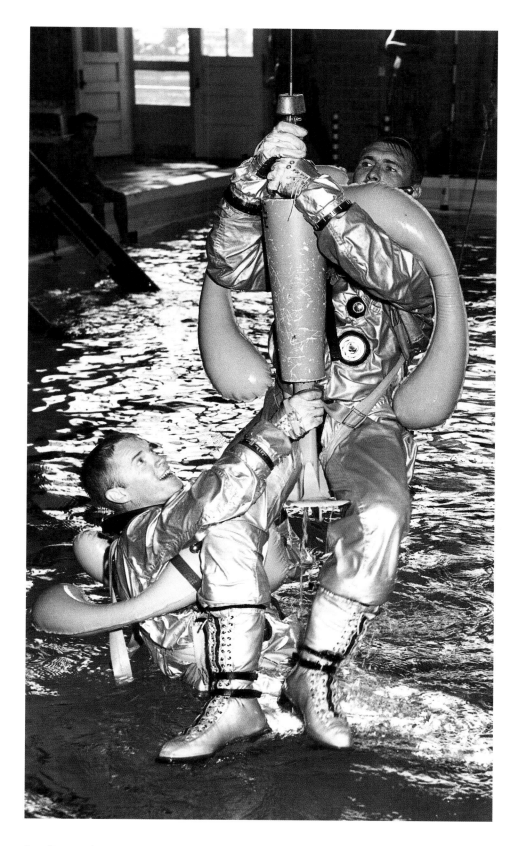

Top, right: *Lieutenant Commander Joseph T. Lawler wears the full complement of equipment carried aloft by naval aviators in 1945, including life vest, parachute, binoculars, and a survival knife. In his right hand he carries a navigation board that slides into the instrument panel of his F6F Hellcat fighter. (U.S. Navy)*

Above: *Commander John Leenhouts pictured on the flight deck of* John F. Kennedy *(CV 67) during the Gulf War. From the most primitive protective equipment worn by the pioneers of naval aviation has emerged the modern armor of the air. (U.S. Navy)*

Left: *Astronauts from the Mercury program to the modern era undergo water survival training under the watchful eyes of U.S. Navy instructors. Here Lieutenant Commander Richard F. Gordon practices climbing onto a helicopter rescue hoist with the assistance of fellow astronaut Russell L. Schweickart during a 1964 training exercise. (U.S. Navy)*

landing. Likewise, this technology was incorporated into the life preserver activation system providing inflation in the event of incapacitation when the aviator landed in the ocean.

Like naval aviation itself, the clothing and equipment worn by personnel is a blend of progress and tradition. Whether it be the leather jacket and flowing scarves of aviation lore, or today's fighter pilot masked behind the darkened sun visor of a colorfully decorated helmet, it symbolizes the uniqueness of those who call the sky and clouds home.

Green & Gold

Green & Gold
Leathernecks of the Air

Commander Peter B. Mersky, USNR (Ret)

A CH-53E Super Stallion emanates an aura of brute power as it launches from Marine Corps Air Station El Toro, California, on 10 May 1999. Crowned by seven rotor blades, the CH-53E can carry loads of up to sixteen tons and accommodate fifty-six Marines and their gear. (Ted Carlson)

Above: *The crew of a DeHavilland DH-4 assigned to D Squadron, First Marine Aviation Force, pictured in France during the final months of World War I. The aircraft mounts two .30-caliber machine guns, the pilot's synchronized to fire through the spinning propeller and the gunner's positioned on a flexible mount, enabling the crew to defend against enemy fighters they might encounter while participating in raids as part of the Northern Bombing Group. (U.S. Marine Corps)*

Left: *First Lieutenant Alfred A. Cunningham, the first Marine designated a naval aviator, stands in front of a Curtiss Jenny, an aircraft produced in great numbers for American fliers before sending them overseas during World War I. Typical of the era, Cunningham sports a leather flight jacket as well as puttees strapped around his lower legs. (National Museum of Naval Aviation)*

Pages 208–209: *The photographer's lens captures the backbone of the Marine helicopter force on the flight deck of the amphibious assault ship* Iwo Jima (LPH 2) *led by a CH-46 Sea Knight, the Corps's primary medium lift helicopter since the Vietnam War. Behind it are an AH-1T attack helicopter, a UH-1N "Huey," and a CH-53E Super Stallion. (Rick Mullen)*

The Beginning

The proud tradition of the U.S. Marine Corps began in November 1775, and through the more than 200 years that followed gained such legendary status that it is impossible to think of this country's military accomplishments without special attention to the seagoing soldiers of the Corps. And within that unique band, there is an even more definitive type of Marine, those who wear the wings of gold. Though barely ninety years old, Marine aviation enjoys a tradition of heroic sacrifice and patriotic dedication that is second to none.

Alfred A. Cunningham displayed a certain courage and longing for adventure before he ever set eyes on an airplane, volunteering to serve in the Army during the Spanish-American war at the ripe old age of sixteen. Eventually receiving his commission as a Marine officer, Cunningham displayed an interest in aviation while assigned to the Philadelphia Navy Yard, and on 12 May 1912 he received orders to report for training at Annapolis, Maryland, thus becoming the first Marine to enter flight training. Other leathernecks followed, and when the United States entered World War I in April 1917, Cunningham organized an aviation company at Philadelphia.

On the ground the performance of the Marines in the trenches of World War I was the stuff of legend, with their fighting abilities at such

Carrying their weapons and packs, Marines stand next to an Atlantic TA-2 of Marine Utility Squadron 6 that will transport them to another base of operations in Nicaragua. Marine aviation, whether engaged in ground attack or providing logistical support, proved especially useful during the Corps's campaigns against the Sandinistas in the 1920s and 1930s. (National Museum of Naval Aviation)

The Marine Flying Field at Quantico, Virginia—the "Crossroads of the Corps"—served as the home of Marine aviation on the East Coast. Flying from its grass field during the 1920s, leatherneck pilots operated an ad hoc collection of aircraft. Those pictured here include (left to right) a DeHavilland DH-4, two Curtiss Jennys, and a Vought VE-7 fighter. (U.S. Marine Corps)

One of the more unusual aircraft evaluated by the Corps during the interwar years was the Pitcairn XOP-1 autogyro. Though the hybrid rotary/fixed-wing aircraft never saw active service, it foreshadowed the day when a sizeable number of Marine pilots flew beneath rotor blades. (National Museum of Naval Aviation)

places as Belleau Wood, France, earning them the nickname "Devil Dogs" from the Germans. As for the tiny Marine air arm, the war's first months were spent on monotonous antisubmarine patrols out of the Azores Islands and on duty at a number of stateside fields. Not until June 1918 did the first Marine aviators arrive in France, but their assignment promised to take them into combat. Flying whatever British DH-4 two-seat bombers they could scrape together, the Marines became part of the Day Wing of the Northern Bombing Group, operating a total of four squadrons in bombing missions against German submarine pens in Belgium. Though they flew in combat for less than a month, the aviators represented the Corps well. By 11 November, the date of the armistice ending the conflict, the First Marine Aviation Force had flown forty-three missions with the Royal Air Force and fourteen on its own, accounting for four German fighters, with claims for eight more. Four Marines had died in action.

One Marine who did not return home was Second Lieutenant Ralph Talbot, who along with his gunner, Corporal Robert G. Robinson, engaged in a running gun battle with eleven German aircraft during a 14 October 1918 mission. Robinson bore the brunt of the initial onslaught, receiving wounds in his arm, chest, and stomach. Before his gun jammed, he managed to down one of the attackers, but his wounds eventually rendered him unconscious. At the controls, Talbot maneuvered his bomber into firing range, unleashing some rounds that found their mark. With his gunner slumped over in the rear cockpit, he headed for home with a German on his tail. "Twisting, turning, zooming trees," his tentmate later related, "he fled with every ounce of power, while above the roar of the motor he could feel the zip of bullets as every part of the plane was struck." Talbot managed to land at a friendly field in Belgium. Robinson recovered from his wounds and received a promotion, but eleven days later Talbot was dead, ironically the victim of an operational accident after surviving such an ordeal against the enemy. Both men eventually were awarded the Medal of Honor.

Between Wars

Just before returning home from Europe following the end of World War I, Cunningham expressed concern over the future of Marine Corps aviation, saying, "I think we could accomplish much more at home getting our Aviation service established under the new conditions of peace." Ironically for the Marine Corps, the ensuing years proved anything but peaceful, for despite reduced resources it found itself deployed in brushfire wars in Central America and guarding American interests in China. Though traditionalists in the ground element of the Corps questioned aviation's importance, events would aptly demonstrate the value of air power. In

This painting illustrates First Lieutenant Christian Schilt's arrival at Quilali, Nicaragua, the first of ten flights he made into the besieged town to evacuate eighteen wounded Marines ambushed by Nicaraguan bandits in January 1928. For his heroic actions in the hotly contested battle zone, Schilt was awarded the Medal of Honor. ("Like an Angel," James Dietz)

Above: *Pilots of the famed Ace of Spades squadron, the insignia visible on their flight jackets, pictured on the flight deck of* Langley *(CV 1) in July 1936. The first leatherneck squadrons deployed on board a flattop in 1931. (U.S. Navy)*

Left: *Boeing F4B-3 fighters of Marine Fighting Squadron Four pictured in formation in June 1933. One of the most successful biplane fighters of the interwar period, the F4B served with the Navy and Marine Corps, and with the Army as the P-12. Many of the senior military aviators of World War II cut their teeth on these nimble little aircraft. Note the bomb racks suspended beneath the fuselage just behind the landing gear. (U.S. Marine Corps)*

Bill Gise · Duke Davis · Pe Sampas · Jack Tyler · Ken Bottinger

Ward Dickey · Al Kryser · Charlie Fike · Herb Becker · Vern Magee · Pete Bartoe · She

Squadron skipper Major Gregory Boyington tops the list of pilots on the squadron roster penned in the original log of Marine Fighting Squadron 214, the "Black Sheep." Also noted are the pilots missing in action, including "Pappy" Boyington. (Al Audleman)

Opposite, bottom: *A Marine pilot beckons new recruits for aviation units in a September 1945 recruiting poster. The aircraft pictured in the background is an F7F Tigercat, a twin-engine fighter that arrived too late for combat service during World War II. (Al Audleman)*

Nicaragua, Marine aircraft helped supply the wide-ranging patrols operating in the jungle in search of rebel forces called Sandinistas. During one operation in January 1928, First Lieutenant Christian Schilt logged ten flights under fire to evacuate eighteen wounded personnel from the besieged town of Quilali, certainly winning the hearts of those on the ground. However, it was the development of what would become one of the primary tactics for air-ground operations that had the most lasting impact. The aviation contingent in Haiti, part of a Marine brigade battling with the so-called Cacos, employed a handful of tired Curtiss JN-4 Jennys in scouting and harassing missions, precursors of the missions that would come to typify Marine air in later wars. Though there are documented instances of diving attacks on enemy troops during World War I, Marine pilots certainly advanced the tactic of dive-bombing during combat in Nicaragua, Haiti, and the Dominican Republic, dropping fragmentation bombs and directing machine gun fire at enemy personnel. Thus, the foundation was laid for the doctrine of close air support, which appeared in the *Tentative Landing Operations Manual* in 1935. Marine aviators would employ this tactic with much success in the island campaigns of World War II, which for the United States erupted with the Japanese attack on Pearl Harbor, Hawaii, on 7 December 1941.

Members of the Second Marine Air Group pictured at San Diego, California, in March 1940. Among these prewar aviators is First Lieutenant Gregory Boyington (far right, second row). Other notable faces include Bill Gise (second row, second from left), Charles Fike (sitting, fifth from left), Vern Magee (sitting, seventh from left) and Sam Moore (sitting, second from right). These men made names for themselves as squadron and air group commanders during World War II. (Colonel William Bauer)

World War II

During the early months of the Pacific war, the Allies could do little to stem the tide of Japanese conquest, though it was the Marine Corps that provided a symbol of defiance for the enemy and an American public starved for any positive news. It came at a spit of land called Wake Island, where for sixteen harrowing days in December 1941, an outnumbered and undersupplied garrison fought a delaying action against overwhelming enemy forces. Personnel of Marine Fighting Squadron (VMF) 211, despite the gradual destruction of their complement of F4F Wildcat fighters, helped repulse the first enemy attempt to conquer Wake, sinking a destroyer and damaging two other vessels. In the end, Marine aviators joined their brethren "grunts," as well as Navy and civilian contract personnel, inflicting many losses on the Japanese invasion force that eventually took Wake.

Another Pacific atoll called Midway was the next great battleground for Marine aviation. Though Navy carrier aircraft scored the blows that achieved ultimate victory, land-based Marine aircrews heroically launched strikes against the Japanese fleet despite overwhelming odds. The experiences of First Lieutenant Daniel Iverson tell the story of

You can ENLIST NOW in the
U.S. MARINE CORPS
for
"DUTY IN AVIATION UNITS"

An SB2U-3 Vindicator of Marine Scout Bombing Squadron 131 pictured during a July 1941 flight. The first monoplane scout-bomber procured by the Navy and Marine Corps, the fabric-covered aircraft was outclassed by its Japanese counterparts when war broke out. At the Battle of Midway in June 1942, agile Zeros decimated a squadron of Vindicators, though one SB2U pilot, Captain Richard Fleming, received the Medal of Honor posthumously for an attack against a heavy cruiser during the battle. (Rudy Arnold collection)

the vicious aerial battle. Half of his flight of SBD Dauntless dive bombers failed to return from a 4 June 1942 mission in which they attacked Japanese carriers without the benefit of fighter protection. Pursued by enemy fighters and diving on a flight deck which appeared as if it were a "ring of fire," Iverson sustained over 200 bullet holes in his aircraft, one round coming so close that its severed the cord of his throat microphone. With a wounded gunner aboard, no hydraulics and one landing gear locked in the up position, he nevertheless managed to land safely.

The survivors of Midway soon found themselves thrust into battle at distant islands in the South Pacific. The first Allied offensive in the Pacific, the battle for Guadalcanal was destined to become the watershed battle in that theater and a hallowed name in the history of the Marine Corps. Elements of the First Marine Division went ashore on 7 August 1942 and quickly captured the airfield on the island, christening it Henderson Field. But the enemy was waiting and soon began an all-out effort to repel the American invaders. Thirteen days later, the same day the first Marine Corps aircraft arrived at Guadalcanal, the Japanese launched their first major effort to capture the airfield, the beginning of a pattern that lasted for three harrowing months. With only a thin defensive perimeter sepa-

Top, left: *Marines operating from Henderson Field on Guadalcanal lived under the constant threat of bombardment from Japanese ships and aircraft. Set afire by a bomb hit on the hangar in the background, this F4F Wildcat fighter survived to fight another day thanks to quick action by men on the ground, some of whom shoveled dirt on the airplane to extinguish the flames. The embattled leathernecks could ill afford to lose any aircraft during the battle for the island. (U.S. Marine Corps)*

Above: *Three important figures of the Guadalcanal campaign pose in 1943, safely back at NAS Anacostia, near Washington, D.C. Major John L. Smith (left) and Captain Marion E. Carl (right) both racked up impressive kill tallies while serving in Marine Fighting Squadron 223, with squadron commander Smith receiving the Medal of Honor. Lieutenant Colonel Richard C. Mangrum led the first squadron of dive bombers to arrive at Guadalcanal, becoming one of the most respected Marine squadron commanders. (U.S. Marine Corps)*

Left: *Pilots of Marine Fighting Squadron 121, some of the heroic members of the "Cactus Air Force," arrayed on one of their squadron F4F-4 Wildcat fighters in February 1943. Captain Joe Foss, wearing the baseball cap in the upper left of this photograph, shot down twenty-six Japanese aircraft during the war. (U.S. Marine Corps)*

rating them from the Japanese, bombarded often by the heavy guns of enemy surface ships, and living amidst the sweltering heat and disease of the jungle island, the performance of the men of the "Cactus Air Force" was nothing short of remarkable. Such was the intensity of the battle that of the fifteen original pilots of Marine Scout Bombing Squadron 232 who arrived at Guadalcanal on 20 August 1942, by the end of September only three remained, the rest having been either killed in action or evacuated because of wounds or fatigue.

Nevertheless, in the cockpits of their war-weary airplanes, they thwarted Japanese attempts to reinforce their garrisons on Guadalcanal by sea, supported the troops on the ground, and out-dueled the enemy in air-to-air combat. Of the eleven Medals of Honor received by Marine aviators during World War II, six went to leatherneck pilots at Guadalcanal, including a posthumous award to Lieutenant Colonel Joe Bauer, who had written to his wife just after Pearl Harbor that "war is a hell of

Following page, top: *A trio of F4U-1A Corsairs of Marine Fighting Squadron 224 stir up dirt on Majuro Atoll as they prepare to launch on a combat mission in August 1944. No plane symbolized Marine Corps aviation more during World War II than the F4U Corsair, in which leatherneck pilots excelled in air-to-air combat over the Solomon Islands and Rabaul. As the bombs suspended beneath these Corsairs reveal, the gull-winged fighters also proved capable ground attack platforms. (U.S. Marine Corps)*

Above: *In a rare wartime color photograph, First Lieutenant Jeremiah O'Keefe proudly announces his tally of seven Japanese aircraft, a mark which is also denoted by the kill flags displayed on his airplane. O'Keefe flew with the Death Rattlers of Marine Fighting Squadron 323, chalking up his kills in April 1945. The close-up of the cockpit provides an excellent view of the "bubble" canopy that appeared on later versions of the Corsair. (Jeremiah O'Keefe)*

Right: *Black Sheep scramble! Pilots of Major "Pappy" Boyington's Marine Fighting Squadron 214 carry their seat pack parachutes as they race to their airplanes. The squadron's fighter aircraft are early model F4U-1 Corsairs featuring "birdcage" cockpit canopies, which were later replaced by "bubble" canopies that afforded better vision. Taken at Turtle Bay airstrip on Espiritu Santo, this is a staged photograph for the benefit of the press, which could not help but be drawn to the squadron and its colorful skipper. (U.S. Marine Corps)*

a thing to face, [but] there is no better way to die than in the process of defending one's country and loved ones."

The subsequent campaign up the Solomon Islands chain relied increasingly upon Marine air power, and its veritable symbol was the Chance Vought F4U Corsair, one of the most successful naval aircraft of the war. Flying long-range escort missions, the "U-bird," so named because of the aircraft's gull wing design, proved the scourge of the Japanese, wracking up scores of kills in air-to-air combat and producing a roll call of fighter aces headed by the likes of Gregory "Pappy" Boyington, Robert Hanson, Donald Aldrich, and Ken Walsh. Corsairs joined the venerable Dauntless and TBF/TBM Avenger torpedo bombers in perfecting close air support. Flying from recently captured airfields or, as was the case in the war's latter stage, the decks of aircraft carriers, the Marines took this skill to the last, bloodiest battles of the war, culminating in the

invasion of Okinawa, Japan. And in the arena of night operations, the Corps played a leading role in the Pacific as well. The Marines commissioned their first night fighter squadron in April 1943, and Marine Night Fighting Squadron (VMF(N)) 513, flying modified PV-1 Ventura patrol bombers, scored its first kill on 13 November 1943. Another patrol bomber, the PB4Y-1 Liberator, equipped Marine Photographic Squadron 254 when it made the first photoreconnaissance mission over the Japanese bastion of Truk Island on 4 February 1944.

In 1939, there were just two Marine Aircraft Groups (MAGs), including only nine squadrons, representing the whole of Marine Corps aviation. By September 1944, Marine air assets encompassed five wings, thirty-one MAGs and 145 squadrons. In 1939, only 232 leathernecks wore wings of gold, but by January 1945, the number had grown to 10,412. These Marine crews shot down 2,355 enemy aircraft, while 367 of their number were killed in aerial action.

Postwar Activities and Development

Radically new forms of aircraft took center stage for the Corps in the years immediately following World War II. Jets began replacing propeller-driven airplanes in fighter squadrons, a testament to the constant search for speed in that particular arena of air combat. Yet, it was the helicopter that had the most lasting effect on the employment of Marine Corps aviation. It was believed that the complicated amphibious operations of the past war would not suffice on a nuclear battlefield; mobility became a top priority. The helicopter appeared to be the answer, for it could deliver troops to a number of different locations on a battlefield and facilitate quick movement of men and supplies from ship to shore.

Marine gunners practice belting ammunition during training at Marine Corps Air Station El Centro, California in 1944. Following in the tradition of Corporal Robert G. Robinson, the Marine gunner who received the Medal of Honor during World War I, enlisted men who manned machine guns on the SBD Dauntless, TBF/TBM Avenger, PBJ Mitchell, and other airplanes displayed unparalleled heroism during World War II. (National Museum of Naval Aviation)

Lieutenant General Roy S. Geiger rose to prominence during World War II as one of the Corps's leading aviator generals. Designated a naval aviator in 1917, he commanded the Marine aviation forces at Guadalcanal during the uncertain days of the pivotal battle. Following the death of Army Lieutenant General Simon B. Buckner on Okinawa in June 1945, Geiger became the first Marine officer ever to command an army. He died on active duty in 1947. (National Museum of Naval Aviation)

Above: *Captain Ken Reusser (left) shows Major Robert P. Keller, skipper of Marine Fighting Squadron 214, the location of a target he successfully destroyed on 4 August 1950. This photo was taken on board* Sicily *(CVE 118), one of the escort carriers from which Marine Corsair squadrons flew missions during the early months of the Korean War. (U.S. Navy)*

Top, right: *Members of Marine Attack Squadron 312 pose for a picture during the Korean War. The Checkerboards flew under the fighter designation during Korea as well, and their distinctively marked Corsairs logged missions from the flight decks of three escort carriers and one light carrier. (National Museum of Naval Aviation)*

Right: *Marine Attack Squadron 121 was one of only three Marine Corps AD Skyraider squadrons in Korea. This squadron aircraft, pictured just before the signing of the armistice in 1953, carries an extraordinary load of bombs. (Howard Heiner)*

Below: *A unique figure in American military aviation, Major John F. Bolt became the Marine Corps's first and only jet ace and naval aviation's only two-war ace in the skies over Korea. As a member of Major Gregory "Pappy" Boyington's Black Sheep squadron during World War II, he shot down six Japanese aircraft in the Pacific. Flying an exchange tour with an Air Force F-86 squadron in Korea, he shot down six MiG-15 jets. (National Museum of Naval Aviation)*

By the end of the 1940s, the Marine Corps was deeply involved in bringing the first helicopters to service, just in time for another war in Asia.

North Korean troops plunged into South Korea on 25 June 1950, surprising the South Korean defenders and their U.S. Army advisors. In a series of delaying actions, the Americans and their poorly equipped allies struggled to fend off the Communist attacks. Aircraft carriers represented the only sustained presence of air power during the war's first weeks, with F4U Corsairs of VMF-214 and VMF-323 operating from the decks of the escort carriers *Sicily* (CVE 118) and *Badoeng Strait* (CVE 116). In the months that followed, Marine aircraft and their crews logged thousands of close air support missions, as well as bomber escort and attack missions, ranging up and down the embattled peninsula. The World War II-era Corsair found a new lease on life as the quintessential close air support platform of the war, applauded by ground soldiers who radioed for help while under Communist guns. As testament to how low the aviators flew to support the men of the ground, one story that circulated in Korea told of Corsairs making a strafing run over an assembly of Marines on a ridge, their advance delayed by an enemy machine gun nest to their front. "Please ask

Left: *An F7F-3N Tigercat pilot observes the hand signals of the plane director prior to launching on a night mission from Kunsan, Korea, in 1951. Along with another World War II design, the F4U Corsair, the twin-engine Tigercat served the night fighter needs of the Marine Corps during the first part of the Korean War. (W.R. Crim)*

Above: *Painted in low-visibility black paint with red numbers, an F3D-2 Skyknight of Marine Night Fighting Squadron 513 undergoes routine maintenance in Korea during 1954. Skyknights enjoyed considerable success in night skies in the last year of the Korean War, and even saw considerable action during the first three years of the Vietnam War. This photograph provides an excellent view of the aircraft's radar. The small antenna is the APS-26 lock-on radar, while the large dish is for the APS-21 search radar. (E.S. Holmberg)*

the people in the front row to be seated," one pilot radioed. "It makes me nervous the see the back[s] of their heads in [my] gun sight."

Korea was the proving ground for jet aircraft, and Marine F9F Panthers, F2H Banshees, and F3D Skyknights saw heavy combat. The Panthers introduced jet close air support, complementing the slower Corsair, while the F2H flew photoreconnaissance missions in such numbers that one squadron shot enough film to circle the globe more than six times. The F3Ds served only with VMF(N)-513 and flew mostly at night, protecting U.S. Air Force B-29 bombers from North Korean MiG-15 interceptors. When F3Ds flew escort, the vulnerable B-29s, masters of the skies over Japan only seven years before, never lost a single plane to Communist defenders. In the early stages of the war, the squadron also operated the F7F Tigercat—a graceful, twin-engine fighter that had arrived too late to see action in the Pacific during World War II—and it was this aircraft that scored the first night kill in Korea for the leathernecks.

The Marines also introduced battlefield helicopter transport in Korea when Marine Helicopter Transport Squadron 161 arrived in September 1951 with the Sikorsky HRS. The HRS's engine was mounted in the nose,

Above: *Major Elswin P. Dunn and his radar operator, Master Sergeant Lawrence J. Fortin, of Marine Night Fighting Squadron 513 shot down a MiG-15 in their Douglas F3D-2 Skyknight on 15 January 1953. The two aviators wear heavy anti-exposure suits for the frigid Korean winter. Note the single red star denoting their kill directly above and between them. (National Museum of Naval Aviation)*

Left: *The Korean War brought the helicopter its first experience in combat operations. Marine Helicopter Transport Squadron 161 used its HRSs to carry supplies and troops to front-line positions, often under heavy enemy fire. By today's standards, the little Sikorsky was underpowered and carried a small payload, but it quickly established the helicopter's usefulness. (U.S. Marine Corps)*

Pilots of an HOK helicopter from Marine Observation Squadron 2 confer with fellow Marines prior to launching on a reconnaissance flight over Korea during Operation Seahawk in June 1960. Support of Marines on the ground is a hallmark of Marine aviation. (U.S. Marine Corps)

Opposite, top: This dramatic photograph staged in 1955 to demonstrate the Marine air-ground team shows AD Skyraiders of Marine Attack Squadron 333 roaring over grunts struggling up from the beachhead after an amphibious landing on the North Carolina coast. Marine pilots pride themselves on their ability to fly close air support missions, and since before World War II aviation has served as a vital element of Marine Corps amphibious warfare doctrine. (National Museum of Naval Aviation)

Sikorsky's HO3S helicopter flew with the Marines, Navy, and Air Force during the Korean War, mostly in observation and rescue duties. This HO3S from Marine Observation Squadron Six evacuates a Navy corpsman from the front lines after he was injured while rescuing a Marine from a minefield in September 1951. Note the stretcher protruding out the side window of the helicopter, and the triangular rigging for the helicopter's rescue hoist. (U.S. Marine Corps)

below and in front of the cockpit behind two clamshell doors, and it could carry 1,500 pounds of cargo at a speed of 90 knots. The first use of helicopters to move troops into a battle zone occurred in October when twelve of the ungainly machines made 156 round trips with 958 men. The HRS also kept up morale during holidays, bringing Thanksgiving and Christmas dinners to the front lines. The Marines used several other types of helicopters for medical evacuation and liaison duties.

The Greatest Crucible: Vietnam

Less than a decade separated the Marine Corps from Korea and the next large-scale involvement in an Asian war, this time in Vietnam. The interlude witnessed the natural progression of aircraft as Marine squadrons rotated duty in the Far East. The first Marine aviators deployed to South Vietnam in April 1962 to bolster the nation's defenses against Communist insurgents from neighboring North Vietnam. Lieutenant Colonel Archie J. Clapp, commanding officer of Marine Medium Helicopter Squadron 362, took his squadron of UH-34 Seahorses and OE Birddog light liaison aircraft to Soc Trang, eighty-five miles southwest of Saigon. In the improbably named Shufly operations, the squadron's mission was to provide transport support to the hard-pressed Army of the Republic of Vietnam. For three years, Shufly squadrons moved their allies in and out of the battlefield, eventually taking on increased combat roles as the Communist Viet Cong guerrillas fired from the jungles and bush at the American helicopters lumbering into landing

Above: *On 19 August 1967, UH-1 pilot Captain Stephen W. Pless (right) and his crew rescued four Army soldiers pinned down on a beach by a superior force of Viet Cong guerrillas. Pless purposefully landed his helicopter between the enemy force and friendly personnel so that the latter could be pulled on board his helicopter. The Marine Observation Squadron 6 pilot was the only Marine aviator to receive the Medal of Honor in Southeast Asia. (National Museum of Naval Aviation)*

Top, right: *First Lieutenant H.C. Brown observes a servicing operation from the cockpit of his UH-34 Seahorse during a Shufly mission in 1963. Note his camouflage fatigues and flak jacket and the machine gun for the door gunner. (H.C. Brown)*

Right: *UH-34 Seahorses land on board the amphibious assault ship* Vancouver (LPD 2) *for refueling during Operation Deckhouse IV on 14 September 1966. Universally known by the Marines as the "HUS," the pre-1962 designation of the aircraft, the UH-34 served as the Corps's front-line assault helicopter during the first part of the Vietnam War. Similar in appearance to its HRS predecessor, with the bulbous nose that housed the aircraft's engine, the Seahorse was certainly ungainly in appearance, but a welcome site for leathernecks on the ground. (U.S. Marine Corps)*

Opposite, top: *An F-8E Crusader of Marine All-Weather Fighter Squadron 235 taxis for a mission from Da Nang, South Vietnam, in 1967. Only four squadrons of Marine Crusaders flew in Southeast Asia during the Vietnam War, and only until 1968. However, during that time, the F-8s unexpectedly proved their worth as bombers, especially in close air support work. Not more than one Crusader fighter squadron was in-country at any one time and the three units that rotated through Da Nang merely transferred their valuable F-8s to the incoming unit. (National Museum of Naval Aviation)*

zones to deliver their charges. It was the beginning of the era of the armed helicopter and the development of true rotary-wing battlefield tactics that would take center stage in the protracted struggle in Vietnam. The men of the helicopter squadrons proved worthy of the test. Over the course of the war, two received the Medal of Honor, and some thirty other pilots and aircrewmen were awarded the Navy Cross for valor in combat. Among them was Major Vince Hazelbaker, who made two night flights on 8 August 1966 to deliver supplies to a surrounded reaction team, in the process coming under intense enemy fire that eventually downed his aircraft and wounded two crewmen. With all of the infantry officers either killed or wounded, the aviator assumed direction of defenses on the ground, holding out until the force could be extracted by helicopter the following morning.

Even before the Tonkin Gulf incident in August 1964 led to heightened military intervention in Vietnam, Marine photoreconnaissance aircraft

operated alongside their Navy counterparts over Laos. With the widening of the war and introduction of sizable ground forces, close air support became a top priority. Operating from bases at Da Nang and Chu Lai, A-4 Skyhawks formed the backbone of the effort, with F-8 Crusader and F-4 Phantom II fighters also pressed into service in this role. In addition, the OV-10 Bronco— a twin-turboprop, two-seat aircraft that carried fixed machine guns, as well as an assortment of rockets and light bombs on fuselage sponsons—was a unique aircraft well suited to its role as an armed scout and light close air support response airplane.

By 1969, the American presence in Vietnam began to diminish. Though the Marine Corps's contribution to the air campaign in North Vietnam proved limited when compared to the number of Navy and Air Force aircraft sent "up north," it increased during the intense bombing effort of 1971–1972. This included deployment on board two carriers, the

Middle, left: *UH-1 helicopters touch down with their loads at Fire Support Base Cunningham during Operation Dewey Canyon in January 1969. Helicopters proved essential in keeping Marine positions supplied with food and ammunition. The Huey served in all United States service branches in Vietnam, often in the offensive role as gunships. (U.S. Marine Corps)*

Middle, right: *The OV-10 Bronco, pictured here in the post-Vietnam markings of Marine Observation Squadron 2, was effective for low-level battlefield surveillance. Still in service during Operation Desert Storm, the slow Broncos proved vulnerable to Iraqi ground fire and senior commanders were occasionally cautious in using them in areas of heavy enemy activity. (Peter Mersky)*

Above: *This Cessna Birddog O-1 from Marine Observation Squadron 6 flies along the coast of Vietnam in August 1967. When the pilot finds a target, he marks it with smoke rockets and calls in Marine jets to destroy it. (U.S. Marine Corps)*

Entering squadron service during the Vietnam War, the A-6 Intruder provided the Marines a true heavy, long-range attack capability, which they employed until the aircraft's retirement following Operation Desert Storm. These Marine All-Weather Attack Squadron 533 crewmen load ordnance onto a squadron aircraft at Da Nang Air Base in August 1967. The 500-pound Mk 82 Snakeyes are equipped with folding tail fins, which extend after drop to retard the bomb's fall. (U.S. Marine Corps)

First Lieutenant Jim Strock assists an elderly Vietnamese woman across the flight deck of Raleigh *(LKA 114) on 4 April 1975, after a CH-46D Sea Knight of Marine Medium Helicopter Squadron 165 airlifted her to safety from her native land. After many years of carrying men into hot landing zones to face enemy fire, Marine helicopter crews ended U.S. involvement in Vietnam by evacuating American citizens and Vietnamese nationals from South Vietnam. (U.S. Navy)*

The first experience operating the AV-8A Harrier at sea occurred on board Franklin D. Roosevelt *(CV 42), an aging carrier logging her last deployment. Marine Attack Squadron 231, the historic Ace of Spades, operated from the carrier in the Mediterranean during 1976. Perhaps one of the most radical and controversial additions to Marine Corps aviation after Korea, Harrier vertical/short take-off and landing jets entered service in 1971. The skittish attack aircraft quickly established an unfortunate mishap rate, but the Marines remained committed to the Harrier. (U.S. Navy)*

first time Marine aviators had launched into combat from a carrier since 1965. Marine Fighter Attack Squadron (VMFA) 333 took its F-4 Phantom IIs on board *America* (CVA 66), and during the cruise the crew of Major Lee Lassiter and Captain John Cummings scored the only MiG kill of the war involving a Marine crew flying a Marine aircraft, shooting down a MiG-21 on 11 September 1972. From the deck of *Coral Sea* (CVA 43), Marine All-Weather Attack Squadron 224 employed their A-6 Intruders to mine enemy harbors and waterways in May 1972, beginning the last intensive campaigns before a cease-fire in January 1973.

It was the Marine Corps that came to symbolize the painful last days of American involvement in Vietnam. The service's helicopters executed Operation Eagle Pull at Phnom Penh, Cambodia, and Operation Frequent Wind in Saigon, airlifting American citizens and South Vietnamese nationals in the face of enemy fire and uncertain weather conditions. During Frequent Wind, the largest helicopter evacuation in history, aircrews logged 1,054 flight hours and 682 sorties. One pilot, Captain Gerry Berry, flew 18.3 hours in one day, and at one juncture one CH-46 Sea Knight and one CH-53 Sea Stallion landed at the U.S. Embassy in Saigon every ten minutes.

Post-Vietnam Developments

The years following America's longest war brought predictable reduction and reorganization, and a need for upgraded weapon systems after the protracted war in Southeast Asia. The most controversial of the new Marine Corps aircraft was the AV-8 Harrier, a single-seat jet attack plane produced by the British firm of Hawker-Siddley. The Harrier was unique in that it could take off and land vertically, bypassing the need for airfields and runways, and possessed the ability to operate directly at the front lines, a feature constantly sought by the Marines. The aircraft's unconventional nature

prompted doubts about the Harrier, especially given the high accident rate during its first years of operation, yet it became the Corps's main light attack/close air support platform. The venerable A-4s and F-4s were retired in favor of the new F/A-18 Hornet, with the Marines eventually operating both single- and two-seat versions of the aircraft.

Modernized versions of the helicopters that flew combat missions over the jungles of Vietnam—the CH-53, UH-1 Iroquois, AH-1 Sea

The Nevada desert merely a blur below it, an AV-8B Harrier of Marine Attack Squadron 331 practices low-level flying during training exercises at NAS Fallon, Nevada, in October 1985. Note the landing gear, which rotate down for landing, on the trailing edges of the wings. (Boeing)

An F-4N Phantom II, its tail brilliantly decorated to denote its assignment to Marine Fighter Attack Squadron 531, sits poised for launch from Coral Sea *(CV 43) operating in the Arabian Gulf on 25 April 1980. Marine squadrons first began operating from the decks of aircraft carriers in 1931, and in today's military posture a leatherneck squadron routinely deploys as part of a carrier air wing. (Art LeGare)*

Page 228: *An A-4M Skyhawk assigned to Marine Attack Training Squadron 102 unleashes rockets over California's Chocolate Mountains, the pilot honing the air-to-ground skills that are a trademark of Marine aviation. First flown in April 1970, the A-4M version of the famed Skyhawk light attack jet was developed specifically for the Marine Corps, and featured more thrust and a brake parachute to facilitate operations from short airfields in forward areas. (Bruce Trombecky)*

Cobra, and CH-46—continued to form the backbone of the rotary-wing force. During the 1980s, the Corps pinned its hopes on a design incorporating tiltrotor technology, which allows a combination of true rotary-wing launch and landing capabilities and fixed-wing straight-line performance. The XV-15 development platform and the V-22 Osprey production aircraft promises to be one of the most important military types of the twenty-first century. Though accidents and operational difficulties have marred its development, the Osprey is scheduled to replace the CH-46 in medium-lift squadrons by 2005.

Top: *Lieutenant Colonel Len Bucko, Executive Officer of Marine Fighter Attack Squadron 323, fires an AIM-7 Sparrow air-to-air missile from his F/A-18 Hornet during a training mission. The Hornet entered operational service with the Marines in 1983, and the Corps currently operates both single-seat and two-seat versions of the strike fighter. (Robert L. Lawson)*

Above: *An AH-1W Super Cobra of Marine Light Attack Helicopter Squadron 367 dispenses flares during exercises over the California desert in 1999. Over the sands of Kuwait during Operation Desert Storm, AH-1Ws destroyed 97 Iraqi tanks and 104 armored personnel carriers without losing a single aircraft to enemy fire. (Ted Carlson)*

Left: *Close-up view of the cockpit of an AH-1J Sea Cobra, the Marine Corps's front-line attack helicopter since the latter stages of the Vietnam War. The pilot flies the aircraft from the rear cockpit, which is raised to provide better visibility, while the copilot in the front seat is responsible for operating the weapons system. (Peyton DeHart)*

Above: *Marines of the 22d Marine Amphibious Unit board a CH-46 helicopter in Beirut, Lebanon, on 26 February 1984, at the conclusion of the multinational peacekeeping operation during which 220 of their comrades lost their lives in the bombing of the Marine barracks. The tandem-rotor Sea Knight replaced the UH-34 as the Corps's medium lift helicopter. (U.S. Navy)*

Above, right: *Without a doubt, the most eagerly anticipated new aircraft in recent years is the MV-22 Osprey, which offers helicopter takeoff and landing abilities combined with fixed-wing performance. With the Corps's aging helicopter fleet made up of designs that saw combat in Vietnam, the Osprey represents much-needed modernization for the air assault mission. However, the design has been plagued by a series of tragic mishaps that have delayed its introduction. (Ted Carlson)*

On Course to Desert Storm

A series of brushfire wars of limited duration and, at times, questionable value and impact, characterized post-Vietnam combat operations. A short conflict in America's Caribbean backyard in October 1983 pitted American military forces against a limited rebel force backed by Cuban advisors on the island of Grenada. Perhaps the most dramatic action involving Marine flight crews occurred on 25 October, when two AH-1 Sea Cobras were shot down. On board one of them, Captain Jeb Seagle was knocked unconscious and awakened with his aircraft in flames. Disregarding his own safety, he pulled his fellow pilot from the burning wreckage, carried the badly wounded aviator to safety, and attended to his wounds. Seagle then gave his life distracting enemy ground forces from his wounded comrade. He posthumously received a Navy Cross for his heroic actions, the first award of this high combat medal since the Vietnam War.

Terrorist activities in the Middle East, generated by the tangled civil war in Lebanon, increased in the 1980s. Marine Corps units participated

Marines unload a container of hot food from a CH-46E Sea Knight helicopter on 27 August 1990 during Operation Sharp Edge in Liberia. An amphibious ready group off the coast provided personnel and logistic support for the U.S. embassy and assisted in the evacuation of civilians when civil war erupted in the nation. (U.S. Navy)

in a few of the American responses, although in an officially passive role on the ground guarding American interests around Beirut. Marine air assets supported this expedition, as well as combat operations against Libya and in Operation Praying Mantis, a short war at sea in April 1988 that pitted U.S. naval units against marauding Iranian surface units attempting to hinder tanker traffic in the Arabian Gulf. In January 1991, during operations in the war-torn African country of Somalia, crews from Marine Heavy Helicopter Squadron 461, flying from *Guam* (LPH 9), transported a Navy Sea-Air-Land (SEAL) team and sixty Marines to rescue U.S. citizens trapped in the U.S. embassy in Mogadishu. That same month, other Marines prepared to confront the first large-scale war of the post-Vietnam era—Operation Desert Shield/Desert Storm.

The War in the Gulf

The Marine Corps sent some 70 percent of its resources to the Middle East for service in the Gulf War—including several Marine Air Reserve units, the first such mobilization of "weekend warriors" since Korea— operating from air bases in Saudi Arabia and Bahrain and from amphibious assault ships such as *Nassau* (LHA 4). The air campaign began on 16 January 1991, and over the course of the war the Marines stretched their limited assets in several directions, participating in the main allied campaign over Iraq, preparing for a possible amphibious landing in Kuwait, and supporting their own ground troops involved in heavy, sustained combat well inland.

Marines served honorably and heroically in the Arabian Gulf. Although U.S. Air Force F-15 Eagle squadrons scored most of the allied air-to-air kills during the war, one of them had a unique twist. Marine Captain Charles Magill, flying an exchange tour with the 58th Tactical Fighter Squadron, shot down an Iraqi MiG-29 on 17 January, thereby

Bottom, left: *Amphibious assault ships like* Nassau *(LHA 4), pictured here with her flight deck packed during Operation Desert Shield, are veritable aircraft carriers for the Marines. AV-8B Harriers and AH-1 Sea Cobras provide lethal attack platforms to support CH-46 Sea Knight transport helicopters and UH-1 Hueys. (Joe Doyle)*

Below: Iwo Jima *(LPH 2), with helicopters of Marine Heavy Helicopter Squadron 461 embarked, steams through the waters of the Arabian Gulf during Operation Desert Storm. (Rick Mullen)*

Bottom: *Its sting arrayed on its wings in the form of bombs and air-to-air missiles, an F/A-18 Hornet of Marine Fighter Attack Squadron 323 is ready to both tangle with enemy fighters and place ordnance on target. (National Museum of Naval Aviation)*

continuing the tradition begun in Korea and maintained in Vietnam of Marine aviators shooting down enemy aircraft flying Air Force fighters. Lieutenant Colonel Michael M. Kurth, skipper of Marine Light Attack Helicopter Squadron 269, received one of only two Navy Crosses awarded to Marines during the war. Having led five AH-1s from the landing zone called Lonesome Dove on 26 February, Lieutenant Colonel Kurth scouted ahead of the advancing ground forces from the cockpit of a UH-1 helicopter. Contending with severely restricted visibility from oil well fires, he repeatedly flew near and beneath power lines to provide laser designation for the Sea Cobra gunships.

The Gulf War ended on 28 February, the ground phase having lasted barely 100 hours. Although the Iraqis had been soundly defeated on the battlefield, political considerations intruded into the final endpoint of the war, and the government in Baghdad was left in place. With the head of the hydra still alive, the Iraqis were free to attack rebel Kurdish elements,

which fled north toward the Turkish border. A massive supply effort called Provide Comfort involved Navy and Marine helicopter crews flying into mountainous terrain, sometimes dangerously close to mobs of desperate, starving Kurds, to deliver vital food and building materials.

The End of the Century

The changing face of the U.S. military following the Gulf War was visible in Marine aviation as squadrons deactivated and women began training for combat roles. By August 1996, the first two female Marine officers had pinned on their wings of gold, one as a pilot, the other as a naval flight officer. The expeditionary nature of Marine aviation remained unchanged, with new missions, new squadrons, new groupings, and new responsibilities, including operations in the Balkans as an ongoing civil war in Yugoslavia spilled over into adjoining areas, and threatened the security and peace of the entire region.

Operating with other North Atlantic Treaty Organization nations, Marine Hornet squadrons were among the first American units on the scene, arriving in July 1993 to begin flying over Bosnia-Herzegovina. They were soon involved in strikes against the aggressive Bosnian Serb forces. Operation Deliberate Force, in early September 1995, involved a sustained, intense campaign against Serb facilities. Marine All-Weather Fighter Attack Squadron 533 flew 180 sorties, while VMFA-312 and VMFA-251 launched on combat missions from *Theodore Roosevelt* (CVN 71) and

Bottom, left: *Women began wearing Marine green during World War I, but it wasn't until the 1990s that females would fly the Corps's tactical aircraft. Pictured in their F/A-18D Hornet, First Lieutenant Ted Schackleton (front cockpit) and First Lieutenant Christine Westrich prepare for a 1998 training hop. (Ted Carlson)*

Below: *Marine air assets were among those deployed to the Adriatic in response to events in the war-torn former Yugoslavia. The crew of this FA-18D Hornet of Marine All-Weather Fighter Attack Squadron 224 prepares to taxi out for a mission into Bosnia from the base at Aviano, Italy. (Peter Mersky)*

Bottom: *While Marine Hornet squadrons operated from fleet aircraft carriers during Operation Allied Force, AV-8B Harriers launched strike missions from the amphibious assault ship* Nassau *(LHA 4). Here a Harrier pilot receives the "thumbs up" signal before taking off. (U.S. Navy)*

An EA-6B Prowler of the Marine Tactical Electronics Warfare Squadron 2 detachment on board America (CV 66) flies a patrol over the Gulf of Sidra during operations against Libya in April 1986. The only electronic countermeasures platform available in any of the branches of the U.S. military, the Prowler is one of the nation's most important air combat assets. (Dave Parsons)

America (CV 66). The four-week air campaign drew the Serbs to the negotiating table, but despite the resolution of a few short-range concerns, it would take an even more sustained operation to stop their terrorism and ethnic cleansing.

Operation Allied Force, launched in spring 1999, became the longest combat operation since Vietnam, eclipsing Desert Storm by more than two months. American and British aircraft, augmented by Italian, Danish, Norwegian, Spanish, and Dutch flight crews flying their first combat operations since World War II, struck Serbian positions daily, delivering their ordnance often in terrible weather over unforgiving terrain. Enemy defenses, while not firing in the wholesale patterns of the Vietnam War, were still dangerous. Marine Hornet and EA-6B Prowler squadrons, flying from Aviano Air Base in Italy and *Theodore Roosevelt*, were active throughout

Just as their predecessors did during the Vietnam War, aircrewmen in the modern Marine Corps still man guns on board the UH-1 Iroquois, the famed "Huey." (Rick Mullen)

One of the highest honors bestowed upon Marine Corps aviation is the privilege of transporting the President of the United States around the Washington, D.C., area in "Marine One." Whether boarding or deplaning, the Commander in Chief always receives a crisp salute from the Marine at the bottom of the ladder. (Rick Mullen)

the campaign. In addition, two F/A-18 squadrons flew strikes from Hungary, while Harriers launched from amphibious ships.

The Prowlers quickly became one of the essential aircraft types of the campaign. Though limited in numbers, they were required on every strike to defend against Serb radar and missiles, much as they did during the Gulf War. By the time of Allied Force, EA-6Bs were the only aircraft in any of the U.S. military services capable of performing the vital electronic countermeasures mission.

A New Century

The Marines have always had to fight to keep their air arm, and it is something of a marvel that they have succeeded, particularly during the periods of force cuts and cost reductions that usually follow major wars. Even today, at the start of the new century, the Marines once again struggle to justify new programs and aircraft, although they desperately require replacements for such ancient types as the CH-46 medium-lift helicopter.

With the arrival of the new century, Marine Corps aviation is changing, too. The Marines eagerly await the first fleet squadrons of MV-22s and the Joint Strike Fighter (JSF), choosing to forego, at least initially, the FA-18E/F Super Hornet. Upgrades of existing aircraft, such as the AH-1Z and UH-1Y, will allow these veterans to continue serving with increased payloads and mission capabilities.

A short takeoff and vertical landing version of the JSF will begin replacing the older AV-8s and F/A-18s by the end of the new century's first decade. Upgrades of the CH-53 fleet will complement the oncoming MV-22 medium-lifter. The Corps is also looking for a replacement for the EA-6B, not an easy task for what has become the "sleeper" aircraft of choice for many military planners.

Always in the vanguard of action, the flying leathernecks enjoy a rich, proud history of defending America and their fellow Marines on the ground. The coming years promise to continue the tradition.

This close-up view of the nose section of an AV-8B Harrier of Marine Attack Squadron 214 operating from Essex *(LHD 2) reveals the bulbous cockpit canopy, an improvement over the AV-8A version of the Harrier. The latest version of the AV-8B is a night-attack variant, which features improved bombing radar in its bulbous nose. (Rick Mullen)*

Marines hit the ground running during training at Camp Pendleton, California, after fast-roping from a hovering UH-1N. Not only skilled in storming a beach from the sea, the modern Marine is equally adept at assaulting an enemy from the air. (Rick Mullen)

Trailing refueling hoses, a KC-130 Hercules prepares to refuel a CH-53E Super Sea Stallion during a 1995 training flight. One of the most long-lived aircraft in the United States armed forces, the Hercules remains a mainstay of Marine transport squadrons. (Rick Mullen)

Guarding Our Shores

Guarding Our Shores

Lieutenant Commander Tom Beard, USCG (Ret)

As a Coast Guard aircrew dashes at a run to their aircraft in response to the search and rescue (SAR) alarm, frequently the only thing they know about the upcoming challenge is that their first turn after takeoff will take them to sea. These crews are daily at war flying from twenty-eight stations bordering the nation's coasts or off ships patrolling treaty waters and polar regions. These are the battlegrounds for 400 aviators and 1,500 aircrew flying 215 aircraft, encountering skirmishes without orders of battle or rules of engagement. Sometimes, with only minutes of planning, they are ready anywhere on the planet. Only their wit and training guides them as they support the average day for the U.S. Coast Guard: saving fourteen lives while assisting 328 others, preserving eight million dollars in property, reacting to thirty-two petroleum and hazardous chemical spills, keeping seven million dollars worth of drugs from reaching American streets, and preventing uncounted illegal immigrants from entering the United States. These aviators and their crews, wearing wings of gold, continue the 210 years of maritime ritual created by the first of this nation's sea warriors, the Revenue Cutter Service sailors. As aviators, they have done so since 1916, emulating three bold pioneers—Commander Elmer F. Stone, Captain Donald B. MacDiarmid, and Captain Frank A. Erickson.

Thomas F. Baldwin, an unlikely man in serendipitous circumstances, nurtured the seeds from which Coast Guard aviation grew. In

Above: A pair of HH-52 Seaguards fly past the face of a towering glacier. Operated by the Coast Guard between 1963 and 1989, the Seaguard was the most successful lifesaving vehicle of all time, with over 15,000 lives saved. About seventy HH-52As, flying from seventeen air stations during one three-year period, accounted for an average of 3,920 search-and-rescue cases, saving 913 lives, and preventing property loss at a value of more than eighty-three million dollars each year. (Captain Kwang Ping Hsu, USCG)

Page 236–237: An HC-130 Hercules flies over the bleak coastline of Alaska during a mission from its home base at Kodiak. The versatile "Herky Birds," flown by Coast Guard aircrews since 1959, can remain airborne for up to fourteen hours, providing long-range support of search and rescue, drug interdiction, environmental protection, and ice patrol missions. (Lockheed)

Opposite: Lieutenant Paul D. Lang received the Distinguished Flying Cross for his rescue of the crew on board the floundering wooden schooner Anne Kristina *on 28 October 1991, during the now famous "Perfect Storm." Aided by night vision goggles, Lang entered a fifteen-foot hover, rising with each oncoming wave as his three-man crew coordinated the rescue. The schooner's nine crew members had to jump one by one into the seas for pickup as the helicopter could not hover over the two twirling spear-like masts. (U.S. Coast Guard)*

Above, left: *Commander Elmer F. Stone, the U.S. Coast Guard's first aviator, achieved widespread fame as pilot of the NC-4 flying boat on its transatlantic flight and established a world speed record for amphibian type aircraft on 20 December 1934. (U.S. Coast Guard Art Collection)*

Above, right: *Captain Carl Christian von Paulsen sparked the reemergence of Coast Guard aviation. In 1925, he arranged to borrow a UO seaplane from the Navy, and operating from a canvas tent hangar on Ten Pound Island, Massachusetts, effectively curtailed rum-running in the region. Based on his initiative and success, the following year Congress appropriated $152,000 for the Coast Guard to buy its own aircraft. (U.S. Coast Guard Art Collection)*

June 1915, Glenn H. Curtiss hired the out-of-work Baldwin, an aging nineteenth-century carnival balloonist, to start a flight school. Baldwin's new aerodrome was adjacent to the Coast Guard Cutter (CGC) *Onondaga*, and among the crewmen who observed the frequent flights was a junior officer named Elmer Stone, who on 1 April 1916 became the Coast Guard's first aviator.

The flamboyant Baldwin, ever the entrepreneur, loaned a Curtiss flying boat to the inquisitive officer, who speculated that it might be a good spotter and a rescue device. *Onondaga*'s commanding officer, Lieutenant Commander Benjamin M. Chiswell, now regarded as the "Father of Coast Guard Aviation," subsequently stated, "I believe it would be the biggest find for the Coast Guard of the century and might be the means of saving hundreds of lives."

The Coast Guard became a part of the Navy as the United States entered World War I. As a result, Elmer Stone was retained in the Navy upon completing flight training, as were the other Coast Guard officers who followed him. Others served as commanding officers of naval air stations while Stone served as a pilot on board the cruiser *Huntington* (ACR 5). Following the war, Stone continued as the Navy's chief test pilot for seaplanes and served as the pilot of the NC-4 flying boat on its famous transatlantic flight in 1919. Following several years during which he served as an engineer, developing catapult and arresting gear for the early aircraft carriers, the Navy finally released Stone back to the Coast Guard in September 1926.

Two months later, Congress appropriated $152,000 for the purchase of the Coast Guard's first aircraft, two Vought UO seaplanes and three

Loening OL amphibians. Heretofore, Coast Guardsmen flew seaplanes borrowed from the Navy. Operations quickly established the requirement for aircraft specifically designed to meet the special needs of the Coast Guard, and in 1928, Stone joined Commander Norman Hall, who started an aviation branch within Coast Guard Headquarters, and Lieutenant Commander Carl von Paulsen in leading the design work on a multimission aircraft. Eventually, the Coast Guard received funds for the construction of "seagoing planes of a type adapted for general coastal service and especially suited to the rescue of those in peril at sea." Two years after Hall, Stone, and others envisioned it, the flying life boat (FLB) was about to become a reality.

The Fokker Aircraft Corporation began building the PJ, the official designation of the FLB, in 1931. According to the pilots who flew it, this robust airplane, which could take off and land in six-foot seas, was "the best seaplane that the Coast Guard ever had." While awaiting delivery of the PJ-1, the Coast Guard also procured three Douglas RD Dolphin commercial amphibians. It was while flying one of these rugged airplanes in 1933 that Lieutenant Richard Burke landed at sea and removed an injured crewman from a trawler 160 miles off the coast of Massachusetts. For this feat he became the first Coast Guard aviator to receive the Distinguished Flying Cross. This and other flights bred confidence in the ability to conduct offshore landings, though future flying boats did not always meet Coast Guard needs. In fact, of all the seaplanes ever procured by the Coast Guard, only the PJ was designed based upon the service's specific requirements.

The forty-nine-year-old Stone suffered a fatal heart attack on 20 May 1936 while inspecting a new naval patrol aircraft shortly after assuming command at Coast Guard Air Station (CGAS) San Diego, California. One

The Fokker Aircraft Corporation of Baltimore, Maryland, later General Aviation and North American Aviation, began building the Flying Life Boat in 1931. This high wing seaplane with pusher engines mounted above plywood wings was designed specifically for operating from the open seas, the only aircraft so built. Its success in offshore landings from 1932 through 1941 was never equaled, even by later, more advanced designs. (U.S. Coast Guard)

A welcome sight for those in distress on the sea is an aircraft with the distinctive Coast Guard emblem on its fuselage. A simplified version of the service's official seal, which dates from 1927, the emblem appears inside the distinctive slash on the paint schemes of Coast Guard Cutters and aircraft. The 1790 date on the emblem commemorates the date on which the Revenue Cutter Service, the forerunner of the modern Coast Guard, was created. (Ted Carlson)

officer who knew him well described Stone as "pop-eyed, bushy-haired, stub-nosed, careless of dress, but as alert as a terrier; a man who cared little for the form, but much for the matter." According to his obituary, Stone was "eccentric perhaps, and something of a trial for his seniors, but he left behind him a rich tradition—the foundation for morals for Coast Guard aviators who follow him."

In the wake of Stone's pioneering work, two other officers directed the Coast Guard along quite diverse avenues in their individual attempts to develop better methods for performing missions. Donald MacDiarmid favored the seaplane while Frank Erickson championed a revolutionary new apparatus known as the helicopter, dividing Coast Guard aviation into two combative camps. Events, namely a world war, finally decided the contentious issue.

Seaplanes and amphibians were still the primary aircraft for the Coast Guard fleet during World War II, flying convoy escort, antisubmarine patrol, and search and rescue for the crews of torpedoed ships and downed aircraft along all the nation's coastal waters. Coast Guard seaplanes

A JF-2 Duck flies over the panoramic vista of a snow-covered mountain. Note the small, square dark window just aft of the lower wing root, the location of two seats for passengers inside the pontoon. The Coast Guard operated Ducks from 1934 to 1948 as a part of its seagoing fleet of aircraft. (U.S. Coast Guard)

reportedly located over 1,000 survivors from torpedoed ships along the Atlantic seaboard and rescued more than one hundred victims by landing in open seas. In one instance a flying boat even retrieved the surviving crew of a sunken German U-boat. Other operations included the North Atlantic and Greenland patrols, including those by Patrol Squadron (VP) 6, a Navy squadron manned entirely by Coast Guard personnel. Flying PBY Catalinas, VP-6 performed search and rescue and flew ice patrols. Coast Guard aviators flew classified long-range electronic navigation siting and survey missions in Alaska and the Pacific, establishing the navigation chains that led Army Air Forces bombers to Japan, and also provided

During World War II the Coast Guard's only PBY-5 Catalina aircraft conducted survey and calibration flights for the new classified Loran radio-navigation system in Alaska and the Pacific, which aided bombers attacking Japan. The plane is shown here anchored in the Garner Island Lagoon of the Phoenix Island Group, British Samoa. It operated alone, often for months, sometimes exposed to enemy fire, with the crew doing all maintenance at anchor. Other Coast Guard crews employed the Navy PB4Y-2 patrol bomber for similar missions. (John M. Shea)

Above: *A 325-pound depth charge visible beneath its starboard wing, a J4F Widgeon conducts an antisubmarine patrol off the coast of the United States. While flying an aircraft of this type on 1 August 1942, Aviation Chief Machinist's Mate Henry C. White and Radioman First Class George H. Boggs, Jr., spotted U-166 on the surface in the Gulf of Mexico off Louisiana. White maneuvered for a quick dive-bombing attack as the submarine submerged, with Boggs releasing the depth charge at an altitude of 250 feet. The bomb exploded alongside the U-boat, sinking it immediately—Coast Guard aviation's first and only U-boat kill of the war. (U.S. Coast Guard)*

assistance to naval ships. Coast Guardsmen also stood ready to engage the enemy. During one particularly notable flight on 1 August 1942, Aviation Chief Machinist's Mate Henry C. White and Radioman First Class George H. Boggs, Jr., flying a J4F-1 Widgeon seaplane, successfully attacked the German submarine U-166, sending her to the bottom of the Gulf of Mexico. This was the only enemy U-boat sunk by a Coast Guard aircraft during World War II.

Despite successes in lifesaving, no comprehensive American air-sea rescue plan or program existed before 1944. Moreover, independent rescue efforts by the Army, Navy, Marine Corps, and Coast Guard resulted in duplication and missed opportunities. The Coast Guard urged the creation of such a plan after creating the elements of an air-sea unit at CGAS San Diego in December 1943. The following February, the Joint Chiefs of Staff responded by directing the Secretary of the Navy to establish the Air Sea Rescue Agency, centered around the seaplane. McDiarmid was chosen to conduct offshore seaplane landing tests under the auspices of the new organization.

Landing and taking off into the wind, at sea, with seaplanes was like crashing into a series of walls. The speeds of the earlier successful seaplanes were slow enough that the aircraft might land or take off into the wind between wave crests. MacDiarmid pursued the idea that landing in the troughs parallel to the major swell system would prevent the dangers

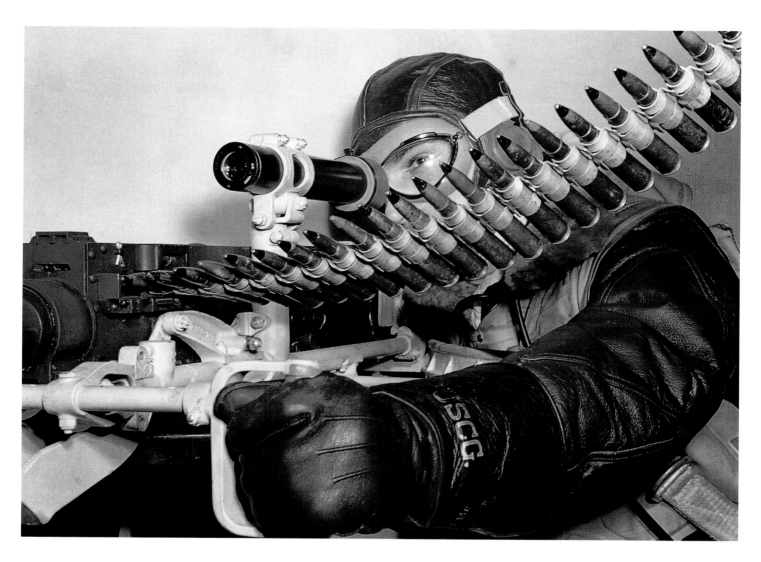

A wartime publicity photograph captures the face of the Coast Guard at war in the form of an aerial gunner, framed by the belted ammunition feeding his machine gun and ready to fire. The Coast Guard operates as part of the Navy during time of war. (National Museum of Naval Aviation)

of crashing into the face of an oncoming wave. He then examined sea surfaces from ocean technology studies, and experimented in offshore conditions near San Diego for three years.

MacDiarmid believed the PBM Mariner was an excellent platform for oceanic SAR. With its long-range ability, it could land at sea anywhere and retrieve downed flyers or victims of shipping disasters. The consensus

Left: A PBM Mariner streams smoke after making a jet assisted takeoff (JATO). The total thrust from the JATO bottles equaled the engine power of one 1950s-era jet fighter, and hastened the ability of flying boats to break the suction of the water and become airborne. (Tom Beard)

Opposite, bottom: Chalk up one for the Coast Guard—a sailor paints the silhouette of a German U-boat beneath the cockpit of the J4F Widgeon that was the only Coast Guard aircraft to sink an enemy submarine during World War II. The aircraft is currently on display in the National Museum of Naval Aviation. (National Museum of Naval Aviation)

among Coast Guard aviators, bolstered by the dynamic MacDiarmid, was that the future of Coast Guard aviation required seaplanes, especially if it were to maintain preeminence in postwar SAR operations. Unfortunately, the performance of the PBM was not impressive during trials. Even landing in line with wave crests, MacDiarmid discovered it was difficult to keep the wing-tip floats from submerging in an oncoming wave. His preliminary testing ended with a crash. The plane skipped off the water on its first contact and lost airspeed, after which the right wing stalled, dropped, and was buried in a wave and torn off. After being spun around, the damaged Mariner sank. The crew escaped without injury, but it was a damning blow to open-sea operations with seaplanes.

While MacDiarmid continued forcing his beliefs, a few senior officers began to lose enthusiasm for open-sea landings. Once, the seaplane zealot confronted an admiral with the appeal to consider the hundreds of times he had made landings in the open seas and leave the decision

to land to his own judgment. Commander Kenneth M. Bilderback, who flew with MacDiarmid, wrote, "The admiral grinned easily and said, 'Mac, I don't think a man who would take an airplane into the sea hundreds of times has very good judgment.'"

MacDiarmid conducted a second series of open water tests with the PBM, and also evaluated the P5M Marlin and the new UF (HU-16) Albatross amphibian between 1949 and 1951. During these tests he planned to meet all known ocean conditions up to the limits of each aircraft's strength and sea capability. For his research, he received the Octave Chanute Award from the Institute of Aeronautical Sciences and the Distinguished Flying Cross from the Navy.

However, the age of large military seaplanes was ending. They were restricted to landing in a few areas while land planes benefited from the many airports built around the globe during World War II. With its range, a land plane could go anywhere, without the extra cost of hauling around a hull sturdy enough to land at sea. The seaplane's limitations brought an end to this craft at a time when Erickson's work with helicopters was just beginning to prove itself as the future of Coast Guard aviation. It all began, however, in the halcyon days of seaplanes.

An interagency board to evaluate rotary-wing craft was established in 1938. Commander William J. Kossler, the Coast Guard's representative, immediately recognized the helicopter as the new flying lifeboat for the Coast Guard. However, the first experimental helicopter, Dr. Igor Sikorsky's VS-300, did not fly in a public demonstration until 13 May 1940, and useful helicopters were years away. Sikorsky's contraption did attract the attention of Erickson, who from his own experiences with seaplanes was acutely aware of their limitations. His helicopter dreams exploded with the first Japanese bombs hitting Pearl Harbor, Hawaii, on 7 December 1941. Literally in the middle of things—Erickson served as the base duty officer that day—he spent the days after the attack flying unarmed Coast Guard amphibians, loaded with rifles and shotguns, looking for the Japanese fleet. Little did he know how the war would affect the evolution of the helicopter.

With no blueprint for future aviation operations firmly established following World War II, the Coast Guard acquired many different surplus aircraft from war service, as evidenced by this photograph of the flight line at CGAS Elizabeth City, North Carolina. Pictured right to left are a PB-1G Fortress (naval version of the famed Army Air Forces bomber), HC-130B Hercules, R5D Skymaster, UF-2G (HU-16E) Albatross, and a UF-1G (HU-16C) Albatross. Aircrews were expected to fly all assigned aircraft. (U.S. Coast Guard)

So confident was Doctor Igor I. Sikorsky in the ability of his helicopter design in the hands of Coast Guard helicopter pilot Commander Frank Erickson that he served as a guinea pig for the demonstration of an early rescue hoist. Sikorsky's son, Sergei, was one of Erickson's mechanics on active duty with the Coast Guard. (U.S. Coast Guard)

Commander Frank A. Erickson, commanding officer of the world's first helicopter school, pictured with Ensign W. C. Bolton, the school's first student, who sits in the cockpit of an HNS-1 Hoverfly at CGAS Floyd Bennett Field, New York, in December 1943. (U.S. Coast Guard)

In 1942, Erickson was unexpectedly ordered to CGAS New York, New York, located close to Sikorsky's Connecticut plant, where he soon witnessed his first helicopter flight. "It was the 26th of June, 1942 a day I will never forget," Erickson wrote. "I was fascinated with both the VS-300 and Mr. Sikorsky . . . I started drafting a report to Headquarters. . . . Since efforts to sell the helicopter as a life saving device had not been successful, I stressed the application of the helicopter as an antisubmarine weapon, which could be operated from ships in convoys." Erickson presumed that if he controlled the development of antisubmarine warfare (ASW) helicopters, he could run simultaneous development projects enabling him to create his ideal rescue craft.

Response to Erickson's letter came one month later. The Navy's Bureau of Aeronautics recommended the requisition of four helicopters then under construction for the Army for study and development of ASW capabilities for the Navy and Coast Guard. The Navy previously objected to helicopter development based partly on Navy Captain Walter Diehl's thesis that this type of craft could not carry a load of any value. A major break came for Kossler and Erickson in January 1943 when the British, enthusiastic about the machine's abilities, ordered 200 HO2Ss and negotiated for another 800 HOS designs from Sikorsky.

Emboldened by this news, Kossler urged Commandant of the Coast Guard Vice Admiral Russell A. Waesche, Sr., to assign helicopters flown by Coast Guard crews to convoy escort duties. Kossler also recommended that the Coast Guard establish a school to train British and other military helicopter pilots, and invited the commandant to witness a helicopter performance in February 1943. The confident Kossler wrote, "The helicopter will solve the submarine menace without the use of a large number of escort vessels for convoys and may play a decisive role in the winning of the war." Erickson noted that "Admiral Waesche was completely sold." Furthermore, the reluctant naval inspector of aircraft casually admitted to the admiral, "The helicopter might be all right—for the Coast Guard." Erickson summed up the demonstration, saying "'Igor's Nightmare,' which had been something of a joke around Bridgeport, even among the workers in his plant, was at last being given serious consideration."

On 15 February 1943, on recommendations from Waesche, Chief of Naval Operations Admiral Ernest J. King assigned responsibility for seagoing development of helicopters and their operations in convoys to the Coast Guard, though the Navy would usurp some of this responsibility until the war ended. On 18 December, King separated pilot training from test and development, directing that, effective 1 January 1944, the Coast Guard would conduct a helicopter training program at Floyd Bennett Field in New York. By this time, Erickson had received his helicopter pilot qualification, having flown solo in June 1943 after only three hours of instruction. However, the following month he crashed the second machine off the production line, a YR-4 assigned to the British, who good-naturedly accused the Yank of destroying their only helicopter on Independence Day. King's directive made Erickson the commanding officer of the world's first helicopter school, giving him the opportunity to pursue his own ambition—conducting test and development in an effort to adapt helicopters to rescue work.

Erickson's first task, however, was to train pilots and instructors to meet a schedule burdened with an influx of British pilots. Coast Guard headquarters would not assign aviators, leaving Erickson to personally recruit volunteers. Career Coast Guard seaplane pilots feared helicopter qualification would harm their chances for promotion. Erickson succeeded only by enrolling current or former enlisted pilots. Lieutenant (jg) Stewart R. Graham, trained by Erickson at the Sikorsky factory, was the only instructor Erickson had for his school when it opened. Graham also attempted to recruit pilots. "I was looked upon as not having all my marbles [and] was ridiculed beyond belief among my fellow flyers that I would jeopardize my well-being to fly such a contraption."

One month after the school opened with a complement of two instructors and one student, a Coast Guard helicopter received national attention. On 3 January 1944, the task set before the much-maligned helicopter was humanitarian service—for the Navy. After *Turner* (DD 648) exploded at anchor off Sandy Hook, New York, a major blizzard blocked delivery of plasma needed for casualties at the local hospital. The storm grounded all aircraft along the eastern seaboard and curtailed road traffic. Erickson loaded cases of blood plasma on an HNS-1

The HH-60J Jayhawk provides the Coast Guard with a long-range rescue platform capable of reaching points up to 300 miles offshore and remaining on scene for rescue operations for a period of forty-five minutes. The Jayhawk continues the Coast Guard's long association with Sikorsky helicopters that began with the first experiments with the HNS during World War II. (Ted Carlson)

The city lights of Miami, Florida, illuminating the night sky. Lieutenants Glen Gileno (left) and Gary Polaski bring their HU-25C Guardian home following a mission over the Atlantic on 10 January 2000. The Night Stalker version of the Guardian, the HU-25C features AN/APG-66 radar, WR-360 forward-looking infrared radar, and encrypted radios, all ideal for the mission of tracking drug smugglers. (Ted Carlson)

trainer and flew through the tempest, delivering lifesaving cargo. The aircraft destined by an obsolete decree as a weapon against submarines, on its first mission assisted in saving lives.

Two days later Graham sailed with British helicopters and pilots on board the British freighter SS *Daghestan* in convoy to England. Following major storms and witnessing ships sunk by submarines in his vicinity, on 16 January 1944 Graham launched from *Daghestan* on the world's first helicopter ASW flight.

One of the most important developments to occur to the helicopter came in August 1944 when Erickson's crew installed the first rescue hoist. Continued development made this hoist standard equipment on nearly all helicopters with the potential of recovering people from the water or, as was demonstrated much later in combat, through jungle canopies. The Navy modified twelve HNS-1 trainers and thirty new HOS-1 helicopters with the new hoists. "Unfortunately," according to Erickson, "most of these helicopters were immediately placed in storage, because they did not fit into the air-sea rescue problem as it was then envisioned by those in control of Coast Guard Aviation."

The world's first helicopter school shut down on 6 February 1945, for lack of assigned students. Of the 103 pilots trained, 71 were Coast Guardsmen, while only eight were Navy personnel. Others were British, U.S. Army, Civil Aeronautics Administration flyers, and manufacturer's test pilots.

Erickson no longer had helicopters with which to continue his openly surreptitious experiments, for all Coast Guard machines were sent to the

Navy or placed in storage. He retained one for the unfinished low-priority ASW dipping sonar program. Erickson had no command, nor would he ever again be given the opportunity for one. Too many senior officers were quite unhappy with his attitude and his steadfastness toward a machine with no perceived benefits. "'Swede' Erickson was always the salesman," reported Captain John Waters, "willing to explain the helicopter's merits to anyone who would listen. His visions of the helicopter's future seemed highly extravagant to many of the fixed-wing clan, and his predictions were often ridiculed behind his back." Erickson's arrogance often defeated his arguments. Chief Warrant Officer Robert J. O'Leary once mentioned to Erickson that he was like a "Jersey cow giving an excellent pail of milk then stepping into it with a (manure) covered foot!"

Rare events did occur that helped boost the helicopter's public popularity, and they did not come from stratagems contrived by Kossler or Erickson. A near tragedy, averted only by the unique abilities of the helicopter, captured international press coverage for the unlikely little machine. The helicopter rescue of eleven Canadian flyers marooned in the snow by two air crashes brought new attention to the unique lifesaving abilities of rotary-wing aircraft. Snowmobiles and ski-equipped rescue airplanes bogged down in the mushy springtime snow, while lakes remained frozen, preventing float-equipped airplanes from landing. Erickson learned about the airmen's plight and had an HNS-1 stashed aboard a C-54 transport and flown to Gander, Newfoundland. Coast Guard Lieutenant August Kleisch lashed five-gallon jerry cans to the pontoons for extra gasoline for the round trip to the survivors's camp. As Kleisch landed, he recalled, "the sight of the machine brought cheers." They had already survived two weeks knowing, unaware as they were of the helicopter, that it would be next winter before new attempts would be tried. Kleisch and the little helicopter persevered, extracting one crew member at a time. The last survivor came out three days later on the afternoon of 2 May 1945. The helicopter had new life.

This Coast Guard recruiting poster, in which a white-hat guides an HH-52 Seaguard to a safe landing, highlighted opportunities in the enlisted ranks of the service. Enlisted personnel serve as mechanics, rescue swimmers, and systems operators on board Coast Guard aircraft, and for a period of time in the service's history also flew as pilots. (U.S. Coast Guard)

Left: *Lieutenant August Kleisch takes off on one of his eleven trips to evacuate downed Canadian airmen, one at a time, following two aircraft crashes in Labrador during May 1945. The pontoon floats are clearly visible on the HNS-1 Hoverfly. (U.S. Coast Guard)*

Opposite, bottom: *A HNS-1 Hoverfly with Commander Frank A. Erickson at the controls conducts early experimental rescue hoist operations, including use of the "horse collar" Erickson designed. One of the single most important developments to occur with the helicopter came on 11 August 1944, with the installation of the first power rescue hoist on an HNS-1. During the subsequent testing period, Coast Guard aviators satisfactorily demonstrated the feasibility of rescuing personnel from the water and of transferring personnel and equipment to and from vessels underway. (U.S. Coast Guard)*

An HNS-1 Hoverfly and HOS-1 helicopter make landing approaches to CGC Cobb, the world's first vessel built as a helicopter carrier. The former SS Governor Cobb, a thirty-seven-year-old coastal passenger steamer with its superstructure cut down, had a 38-by-63-foot flight deck added aft. Commander Frank A. Erickson made the first landing on Cobb's deck in Long Island Sound on 29 June 1944. (U.S. Coast Guard)

A Coast Guard HO2S-1 enters a hover while lowering the sound pickup sphere during early sonar tests. The sonar operator sat in the front seat, while the pilot flew the aircraft from the aft section of the cockpit. The first dipping sonar tests occurred in an XHOS-1 flying from CGC Cobb in April 1945. Subsequent tests in Key West, Florida, revealed the sonar's capabilities in detecting submerged submarines. (U.S. Coast Guard)

Over the next two years, the helicopter began to assume a greater role in naval operations. In 1946 a Coast Guard helicopter and crew sailed on board *Midway* (CVB 41) during Operation Frostbite in the Davis Straits, the first use of a helicopter for plane guard duty. Within the year, helicopters were placed on all icebreakers, followed soon by aircraft carriers. The Navy moved into helicopter operations on 1 July 1946 with the commissioning of Experimental Squadron 3 at Naval Air Station New York, the site of Erickson's first helicopter school. And as part of the Navy's Operation Highjump—the photographic exploration of Antarctica from December 1946 to March 1947—Coast Guard crews flew the first helicopters on that continent.

Erickson moved to Coast Guard Air Station Elizabeth City, North Carolina, with Graham and a small crew to occupy an abandoned hangar to complete the ASW experiments and test any helicopters he could acquire. It was, in effect, an exile with a title—Helicopter Test and Development Unit. However, acceptance of this machine within the Coast Guard was diminishing despite a demonstration of the capabilities of the helicopter when a Belgium airlines DC-4 passenger airliner crashed near Gander on 18 September 1946. As on the previous rescue, the Coast Guard's then only two helicopters were loaded on board transports and flown to Canada.

At the end of the decade, as his projects withered from lack of support and the Coast Guard purchased no helicopters, Erickson was assigned duty with the U.S. Air Force to advise on helicopter development and operations during the Korean War. In 1951, Graham began assisting the Navy in developing helicopter ASW, his work concluding with the establishment

of Helicopter Antisubmarine Squadron 1, the Navy's first helicopter ASW squadron. The Navy then ordered Graham to Naval Air Test Center Patuxent River, Maryland, as head of the Rotary Wing Section within the Tactical Test Division. By the time the Korean War was over, most of the services had accepted the helicopter, established schools, and were making operational decisions based on its use. Ironically, the one exception was the Coast Guard.

In an equally ironic turn of events, MacDiarmid qualified as a helicopter pilot in June 1953, making him the target of attacks by contemporaries who had endured many years of his scorn and cynical attitude toward the machine. "I hear via the grapevine," Waters wrote MacDiarmid in a flippant note, "that you are now a helicrapper [sic] pilot, and have conceded that Erickson was right all along."

Just a year later, on 28 June 1954, Captain Erickson retired following a series of demeaning duty assignments away from flying, seemingly calculated to keep him away from command or any future development work on his beloved helicopter. He was disappointed at failing to promote his dream. However, still optimistic, he predicted in a letter to his brother, "Coast Guard Aviation will be an all-helicopter outfit before long except for a few land planes used for logistic purposes." A performance the following year seemed to prove he was correct in his thinking.

The event that changed the direction of Coast Guard aviation began two days before Christmas 1955. Yuba City, California, was struck by a

Lieutenant Stewart Graham, flying an HNS-1 Hoverfly, lands with one victim from the Belgium airlines DC-4 passenger airliner that crashed near Gander, Newfoundland, in September 1946. The entire crash site was a marsh-covered muskeg that could not support the weight of people or a helicopter. Platforms were built at selected helicopter landing sites from lumber dropped by a PBY Catalina flying boat. The survivors were flown from the crash site platform to a lake's edge by helicopters, then were floated out on life rafts to a waiting PBY. (U.S. Coast Guard)

Chief Aviation Electronics Technician Jeffrey Bailey, a surveillance system operator, monitors a communications and radar panel in the cabin of an HU-25C Guardian during a 10 January 2000 mission from CGAS Miami, Florida. The sophisticated equipment on board the Guardian allows the aircraft commander to coordinate operations from the air. (Ted Carlson)

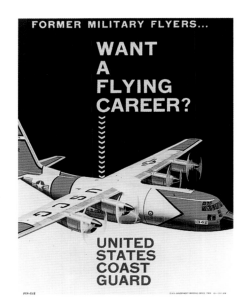

Dating from 1963, this recruiting poster highlights the program in which the Coast Guard added to its aviator ranks by giving a "direct" commission to qualified aviators from other military services. (U.S. Coast Guard)

Opposite: A rescue swimmer dangles from the hoist of an HH-65A Dolphin during a practice search and rescue operation in the Atlantic. A computerized flight management system on board the helicopter includes an automatic flight control system that will bring the aircraft to a hover just fifty feet above a selected target, a tremendous asset to recovery operations in unfavorable weather. (Ted Carlson)

An HU-25B sweeps over burning Kuwait, waging war on the environmental disaster that arose in the wake of the Gulf War. Two Coast Guard HU-25Bs specially equipped with water-surface, oil-scanning AIREYE radars flew to the Arabian Gulf in February 1991, just three weeks after notification of their mission. A time-honored tradition established at the beginning of Coast Guard aviation is the crew that flies the aircraft repairs it. Thus, the typical support line required by other services is thin or non-existent in the Coast Guard, making for rapid deployments anywhere in the world. ("Oil Fires of Kuwait," Dante H. Bertoni, USCG Art Program)

huge flood on 23 December when a storm-weakened river dyke burst. One Coast Guard HO4S helicopter from CGAS San Francisco, the only one in the region with a hoist and rescue basket, pulled 138 victims to safety, the first fifty-eight of them in darkness.

Among the pilots participating in the operation was Lieutenant Henry J. Pfeiffer. Flying in the storm-darkened night between trees, high-tension lines, television antennas, and telephone wires, aided only by a handheld light, he hovered just feet above rooftops and picked up stranded families huddled in the stinging blast from the rotor's downwash. In the helicopter's cabin, Chief Machinist's Mate Joseph Accamo lowered the basket and began the routine that would repeat itself throughout the night and day. From housetop, to treetop, to power pole—anywhere people took refuge—the helicopter hovered and winched up terrified victims. It was an incredible performance.

Erickson's prediction soon came to pass. The Coast Guard transferred its remaining seaplanes to the Navy in 1961, replacing them with long-range C-130 Hercules patrol planes. HU-16 amphibians would serve another two decades, but by the early 1970s were restricted from water landings. The next order for an aircraft to meet the Coast Guard's role at saving lives at sea was a compromise. It was an amphibious helicopter, the Sikorsky HH-52 Seaguard.

One can only guess the number of lives saved the world over with Erickson's dream. The helicopter today is an icon to human rescue and the Coast Guard's gift to aviation worldwide. But it is the combination of the long-range and medium-range fixed-wing aircraft and helicopters that enable today's Coast Guard to meet its aerial response requirements. Future plans still include the indomitable C-130 and more helicopters, with perhaps newer tilt-rotor aircraft and possible use of unmanned vehicles. Stone's seaplane is now only a fading memory, but a part of his vision and that of MacDiarmid and Erickson still touches the lives of the Coast Guardsmen of the air.

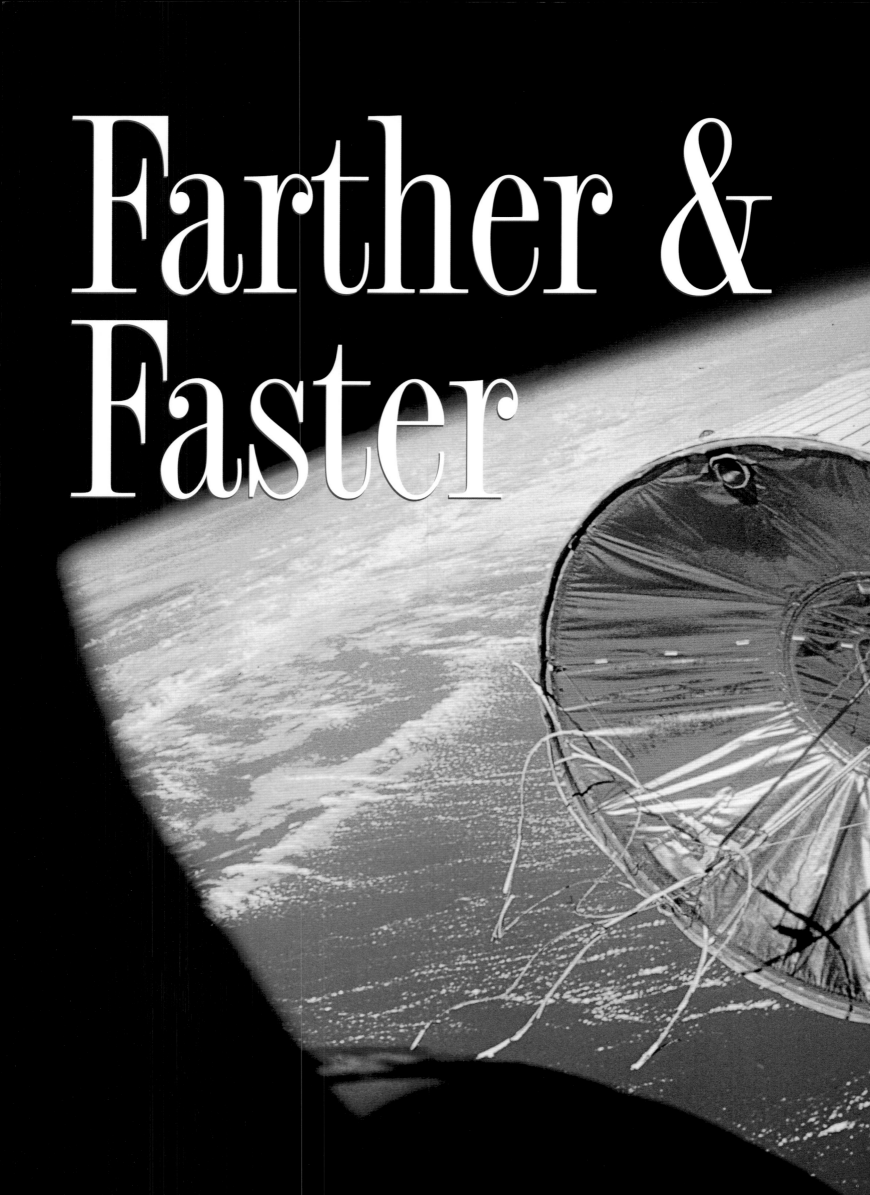

Farther & Faster

Farther & Faster

Tom Wildenberg

Neil Armstrong set foot on the moon only sixty-six years after the Wright brothers made their flight over another desolate landscape on earth, a period of progress unequaled in human history. Yet, it is not a surprising feat if one takes into account that in the arenas of land, sea, and sky, only the latter knows no bounds, the heavens stretching millions of miles from the earth. Thus, a unique spirit of discovery has always marked mankind's efforts to conquer the air, including those of the men and women of naval aviation.

For the naval service's pioneer airmen, this spirit included a distinct element of risk. Such was the array of primitive aircraft assigned to them during the formative years that almost every trip could be classified as a test flight. Many paid for their efforts with their lives, notably Lieutenant Richard C. Saufley, who two months after establishing an American altitude record of 16,072 feet perished during an endurance flight, crashing near Pensacola, Florida, on 9 June 1916, after more than eight hours in the air. Others saved lives with their determination, among them Marine Captain Francis T. Evans. In 1917, while attempting to ascertain the best way to recover from a spin, which plagued students at Naval Air Station Pensacola, he traced an arc through the sky in an N-9, thus accomplishing the first-ever loop in a seaplane. The determination of these early pilots passed down from one generation of naval airmen to another, thus continuing the tradition of pushing the envelope.

For centuries the Atlantic Ocean represented the ultimate challenge for seafaring men, the tumultuous barrier separating the old and new worlds. Bridging the Atlantic almost instantly represented the ultimate test of fortitude and endurance for the early aeronauts as well, among

Top, left: *Formal portrait of Lieutenant (jg) Richard Caswell Saufley, Naval Aviator Number 14. While still a student pilot, he flew as an observer in combat flights over Vera Cruz, Mexico, and later participated in experiments with one of the first automatic pilot devices. In a not uncommon occurrence during the early days of naval aviation, he crashed to his death in Pensacola Bay on 9 June 1916. (National Museum of Naval Aviation)*

Top, right: *An N-9 seaplane pictured near the top of a loop during a training hop over NAS Pensacola, Florida. Performing this maneuver for the first time never ceased to provide a thrill for student aviators, who in surviving letters home describe the feeling of looking down at the blue waters and white sands as being like no other. (National Museum of Naval Aviation)*

Above: *The fourth Marine Corps officer to receive his wings as a naval aviator, Captain Francis T. Evans performed the first-ever loop in a seaplane in the skies over NAS Pensacola, Florida, on 13 February 1917. "Well, never again! Sweeheart unless I have to do it, (sic)" he wrote his future wife the following day. "I know it can be done so I'm satisfied." (National Museum of Naval Aviation)*

them men who wore wings of gold. Seaplanes and flying boats formed the centerpiece of the Navy's air efforts during World War I, and the pressing tactical requirements of wartime spawned an effort to build long-range airplanes capable of combating the German U-boat menace. The Navy signed a contract with Glenn Curtiss to build four flying boats for this purpose, lending some of its own engineering officers to the joint endeavor. The result was the flying boat model designated NC for Navy-Curtiss.

Mammoth in size, the NCs (or Nancy boats as they were affectionately nicknamed) boasted wingspans of some 126 feet, the size of those on a modern commercial airliner. The first of these enormous airplanes, NC-1,

made her first flight in October 1918. A month later she took off with fifty-one people (including a stowaway) establishing a new record for carrying passengers aloft, though by then an armistice had ended World War I and seemingly any apparent requirement for the new airplane.

Eleven days before the armistice was signed, Commander John H. Towers, one of the Navy's pioneer airmen, proposed the employment of the NC boats in an effort to regain the lost prestige of America's leadership in aeronautics. Nothing would restore it more than flying the Atlantic. Towers's idea coincided with the sudden resurgence of public interest in a transatlantic flight stimulated by a large cash prize offered by a London newspaper.

Preparations for the undertaking took months, and a hangar fire necessitated one airplane's removal from the flight. Additionally, such was the urgency of beating others across the Atlantic that the crew of NC-4 made only two test flights in their aircraft before departure. On 8 May 1919, the three remaining seaplanes—NC-1, NC-3, and NC-4—took off under Towers's command from NAS Rockaway, Long Island, New York, for the 3,600-mile flight to Lisbon, Portugal, by way of Newfoundland, Canada, and the Azores Islands. Only NC-4, under the comand of Lieutenant Commander Albert C. Read, was able to negotiate the trying weather conditions of the North Atlantic, overcoming mechanical difficulties during the early stages of the flight that had prompted the press to label her the "lame duck." The others, weather having hampered their navigation, were forced to land at sea. Although the crew of NC-1, Towers's

First Across: the Navy/Curtiss NC-4 pictured in flight following her return to the United States after the successful transatlantic flight of May 1919. The famed flying boat toured the eastern seaboard, Gulf Coast, and Mississippi River before being disassembled and placed in storage. She was not seen again until 1969, at which time she was displayed on the Mall in Washington, D.C., to commemorate the fiftieth anniversary of her landmark flight. (National Museum of Naval Aviation)

Opposite, center: Navy and Curtiss Engineering Corporation personnel inspect the newly completed NC-1 flying boat at Garden City, New York, on 3 October 1918. The maze of struts and wires attest to the craftsmanship involved in manufacturing the giant flying boat. For the transatlantic flight attempt the following year, the three Liberty engines were supplemented by a fourth pusher motor facing aft . (National Museum of Naval Aviation)

command plane, managed to make it to the Azores under a jury-rigged sail, NC-3 was not so fortunate. She foundered in the high seas, and a passing ship rescued her crew before the flying boat sank.

It was only after his safe arrival that Read could express the risks that the three crews had taken. "Now that its [*sic*] over," he wrote his wife, "I realize that we were taking much greater chances than any of us had thought." NC-4 subsequently flew from Portugal to England, where Read and the crew of all three aircraft received a tumultuous welcome, the beginning of a whirlwind series of dinners and receptions in England, France, and America. Though the flight of the NC boats was overshadowed by Charles Lindbergh's solo crossing of the Atlantic eight years later, the honor of being first across belonged to the United States Navy.

Navy flying boats continually demonstrated their endurance in the following two decades. Almost six years to the day that NC-4 departed on its transatlantic journey, the Naval Aircraft Factory PN-9, a metal-hulled "big boat," successfully completed a test flight over Philadelphia that lasted twenty-eight hour, thirty-five minutes, and twenty-seven seconds. Occurring in the wake of the Army Air Corps's successful around-the-world flight, the

This NC-4 flying boat heads into storm clouds over the North Atlantic during the longest and most harrowing leg of the flight from Newfoundland to the Azores Islands. The few photographs taken of the aircraft in flight during the transatlantic crossing consist of fleeting images taken from the decks of station ships strung out along the route. ("Into the Clouds," Ted Wilbur)

Top, left: *Among the naval hierarchy that welcomed the NC fliers back to the United States in July 1919 were Secretary of the Navy Josephus Daniels (seated at left) and his assistant, future President of the United States Franklin Roosevelt. Four of the officers behind them—A.C. Read, Pat Bellinger, John Towers, and Marc Mitscher—served as admirals under Roosevelt during World War II. (U.S. Navy)*

Above: *Commander John Rodgers (center), Naval Aviator Number 2, commanded the ill-fated PN-9 during its attempted flight from San Francisco to Hawaii in September 1925. Part of a distinguished naval family that traced its service to the War of 1812, Rogers perished in an airplane crash in August 1926. (U.S. Navy)*

Left: *The PN-9, battered from nine days at sea, pictured after being located by a U.S. submarine. Note that the fabric has been removed from the lower wing to make sails. (U.S. Navy)*

PN-9's performance prompted its assignment to a proposed flight from San Francisco, California, to Hawaii.

Some four months later, Commander John Rodgers and a crew of four boarded the airplane and took off from San Francisco Bay for the 2,400-mile overwater flight to Honolulu. The first few hours in the air went according to plan, though as the crew ventured further out over the Pacific, the plane's fuel supply began to dwindle more rapidly than expected. On 1 September, after twenty-five hours and twenty-three minutes in the air, the PN-9 consumed its last drop of fuel, leaving Rodgers no choice but to set the plane down at sea, some 460 miles short of his goal. Lost at sea for ten days, the crew put its nautical training to work, rigging sails from the fabric of the aircraft's lower wing and setting course for the Hawaiian Islands. The submarine *R-4* finally spotted them ten miles off the coast. Despite the failure to reach Hawaii, the 1,841.12 statute miles covered before the forced landing was recognized as a new world's distance record for seaplanes.

By the 1930s Navy patrol squadrons, built around Consolidated P2Y and PBY flying boats, routinely ranged far and wide in mass formation flights, logging distances of over 3,000 miles between bases in San Diego,

Opposite, top: *Sailors inspect the NC-4 flying boat a few days after her arrival in Lisbon Harbor following her successful flight across the Atlantic Ocean on 29 May 1919. Two days later the NC-4 flew to England, symbolically landing at Plymouth, the location from which Englishmen set sail to colonize the New World. (U.S. Navy)*

P2Y-1 flying boats of Patrol Squadron 10F fly past Diamond Head as they near the completion of their record nonstop formation flight from San Francisco, California, to Pearl Harbor, Hawaii. The 10–11 January 1934 flight, in which the squadron flew 2,399 miles in twenty-four hours and thirty-five minutes at an average speed of 94.5 mph involved flying through fog and haze over the vast Pacific without the benefit of automatic pilot or radar. (U.S. Navy)

Members of the Navy team assembled for the National Air Races in Detroit, Michigan, pictured on the hull of an F-5L flying boat. Lieutenant Adolphus W. Gorton, who captured the Curtiss Marine Trophy Race at the event, is seated third from right. Many of the aviators pictured established world records during the 1920s. (National Museum of Naval Aviation)

California; Norfolk, Virginia; Coco Solo, Canal Zone; and the Hawaiian Islands. Overwater flights of this nature remained risky due to the uncertainties of weather and the absence of navigational aids, and their successful completion reflected on both the designs of the aircraft and the men in their cockpits. They also foreshadowed the important role flying boats would play in the wide-ranging war in the Pacific during 1941–1945.

Though the distance flights brought great credit upon naval aviation, what most captured the attention of the aviation-crazed public of the 1920s and 1930s was air racing. Air meets were almost as old as aviation itself, and the "barnstorming era" following World War I witnessed pilots, among them young Lindbergh, flying from town to town giving flight demonstrations. The great air races of the interwar years developed into more formal affairs, yet were still products of the flamboyant era in which they occurred. Victory brought prize money, ornate trophies, and national acclaim to the winners. For naval aviation the races spurred the technological development of engines and airframes, and provided a forum for their evaluation. More importantly they provided a stage upon which airmen could showcase their talents and the capabilities of the Navy's air arm. Among the qualities of Rear Admiral William A. Moffett, who took the helm of the newly formed Bureau of Aeronautics on 1 September

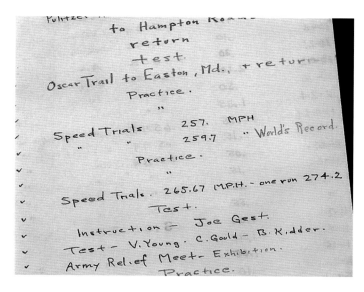

1921, was a particular savvy for politics and public relations. He quickly recognized the platform that air racing provided and the following year a Navy team entered the National Air Races, which included among its events the Curtiss Marine Trophy Race and the more prestigious Pulitzer Trophy Race for unlimited class airplanes.

The Curtiss race, which was reestablished in 1922 as an aerial water derby for seaplanes, proved ideally suited for naval aircraft. A crowd of 200,000 spectators in Detroit, Michigan, watched Lieutenant Adolphus W. Gorton capture the prize in this grueling event, flying eight laps over a twenty-mile course with an average speed of 112.6 mph. Gorton's aircraft, the TR-1 floatplane—a specially modified version of the TS fighter, the Navy's first aircraft designed specifically to fly from an aircraft carrier—benefited from its revolutionary Lawrence J-1 air-cooled radial engine. The Navy sponsored the Curtiss Marine Trophy Race until 1930, with the top Navy and Marine Corps pilots of the day battling one another for the top prize.

Naval aviation also competed against the world's best at the Schneider Trophy races, Europe's most prestigious event and one renowned for the extremely high speeds required for victory. In September 1923 Moffett sent a team of four pilots under the command of Lieutenant Frank W. Wead to England to race in what had previously been a strictly European contest.

Top, left: *The Curtiss CR-3 racer in which Lieutenant David Rittenhouse captured first place in the 1923 Schneider Cup seaplane race. The aircraft featured an aluminum propeller instead of a traditional wooden one, which allowed for higher engine speeds. Note the streamlined appearance of the fuselage and how low the pilot sat in the cockpit. (U.S. Navy)*

Top, right: *Lieutenant Al Williams, the Navy's premier racing pilot of the 1920s, stands on one of the pontoon floats of a Curtiss R3C-2 racer, one of the Navy entrants in the 1925 Schneider Trophy race. The engine panels have been removed for maintenance, revealing the inner workings of the airplane's 565 horsepower Curtiss V-1400 power plant. (National Museum of Naval Aviation)*

Above: *A pair of Al Williams's flight goggles worn by the daring aviator during the golden age of naval aviation. (Robert K. Ander)*

Much to the consternation of the British, the Navy's two Curtiss CR-3 racers finished well ahead of the rest of the field. The winner, Lieutenant David Rittenhouse, reached an average speed of 177.38 mph over the triangular course that stretched 37.2 nautical miles. Lieutenant Rutledge Irvine finished not far behind him, taking second place with a speed of 173.46 mph.

Another factor that fueled the Navy's participation in air racing during the 1920s was interservice rivalry with the Army. Thus, the Pulitzer Trophy Race for land planes assumed importance as naval aviators pitted themselves against their Army counterparts. The Navy could muster only a third place finish in its first run at the Pulitzer on 8 October 1922, though Lieutenant Al Williams demonstrated exemplary airmanship when he continued flying after the fire extinguisher in his Curtiss CR-2 racer exploded, scattering pieces of shrapnel throughout the cockpit. Although he lost his flying goggles and part of his helmet, and was made violently sick by the fumes, he still managed to finish fourth. The following year, Navy flyers achieved a clean sweep in the Pultizer, taking first, second, third, and fourth places. Williams, flying the latest Curtiss R2C-1 racer, led the pack with a blistering run that eclipsed 243 mph. A month later he established a world's speed record of 266.5 mph, earning him the sobriquet as the Navy's "speed king."

The triumphs of the interwar years marked tangible demonstrations of advancements in aircraft technology that served the Navy well in the greatest air war in history. Following the end of World War II, it did not take naval aviation long to once again establish marks in record books. On 1 October 1946, the "Truculent Turtle," a Lockheed P2V-1 Neptune manned by Commanders Thomas D. Davies, Eugene P. Rankin, and Walter S. Reid, accompanied by Lieutenant Commander Roy H. Tabeling, landed at Columbus, Ohio, after a fifty-five hour, seventeen-minute flight from Perth, Australia. The aircraft covered a total of 11,236 miles, a record for a nonstop flight without refueling that stood for sixteen years until broken by a jet-powered B-52 Stratofortress. In addition to demonstrating the new airplane's long-range capabilities, the flight brought

The record-setting P2V-1 Neptune "Truculent Turtle," its insignia visible on the nose, takes off from Floyd Bennett Field, New York, on 8 May 1949 to commemorate the thirtieth anniversary of the transatlantic flight of the NC-4. (Edgar Deigan)

The crew of the "Truculent Turtle" charts their course prior to attempting a record distance flight. Pictured left to right are communications officer Lieutenant Commander Roy H. Tabeling, patrol plane commander and pilot Commander Thomas S. Davies, copilot Commander Eugene P. Rankin, and copilot and navigator Commander Walter S. Reid. The flight had no set termination point following takeoff from Perth, Australia; the fuel state determined when the pilots landed the airplane. (U.S. Navy)

much-needed publicity at a time when naval aviation's continued existence was seriously threatened by the impending creation of the U.S. Air Force.

That same year, other naval aviators resumed operations in one of the most hostile environments on earth—the Antarctic. Naval aviation's tradition of exploring the world's polar regions dated back to 1925, when Navy seaplanes participated in the MacMillan Arctic Expedition. The officer in charge of the aviation detachment during that effort, the controversial Lieutenant Commander Richard E. Byrd, subsequently gained international renown with flights over the North and South poles.

President Calvin Coolidge presents the Medal of Honor to Commander Richard E. Byrd in recognition of the first flight over the North Pole during a ceremony at the White House in February 1927. Standing behind the chief executive is Machinist Floyd Bennett, who as pilot on the flight also received the nation's highest military decoration. It is ironic that it fell to President Coolidge, who purportedly once stated that the United States should buy one airplane and let the aviators take turns flying it, to recognize this epic feat in aviation. (U.S. Navy)

Following his flight over the North Pole in May 1926, Commander Richard E. Byrd attempted to do the same at the opposite pole employing a Ford Trimotor that he christened "Floyd Bennett," after the late pilot on his North Pole flight. He did so in the aircraft during a nineteen-hour flight on 28–29 November 1929. Note the skis on the aircraft that allowed for operations from the ice and snow of the Antarctic. (U.S. Navy)

He also led numerous polar expeditions, including Operation Highjump during 1946–1947, a massive effort designed to explore and photograph the coastline and a large area of the interior of Antarctica. Following in the tradition of Byrd, on 31 October 1956, a Navy R4D Skytrain nicknamed "Que Sera Sera"—piloted by Lieutenant Commander Gus Shinn and carrying Rear Admiral George J. Dufek, Commander, Naval Support Forces, Antarctica—landed on the ice at the South Pole. The seven men who disembarked from the aircraft were the first to stand at the spot since Captain

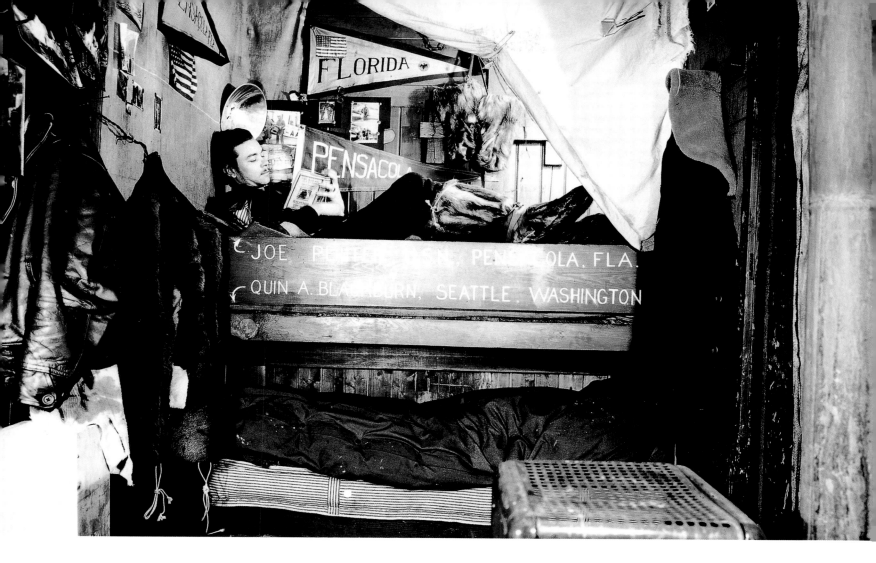

Life at Antarctica's Little America II base camp during the 1934 Byrd Antarctic Expedition proved rustic for the participants. Naval aviation pilot Joe Pelter relaxes with a book in his bunk, still wearing his mukluks in order to keep his feet warm. (National Museum of Naval Aviation)

In 1926 the Navy joined with the Department of the Interior in inaugurating a series of operations devoted to the aerial mapping of the territory of Alaska. Air assets included three Loening OL amphibians that carried the aerial photographers over the Alaskan wild. Note the clever insignia chosen for the survey, the centerpiece of which is a seal with wings. (U.S. Navy)

Nonperishable goods line the walls of the mess hall at Little America II in the Antarctic as members of the 1934 Byrd Antarctic Expedition celebrate Mid-Winter Night on 22 June 1934. Though the meal looks appetizing, for these men working thousands of miles from civilization the highlight of the evening was certainly the Paramount Penguin Theater feature starring Marlene Dietrich. (National Museum of Naval Aviation)

Above: *The U.S. Navy resumed operations in the Antarctic following World War II, launching Operation Highjump in December 1946. In a unique evolution, six R4D-5 Skytrain transport aircraft not designed for shipboard operations launched from the deck of* Philippine Sea *(CV 47) and subsequently flew mapping flights. Note the high-visibility markings on the aircraft, necessary for spotting purposes in the snow and ice. (U.S. Navy)*

Right: *Ground support personnel warm the engines of the famous "Que Sera Sera" on 26 September 1957. The R4D-5L Skytrain, which on 31 October 1956 became the first aircraft to land at the South Pole, is now on display at the Nation Museum of Naval Aviation. (U.S. Navy)*

Opposite, top: *A durable workhorse, the LC-130 Hercules proved ideal for operations in support of Antarctic Development Squadron 6 during the squadron's final years of service in support of Operation Deep Freeze. (National Museum of Naval Aviation)*

Robert F. Scott of the British Royal Navy reached it in January 1912. The landing at the pole occurred as part of Operation Deep Freeze, established by the Navy to provide logistical support for scientific research studies of the Antarctic. Deep Freeze continued until February 1999, when Antarctic Development Squadron (VXE) 6 made its final Antarctic flight, ending naval aviation's forty-four years of continual presence on the ice.

During the 1940s, military aviation entered a new realm with the advent and rapid advancement of jet engine technology. The Navy joined with the National Advisory Committee for Aeronautics in investigating the flight characteristics of the new rocket- and jet-powered aircraft just coming off the design boards, procuring a cylindrical airplane whose appearance and purpose prompted one reporter to call it the "Crimson

Lieutenant Commander Arthur W. Radford (seated eighth from left) commanded the Second Alaskan Aerial Survey from February to November 1929. Later surveys focused specifically on the Aleutian chain, to the great benefit of U.S. Navy operations there during World War II. (National Museum of Naval Aviation)

271

TEST PILOT TRAINING

Above: *Class 12 at the U.S. Naval Test Pilot School at the Naval Air Test Center in Patuxent River, Maryland, in 1954, included Major John Glenn, USMC (second row fifth from left), the first American to orbit the earth. Other graduates included future Chief of Naval Operations Lieutenant Tom Hayward (top row center) and Vietnam War Medal of Honor recipient Lieutenant James B. Stockdale (top row right). (Vice Admiral James Stockdale)*

Opposite, top: *Aviators assigned to the Flight Test Division of the Naval Air Test Center in Patuxent River, Maryland, flew the Navy's newest aircraft designs, "wringing them out" in an effort to determine their operational envelopes before they entered fleet service. The May 1959 flight test pilots included future admirals Paul Gillcrist and Don Engen and Apollo astronaut Dick Gordon. (U.S. Navy)*

Right: *Major Marion Carl, USMC, (left) and Commander Turner F. Caldwell stand next to the D-558-1 Skystreak on the dry lake bed at Muroc Army Airfield, which later became the famed Edwards Air Force Base. Called the "Crimson Test Tube" by reporters, the cylindrical D-558-1 was designed as a subsonic high-speed research aircraft, and contained 634 pounds of instruments for collecting data. (Boeing)*

Test Tube." The D-558-1 Skystreak made its debut in April 1947, and over the course of the ensuing months assaulted the record books. On 6 August, Commander Turner F. Caldwell pushed the subsonic Skystreak to 640.7 mph, setting a new world's record for speed over a measured course, a mark bettered by fellow test pilot Major Marion Carl, USMC, just days later. Though overshadowed by Chuck Yeager's eclipsing of the sound barrier in the X-1 in October 1947, for a brief moment the fastest man alive wore

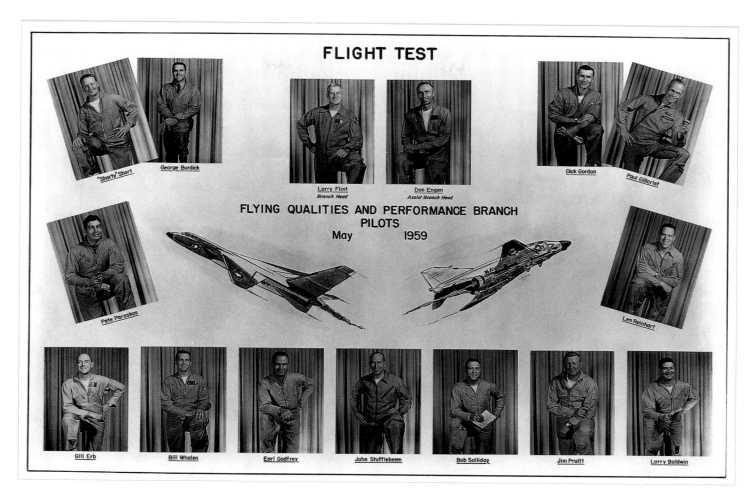

FLIGHT TEST

"Shorty" Short George Burdick

Larry Flint
Branch Head

Don Engen
Assist Branch Head

Dick Gordon Paul Gillcrist

FLYING QUALITIES AND PERFORMANCE BRANCH
PILOTS
May   1959

Pete Paraskos

Len Reinhart

Gill Erb Bill Whalen Earl Godfrey John Stufflebeem Bob Solliday Jim Pruitt Larry Baldwin

wings of gold. The Skystreak's successor, the rocket-powered D-558-2 Skyrocket, was designed to test supersonic flight at high altitude. It was soon setting new speed and altitude records, including a mark of 83,235 feet achieved by Carl on 20 August 1953.

The dawning of the jet age marked an exciting time for military aviation that brought scores of diverse aircraft off drawing boards. For those who wanted to fly the Navy's hottest new airplanes, the Naval Air Test Center at Patuxent River, Maryland, was the center of the flying universe, and home to the U.S. Naval Test Pilot School. Its graduates were at the forefront of the technological revolution that took them to levels few could have imagined. Among their early triumphs was the evaluation of the first operationally equipped airplane in history to fly faster than 1,000 mph, the Navy's F8U-1 Crusader. On 21 August 1956, an F8U-1 piloted by Commander Robert W. Windsor, Jr., captured the Thompson Trophy with a new national speed record of 1,015.428 mph over the 15-kilometer course at the Naval Ordnance Test Station at China Lake, California, snatching the record from the Air Force. The Crusader's spectacular capabilities were demonstrated once again in July 1957 during Project Bullet. With Major John H. Glenn, USMC, in the cockpit, a photographic reconnaissance version of the aircraft took off from Los Alamitos, California, headed for Floyd Bennett Field, New York. When he landed three hours, twenty-three minutes and fifty seconds later, Glenn owned the transcontinental speed record.

The performance of the F8U's successor, the F4H-1 Phantom II, was even more spectacular. Between 1959 and 1962 this Mach 2 airplane

Commander Robert W. Windsor (right) poses with the Thompson Trophy he captured for the Navy after establishing a new national speed record of 1,015.428 mph in an F8U-1 Crusader in 1956. During the record run, Windsor covered 400 miles during repeated runs over the 15-kilometer course, including supersonic turns. The aircraft carried a full armament of 20mm cannon and dummy ammunition, making the aircraft the first operationally equipped aircraft to eclipse the 1,000 mph mark. Accordingly, the Navy dubbed the record flight Project One Grand. (National Museum of Naval Aviation)

Top: *Major John H. Glenn, USMC, pictured in the F8U-1P photoreconnaissance plane in which he established a transcontinental speed record between Los Alamitos, California, and Floyd Bennett Field, New York, on 16 July 1957. Glenn completed three in-flight refuelings during the record run, which traveled from west to east to take advantage of the jet stream. (U.S. Navy)*

Above: *While Project Top Flight carried the F4H-1 Phantom II to dizzying heights, Project Sageburner demonstrated the aircraft's low-altitude speed capability. On 28 August 1961, a Fighter Squadron 101 Det A Phantom zipped across the desert landscape of White Sands, New Mexico, in setting a low-altitude speed record with an average of 902.769 mph over a three-kilometer course. (Boeing)*

Right: *Lieutenant Richard Gordon and Lieutenant (jg) Bobbie R. Young pictured in their high-pressure suits after capturing the Bendix Trophy for their 2,421.4-mile flight from Los Angeles to New York in a time of two hours and forty-seven minutes. Average speed for their 24 May 1961, flight was 870 mph. Gordon joined the National Aeronautics and Space Administration as an astronaut in 1963. (Boeing)*

established fifteen world's records. The incredible performance began with an assault on the altitude mark, broken on 6 December 1959 when Commander Larry E. Flint reached 98,560 feet. Eighteen months later, on 12 April 1962, Lieutenant Commander Del W. Nordberg culminated the run by capturing the world's time-to-climb mark at 30,000 meters in 371.43 seconds—almost 3 miles per minute straight up! Such was the power of the new airplane that on 25 September 1960, its 1,390.21 mph run over a 100-kilometer closed course bettered the existing mark for that distance by more than 200 mph.

In the meantime, others reached farther into the heavens. The challenge of exploring worlds beyond our own captivated the nation after the Soviet Union's successful launching of a satellite into orbit in October 1957. Over the ensuing years, rocket-propelled aircraft began to enter the threshold of space, and the National Aeronautics and Space Administration (NASA) launched a space program that ultimately put a man on the moon and continues to explore our galaxy. It included a number of prominent naval aviators who made the transition from aeronaut to astronaut. The first of these was Lieutenant Commander Forrest S. Petersen, the only Navy test pilot assigned to NASA's X-15 program. On 10 August 1961, Petersen became the first naval aviator to fly at four times the speed of sound, taking the rocket-powered X-15 airplane to Mach 4.11. He then bettered that mark on 28 September with a speed of Mach 5.3. In addition, of the seven men chosen for Project Mercury, NASA's first manned space flight program, four—Lieutenant Commanders Walter Schirra and Alan B. Shepard, Lieutenant Malcolm Scott Carpenter, and Lieutenant Colonel John H. Glenn, USMC—were naval aviators. Shepard became the first American in space when his *Freedom 7* space capsule achieved suborbital flight on 5 May 1961, reaching an altitude of 116 miles. On 20 February 1962, Glenn made America's first orbital flight, circling the earth three times in his space capsule *Friendship 7*.

As the space program expanded, so too did the number of astronauts who wore wings of gold. Commander John W. Young, a former record-setting pilot in the F4H Phantom II, was on board Gemini 3, the first manned flight of the space program involving a two-man capsule, when it was launched into orbit in 1965. Young was joined in the Gemini program

Top: *The crew of Project Sageburner's record low-altitude speed run was pilot Lieutenant Huntington Hardisty (left) and radar intercept officer Lieutenant Earl H. DeEsch. Hardisty eventually rose to the rank of admiral, retiring as Commander in Chief, U.S. Pacific Command. (Boeing)*

Above: *The names of the Mercury 7 astronauts became household words following their selection in April 1959. All told, the four naval aviators in the group logged eight trips into space, including the first American space flight by Alan Shepard and the first orbital flight by a U.S. astronaut by John Glenn. Wally Schirra became the only astronaut to fly at least one mission in the Mercury, Gemini, and Apollo programs. (NASA)*

Above: *The first female naval aviator chosen as an astronaut, Lieutenant Commander Wendy Lawrence logged her first mission in space on board the Space Shuttle* Endeavor *in March 1995. (NASA)*

Left: *A helicopter rescue hoist pulls astronaut John Young from the waters of the Atlantic after the splashdown of the Gemini 10 space capsule in July 1966. Young later flew as a crew member of Apollo 10, and commanded the Apollo 16 mission to the moon in April 1972. He also served as commander of the first flight of the Space Shuttle in April 1981. (National Museum of Naval Aviation)*

by others with naval aviation backgrounds, among them James Lovell, Eugene Cernan, Pete Conrad, and Neil Armstrong, whose names would become well known during the next phase of the American space program, the quest to land on the moon.

The Apollo program endured a tragic beginning when a fire erupted during a test of the Apollo 1 command module, killing all three members of the crew, including Lieutenant Roger B. Chaffee, the Navy's first casualty of the space program. Although the program was delayed while the spacecraft was completely redesigned, it did not prevent the U.S. from beating the Russians to the moon. On 20 July 1969, Armstrong, a former naval aviator who had distinguished himself as a fighter pilot in Korea, became the first man to set foot on the lunar surface. Of the five Apollo flights that followed, naval aviators commanded four of them. In addition, seven of the twelve American astronauts to set foot on the moon were Navy-trained. An all-Navy crew was the first to live and work aboard Skylab, the American orbiting laboratory launched in May 1973, and John Young and Robert Crippen manned the Space Shuttle *Columbia* during its maiden flight on 12 April 1981. The Navy's participation in the space shuttle program has continued since that time. There has been

Opposite: *Astronaut Jim Lovell, commander of the ill-fated Apollo 13 mission, undergoes space suit checks just hours before blasting into space on 11 April 1970. An explosion on board the command module just under fifty-six hours into the mission ended the crew's hopes of reaching the moon and triggered a harrowing drama as they heroically brought their crippled spacecraft back to earth. (NASA)*

The Space Shuttle Columbia *kicks up sand from the dry lake at Edwards Air Force Base, California, after returning from its maiden voyage into space on 14 April 1981. The flight, which consisted of thirty-six orbits around the earth, inaugurated a space shuttle program that today serves as an essential element in the construction of the International Space Station. (NASA)*

Astronauts John Young (left) and Robert Crippen display a model of the Space Shuttle Columbia, *which they piloted on its maiden flight into space. Between them, the pair eventually commanded four later Space Shuttle missions, Crippen in* Challenger *and Young on board* Discovery. *(NASA)*

tragedy, namely the *Challenger* explosion in January 1986 that killed all on board, including Navy Captain Michael Smith, but overall naval aviation's participation in the shuttle program represents a series of triumphs. These include the selection of Commander Wendy Lawrence as the first female naval aviator in space, and the leading role of Captain Robert Gibson, commander of the first space shuttle to dock with the Russian space station *Mir*.

Many years separate the first naval aviator, Lieutenant Theodore G. Ellyson, sitting precariously without a seatbelt on a Curtiss pusher preparing to leave the ground for his first flight, from his successors, the rumbling of igniting rockets shaking them to the core as they prepare to blast into space. The technological advancements that bridge the period are nothing short of incredible. Ellyson measured his progress in feet and on those first flights never eclipsed 60 mph, while space shuttle astronauts fly miles above the earth and orbit it at dizzying speeds. Yet, though their platforms may differ, the spirit that guided Ellyson is very much a part of those who follow him, one that pushes the individual and the collective group to explore the bounds of flight and exceed them, indeed to always go farther and faster.

A formation of U.S. Naval Test Pilot School aircraft—an F/A-18 Hornet followed by two TA-4 Skyhawks and a T-2 Buckeye flanked by a pair of T-38 Talons—flies over NAS Patuxent River, Maryland, circa 1987. Since it opened in 1943, Pax River has been a centerpiece in the Navy's efforts to test the limits of flight. (U.S. Navy)

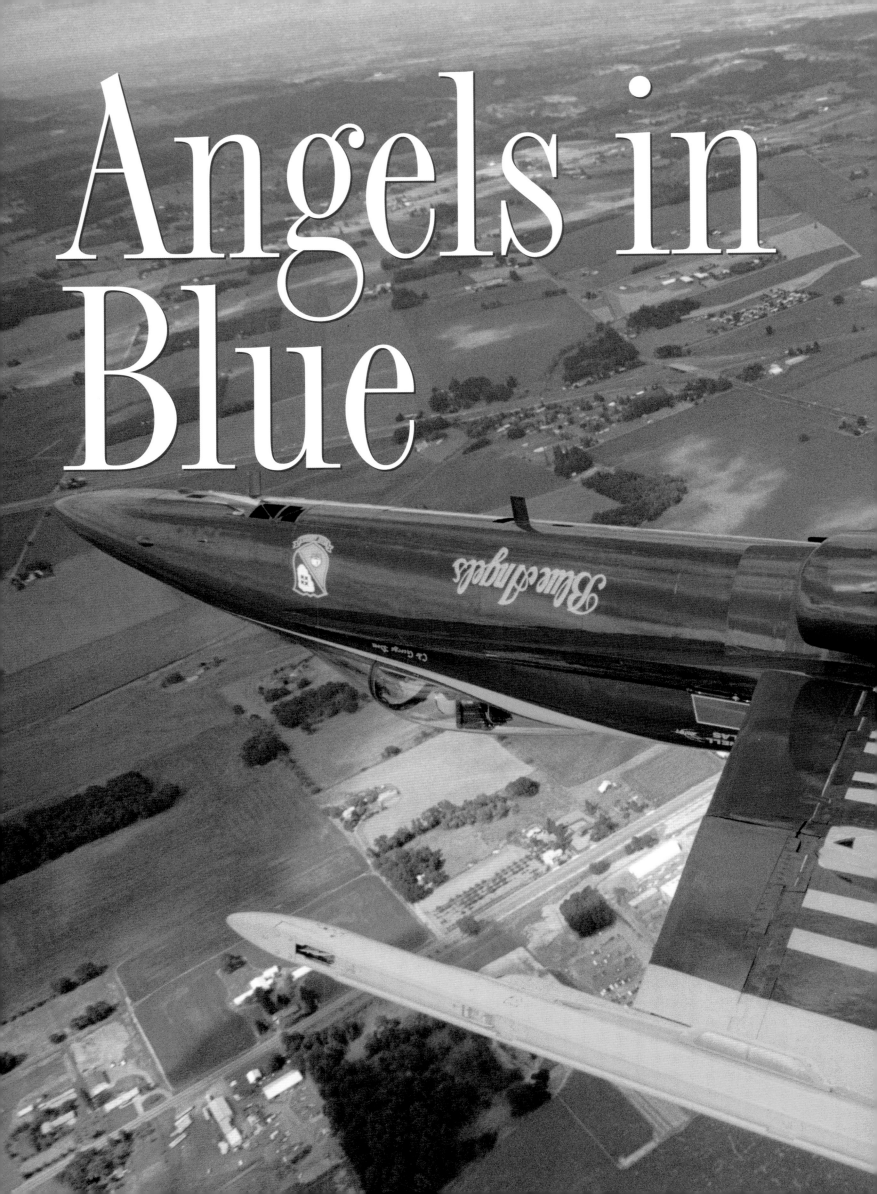

Angels in Blue

Angels in Blue

Captain Pat Walsh, USN

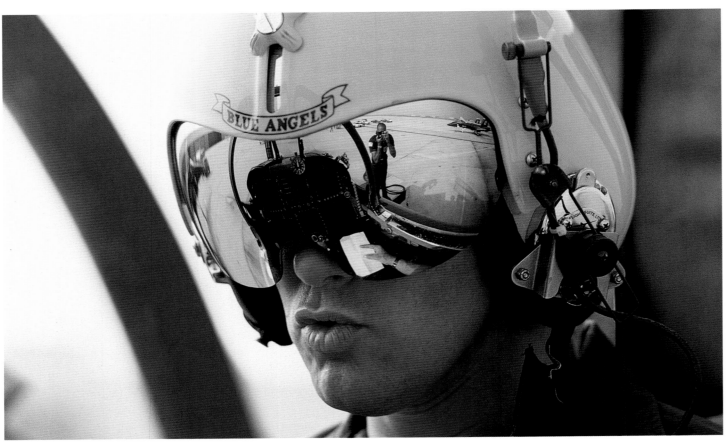

Pages 280–281: *The panoramic vista of the landscape below fills the canopies of two Blue Angels F/A-18 Hornets as they fly inverted during one of the thrilling maneuvers that have made the U.S. Navy Flight Demonstration Squadron world famous. Known as the "Boss," Blue Angel Number One commands the squadron and leads the diamond and delta formations during an airshow. (U.S. Navy)*

Above: *The distinctive yellow flight helmets worn by Blue Angel demonstration pilots include microphones so that they can maintain communication with one another. The flight leader calls formations and maneuvers using a precise cadence that ensures perfect execution. (Mark Hopkins)*

The sun glints off the canopies of Blue Angels F/A-18 Hornets aligned on the flight line just prior to rolling out onto the runway to commence another flight demonstration. Precision on the ground breeds precision in the air. Thus, even at a standstill Blue Angel aircraft sit in tight formation. (U.S. Navy)

O f the hundreds of naval aviators on active duty in the U.S. Navy and Marine Corps in any given year, only six man the cockpits of the distinctive blue and gold jets of the Blue Angels each year, flying as demonstration pilots at airshows. While their brother and sister fliers protect the nation's interests abroad, often thousands of miles from friendly shores, it is the Blue Angels, traversing the skies at airshows throughout North America, that represent naval aviation to the public, thrilling spectators with dazzling flight maneuvers. Between 1985 and 1987, I had the high honor and distinct privilege to fly as a member of the Navy Flight Demonstration Squadron. In three years we performed in front of 18 million people and crisscrossed the country from Maine to Hawaii and from Florida to Canada. In addition to representing naval aviation at each show, the team strove to achieve a private goal: we simply wanted the public to say at the end of the performance that the team, the aircraft, and the show "looked the same as it did last year." This seemingly innocuous remark was revealing because it meant we had achieved the same standard of performance set by the team from the previous season. It was, however, a lofty goal that required our 100 percent commitment to each other, in each maneuver of every show for an entire year. Unknown to most was the profound impact that this quest for excellence had on all of us personally. When officers were not involved in an endless number of rehearsals, briefings, or debriefings, we joined the efforts of our enlisted team members to serve as "ambassadors of goodwill" at local civic and community functions. Together, these events in the air and on the ground became part of the weekly rhythm that, in total, made my tour of duty with the Blue Angels an extraordinary and life-changing experience.

Lieutenant Pat Walsh pictured in the cockpit of his A-4 Skyhawk during his time flying as the Slot pilot while a member of the U.S. Navy Flight Demonstration Squadron. Blue Angel demonstration pilots must be career-oriented officers with a minimum of 1,500 flight hours and aircraft carrier qualification. (U.S. Navy)

WINGS OF ANGELS—THE FIRST DECADE: *On 15 June 1946, a formation of F6F Hellcats roared down the runway at Naval Air Station Jacksonville, Florida, and into the sky, rolling and looping in graceful precision for some twenty minutes above the crowd gathered below. The brainchild of Fleet Admiral Chester W. Nimitz, the exhibition in this first year of peace was to demonstrate to the American public the capabilities of naval aviation that had been so vital in winning World War II. It marked the beginning of today's world famous Blue Angels Flight Demonstration Squadron.*

With a 19:1 kill ratio against Japanese aircraft during World War II, the Hellcat proved an ideal choice as the first platform for the Blue Angels, the moniker chosen for the team after members saw an advertisement for a nightclub of the same name in the New Yorker *magazine. However, the team flew the venerable aircraft only until August 1946, at which time they received the F8F Bearcat. The last propeller-driven aircraft flown by the Blue Angels, the diminutive fighter possessed speed, maneuverability, and a rate of climb that proved ideal to air show flying.*

The Blue Angels entered the jet age in 1949, taking delivery of the F9F Panther, one of the Navy's newest front-line fighters. Not only did they fly the airplane until 1954, they took it into combat when the team was disbanded for service in Korea during 1950–1951. The Panther's swept-wing successor, the F9F Cougar, became the fourth demonstration aircraft in the team's history. The Cougar served into the 1957 show season. Not only did both of the jets allow for higher speeds, the fact that there were no spinning propellers to worry about enabled the team to fly even tighter formations.

Left, top to bottom:
Blue Angel F9F-8 Cougars trail smoke from their wingtips as they pass over a beach near their home at NAS Pensacola, Florida, during the mid-1950s. The releasing of smoke is still practiced today, allowing spectators to trace the path of the formation. (National Museum of Naval Aviation)

A crowd gathers as Lieutenant (jg) George Hoskins climbs aboard his F8F-1 Bearcat at Stapleton Airport in Denver, Colorado, prior to flying a demonstration on 8 May 1949. (U.S. Navy)

Opposite: *The distinctive diamond formation that is a hallmark of the Blue Angels first appeared with the advent of the F9F Panther, with which the team entered the jet age in 1949. Spinning propellers on the noses of previous aircraft made the formation too hazardous. (U.S. Navy)*

Right, top to bottom:
Blue Angel F8F-1 Bearcats make a formation takeoff at NAS Atlanta, Georgia, during a demonstration in 1948. The small, piston-engine aircraft was full of pep, and made an excellent demonstration aircraft. However, jet aircraft represented the future and the Bearcat flew on borrowed time. (U.S. Navy)

The F6F Hellcat, the platform upon which naval aviation swept the skies of enemy aircraft in the Pacific during World War II, was the ideal aircraft to outfit the U.S. Navy's flight demonstration team when it was formed in 1946. The team's mission was to provide the public a firsthand look at the capabilities of the Navy's air arm. (National Museum of Naval Aviation)

The diamond formation passes over NAS Pensacola, Florida, home base of the Blue Angels since 1955. During the show season, the squadron typically flies practice shows over Pensacola in preparation for their performances throughout the United States. (U.S. Navy)

As is the case in fleet squadrons, the backbone of the Blue Angels is the enlisted personnel on the ground who keep the aircraft flying, or in this case, make sure the appearance of the blue and gold jets is ship-shape. (U.S. Navy)

Each season began with approximately 150 winter training flights or sorties at Naval Air Facility El Centro, California, where the sunny blue skies served as the perfect setting for the intense training regimen the team endured for the first three months of each year. Three new pilots joined the team annually, and such was the rotation of positions among the formation and solo pilots that those who had a year of air-show experience occupied a position from which to model and judge the performance of each maneuver.

Initially, the syllabus divided us into pairs to begin the methodical process of building a team in the air. We devoted the early flights to the synchronization of basic stick and throttle movements, so important to maintaining the precise formations that were the team's trademark, as well as the development of a common understanding of how to make a safe escape from the formation. The flight leader, known simply as the "Boss," announced each movement of the formation with an exaggerated and deliberate cadence over the radio, which required a timely reply from each participant. Slowly, the flight of two aircraft that began twenty feet apart and used 2,000 feet as a minimum altitude, became four aircraft that maneuvered dynamically six feet apart and then lowered the formation to 700 feet. Finally, as the performance season approached, the solo pilots joined the formation, which then followed the Boss in maneuvers that began at "show altitude" between 150 and 200 feet.

I flew in the Left Wingman or Number Three position for one year, where my sole responsibility was to balance the formation set by the Right Wingman. The next year, my responsibilities broadened with assignment as the Slot pilot, which I occupied for two show seasons. Tucked in behind the leader and flanked by the two wingmen, the Slot pilot provided oversight for training and safety and filled out the Diamond silhouette. During most maneuvers, I was in a position to evaluate the entry airspeed and altitude of the Boss throughout the maneuver. This position "in the back of the bus" also allowed me to scrutinize the formation pitch rate and rate-of-roll during overhead and rolling maneuvers. My position in the formation was underneath the Boss's fuselage, which made it relatively simple to match his profile. Although stepped down from the flight leader, my jet was also below and between the wingmen so that their wingtips were behind me. It is testament to the teamwork and training that I did not have to even look up or behind in order to judge the proximity of our wings; they were so close that I could feel or sense their positions.

Though the Diamond formation is the standard for most Blue Angel maneuvers, flying in echelon, in which each aircraft is stepped out and back from the one in front of it, proved most challenging. In echelon formation, the back-up function performed by the Slot pilot took on an additional degree of difficulty because of the amount of concentration required to maintain position three aircraft removed from the Flight Leader's aircraft. Each correction or movement by the Number Two or

Just as he would on a carrier deck, a plane captain employs hand signals to communicate with a Blue Angels pilot as the squadron's F/A-18 Hornets prepare to launch for a demonstration. In this way, both plane captain and pilot ensure that control surfaces like the flaps and vertical and horizontal stabilizers are in working order. (U.S. Navy)

A popular element of each Blue Angel flight demonstration is the high-performance takeoff by one of the solo pilots. The thunderous roar from the engines and the vapor cloud that forms over the wings as the F/A-18 Hornet climbs skyward are impressive no matter how many times one witnesses it. (U.S. Navy)

Number Three pilot in echelon meant a correspondingly larger one by the succeeding pilot, which by the time it reached me required even greater stick and throttle movements to maintain position. From the perspective of the spectators far below, the formation appeared rock steady. However, in the air corrections would build up to a point where the movement within the formation more resembled that of a snake. In the Left Echelon Roll, all four aircraft were stacked down and left. The maneuver rolled into the echelon, which could make the moment as entertaining as it was exciting for the Slot pilot. Jokingly, we often remarked that in echelon, we would "remember who our friends were."

My favorite maneuver, the Diamond 360, exemplified the commitment to professionalism that we made to the team as well as to each other. We introduced it early in the sequence from right to left in front of the crowd, in an angle of bank that made the four aircraft appear to be welded together. In my first year, I flew on the inside of this arcing turn looking up at the Boss who led the formation at 150 feet altitude. The narrator announced to the crowd that my position was twenty-four inches from the lead's wingtip to my canopy. I could not measure it, but simply used the sound of the Number One jet engine to set the formation. I knew that I was close to position when I could hear a high-pitched whine from the engine. I judged the distance between the wingtip and the canopy based on the sound of the aircraft rather than visual cues

Above: *Though the diamond formation is the standard one flown by the Blue Angels, some maneuvers involve flying in echelon formation, with the aircraft stepped down, out, and back from the flight leader's bird. (U.S. Navy)*

Opposite: *The portrait of precision that is the Blue Angels diamond formation as seen from the cockpit of the slot pilot's aircraft during a training flight near El Centro, California. The Blues give new meaning to the definition of a tight formation.. (U.S. Navy)*

Both enlisted sailors and Marines man the ground support echelon of the Blue Angels, working in front of the crowd at show sites or serving behind the scenes maintaining the aircraft, assisting in recruiting, or ensuring the smooth administrative functioning of the squadron. (U.S. Navy)

Above: *The Blue Angels's signature formation, the Diamond, passes in front of the crowd during a flight demonstration. The pilots fly with such grace and precision that from the ground it appears as if the aircraft are a single unit. (U.S. Navy)*

Right: *Throughout the show season the Blue Angels routinely take members of the news media and visiting dignitaries on exhibition flights in the two-seat Number Seven 7 jet, orienting them to some of the maneuvers flown by the squadron. A plane captain straps Senator John Glenn into the rear cockpit of a TA-4F Skyhawk on 29 August 1986, prior to an orientation flight that proved most memorable for the author, Lieutenant Pat Walsh. (U.S. Navy)*

Below: *A plane captain salutes the line of Blue Angel pilots marching toward their aircraft prior to manning up for an airshow. Each demonstration begins in this manner and displays for the crowd the military order that is the foundation for the success of the Blue Angels. (U.S. Navy)*

from the fuselage. There were other peripheral cues that we would use, almost subconsciously, to monitor each other while we were flying. For example, in the Line-Abreast Loop, we could look through the formation and see the grimaces on each other's faces as we fought to hold onto our momentarily proper positions in the maneuver.

Although it was a very intense and professional environment, flying with the Blue Angels had its lighter moments. One year during a stop in Cleveland, Ohio, I had the privilege of flying John Glenn, the first American to orbit the earth and then a U.S. Senator from Ohio, in the back of our two-seat TA-4F Skyhawk. It was the last season in which the Blue Angels flew the venerable A-4, the first versions of which had been

Silhouetted against a bright sun, the two solo jets pass over other members of the squadron on the ground, who are monitoring the pilots as they hone their skills during a flight training. (U.S. Navy)

introduced in the 1950s, and it was not unusual to have an occasional mechanical problem with the airplane. Given my passenger's stature, the flight was a big event, attended by thousands of well wishers, hundreds of dignitaries, and several camera crews and reporters. Shortly after takeoff, we set up in front of the crowd for the Diamond Loop, entering the maneuver at 400 knots. All was normal, but as we reached the apex of the loop, the cockpit became eerily quiet. When I added power, I felt a pressure surge followed by an ear-piercing, deafening KABOOM as the cabin pressurization turbine gagged and spewed out condensation, smoke, and a few pungent fumes. Immediately, I looked in the rear-view mirror and could not see the familiar face that had been in my back seat when we

took off. Where did he go? How could I have possibly lost him? It turned out that this was not the first failure of a cabin pressure regulator that he had experienced. After a few nail-biting moments Senator Glenn emerged from his crouched position in the back seat, looked up and smiled. When the cockpit had lost pressurization, he had simply bent over to clear his ears, but I could not see him. In the meanwhile, I fretted over how I would ever explain to all of the reporters on the ground how I had lost an American hero. The team enjoyed this story at my expense for many years.

Although it is difficult to match the thrill of flying an air show, the special benefits of wearing the blue and gold flight suits of the Blue Angels came on the ground, whether signing autographs for bright-eyed kids after landing or visiting hospitals. Invariably, for each of us, someone or something served to center us and help prioritize values in our professional lives. It usually occurred when officer and enlisted members of the team made themselves available to participate in the local community on television or radio, in schools, or at charitable events. For me, it came during my second year on the team, when an airshow sponsor arranged for the Blue Angels to provide a team representative to visit a Veterans Administration hospital. As part of the arrangement, I attended the Friday morning event in uniform.

An escort met me at the facility early in the morning and together we walked up the staircase from the parking lot to the old, red brick structure. I can still hear the creak of the wooden floor that accompanied

Above: *The two solo jets appear to be one while executing a maneuver known as the Fortus. In actuality, the Number Six jet is below the right wing tip of the inverted Number Five as the pair passes in front of the crowd in the landing configuration. (U.S. Navy)*

Senator John Glenn and his wife Annie laugh with members of the Blue Angels, including Lieutenant Pat Walsh (standing second from right), following the former astronaut's 29 August 1986 flight with the demonstration squadron. (U.S. Navy)

each step as we made our way down a hallway toward several patients sitting on beds waiting for us.

There were five men. They rose to their feet when we walked into their section of the room. They represented several generations of conflicts—two were from the Vietnam War, one was from the Korean War, and two from the great World Wars. All of them wore medals, pinned on their pajamas over their hearts. One had difficulty standing and balanced

Opposite, bottom: *Positioned line abreast, Blue Angel F/A-18 Hornets plummet straight down toward earth. The squadron employs this formation in executing one of the more graceful maneuvers in any airshow, the Line-Abreast Loop that reaches its apex at an altitude of about 7,500 feet. (U.S. Navy)*

WINGS OF ANGELS—TIGERS TO HORNETS:

Keeping pace with the rapid advancement in jet aircraft technology, the Blue Angels transitioned into Grumman's supersonic F11F Tiger halfway through the 1957 show season. The team continued to fly shows in their trusty Cougars while they practiced with their new mounts and on 4 July 1957, after almost three months of work in their Tigers, the Blue Angels flew them in public for the first time at Newcastle Air Force Base, Delaware. The airplanes served the team well into the 1960s, their sleek appearance and roaring afterburner seemingly tailor-made for the team's aerobatics. The F11Fs equipped the Blue Angels when they flew their milestone 1,000th demonstration in 1963, and were also flown during the 1965 European tour, the team's first visit overseas.

The final show of 1968 marked not only the farewell to one more demonstration season, but also the end of twenty-two years of flying Grumman-built aircraft. The selection of the McDonnell-Douglas F-4 Phantom II as the team's sixth demonstration aircraft prompted the Blue Angels to adjust their show routine to the larger and more powerful airplane, and they inaugurated the Phantom-era on 15 March 1969. Nicknamed the "Flying Anvil" and the "Big Iron Sled," the Phantom's lines were not nearly as graceful as that of the Tiger, but the Blue Angels made them look beautiful. The F-4 equipped the Blue Angels until 1974 and during a portion of that period the U.S. Air Force's Thunderbirds also performed in the Phantom, the only time in history that the demonstration squadrons of the Navy and Air Force have flown the same aircraft.

While the supersonic F-4 brought raw power to an airshow, the nimble flight characteristics of the A-4 Skyhawk, with its slender fuselage and compact delta wing, made it much more maneuverable than the Phantom. Not surprisingly, the Blue Angels flew Skyhawks for twelve years until they were replaced by the F/A-18 Hornets after the 1986 season. The flight demonstration squadron still flies the Hornet, the longest serving aircraft in the history of the Blue Angels.

Left, top to bottom:
The small size and nimble performance of the A-4F Skyhawk made it an ideal platform for the precision formations that have made the Blue Angels famous. (U.S. Navy)

An F-4J Phantom II thunders past the crowd during a high-speed pass at Nellis AFB, Nevada, on 22 November 1970. (Robert L. Lawson)

Opposite: *Blue Angel Number Six flies inverted over the desert landscape at Nellis AFB, Nevada, during a demonstration on 14 November 1967. The F-11A Tiger, with its sleek lines and screaming afterburner, always provided a good show. (Robert L. Lawson)*

Right, top to bottom:
A head-on view of a Blue Angel A-4F Skyhawk reveals the aircraft's slender, compact profile and delta wing. The squadron flew A-4s from 1974 to 1986. (Andy Neimyer)

A sea of hands seeking his autograph surrounds Lieutenant Mark Perrault at a 1958 airshow. Ambassadors of the Navy in the air and on the ground, members of the squadron interact with the public to a great degree. (National Museum of Naval Aviation)

himself on a single crutch—the lower half of his pajamas were pinned to cover a missing limb. Overwhelmed by the sight of these men, I found myself asking, "Why do you stand so rigidly?" One man, apparently a spokesman for the group, stepped forward and said, "We stand proudly for what you represent."

A number of years have passed since I met this group in the Veterans Administration hospital at Fargo, North Dakota. Yet, even today, I carry with me a vivid memory of a Friday morning in the summer of 1986, of five men whose life experiences in service to their country were profound and beyond comprehension. I do not remember their names. I did not know their rank as enlisted or officers; I do not remember their branches of service; I do not even remember the jobs that they held. I only remember feeling humbled by their presence. I could sense their commitment, their dedication, and their selflessness and see in their eyes the courage, valor, and bravery to face unbeatable odds. I could listen to their stories and learn of their love of country; I could tell by the firmness of heartfelt handshakes their honesty, integrity, and strength of character. Although they would not admit it, I knew by the lines on their faces the depth of their youthful sacrifice. When I imagined the spirited lives of these very proud servicemen, it reminded me of the words of Lord Byron: "The days of our youth were the days of our glory."

My time with these men was one small sojourn in a weekly rhythm that repeated itself hundreds of times in the course of the Blue Angel show season. After the autumn air shows fade into distant memory, the season becomes part of naval aviation lore. Then one-half of the officers and enlisted sailors quietly resume positions of leadership and service in the fleet. By mid-November, these experienced team members have vacated their positions to make room for a new group to wrestle with a new set of challenges in the air and on the ground. Few in the audience will distinguish one Blue Angel show season from another. Our country, however, will remember what they will do in the days that follow as part of the larger Navy and Marine Corps team on watch around the world.

In the years since my tour with the team, I have often thought of the everyday heroes whom I met on a bright summer day in Fargo. Whenever I return from a cruise, friends and loved ones ask, "What did you do out there?" Before I describe the excitement of flying, the tedium and monotony of life at sea, or the fun and wonder of visiting a foreign port, I stop to think of those men. Veterans are the conscience of a nation—to lose sight of them or what they have done would contribute to a nation without a conscience. And as Winston Churchill once said, "A nation without a

Their shadows visible on the runway below, the flight leader and his wingmen execute a formation takeoff, raising their landing gear just moments after getting airborne. Typically, the Slot pilot is positioned to the right of the Number Two aircraft, and slides into position behind the Number One jet after the formation gains altitude. (U.S. Navy)

297

To the over millions of people who have watched the Blue Angels perform, the jets are sometimes distant silhouettes high in the sky. This reverse perspective of a Blue Angel airshow reveals a pilot's-eye view of one of the U.S. Navy Flight Demonstration Squadron's high-flying maneuvers as the formation heads toward the ground. (U.S. Navy)

The two solo pilots display a different type of precision than that demonstrated by the pilots in the Diamond formation. Maneuvers like the Knife Edge Pass involve the aircraft converging at high speeds and passing within close proximity of one another. (U.S. Navy)

Blue Angels Number Five and Number Six cross paths, demonstrating the precise timing and consistency that is required from the solo pilots during their low-altitude maneuvers. The need for exactness is illustrated by the fact that for every second of approach error, a maneuver moves off center by one-eighth of a mile. (U.S. Navy)

conscience is a nation without a soul . . . and a nation without a soul cannot function." So, in response, I will repeat the message that my friends in Fargo told me that morning—that we stood proudly for what America represents.

Rarely in our professional careers do we have an opportunity to have a direct impact on the lives of others. As a Blue Angel, I wore a crisp, blue flight suit, flew gleaming jets, and witnessed panoramic vistas that many

A LEGACY OF VALOR: *Given the demands of demonstration flying, Lieutenant Commander Roy M. Voris, the first leader of the Blue Angels, chose only bachelors as members of the first flight demonstration team. Additionally, the first Blue Angels were all combat veterans of World War II, Voris being the most notable having become an ace in aerial combat against the Japanese. Although bachelorhood is no longer a requirement, the combat legacy of pilots who have served with the Blue Angels continues to this day.*

During the decade following World War II, most of the officers-in-charge who led the team's jets in their aerial ballet were distinguished combat pilots. In addition to Voris, three other team leaders—Lieutenant Commanders John Magda, Ray Hawkins, and Zeke Cormier—were fighter aces and another, Lieutenant Commander Ed Holley, received a Navy Cross as a wartime dive bomber pilot. Another leader, Lieutenant Commander Raleigh Rhodes, spent much of the war as a prisoner of war, having been shot down during an air battle off Guadalcanal.

The outbreak of the Korean War turned all of the members of the 1950 team into combat veterans. Disbanded less than two months after North Korean forces invaded South Korea, the team formed the nucleus of Fighter Squadron 191 and went to war on board Princeton *(CV 37). Adopting the name "Satan's Kittens," the squadron executed the first bombing attack by jet aircraft in the history of the U.S. Navy. Yet, their time in combat exacted a price when John Magda was lost on a combat mission in May 1951. He was the first Blue Angel lost to enemy fire, but sadly he would not be the last.*

America's protracted struggle in Vietnam impacted all of naval aviation, including the Blue Angels. Many of the demonstration pilots who had served in the 1950s and early 1960s commanded squadrons and air wings during the course of the war. In addition, during the Vietnam era, the pilots who rotated on and off the team were most often combat veterans. For example, the 1969 team included flight leader Lieutenant Commander Bill Wheat, Number Three pilot Ernie Christensen, and narrator Rick Adams, all of whom had been forced to eject from their aircraft over Vietnam. Adams punched out twice, and the second time he was rescued just thirty miles from the North Vietnamese capital of Hanoi. Sadly, the Blue Angels lost three pilots in Southeast Asia, including Commander Harley Hall. The popular skipper

of the team during the 1970–1971 show seasons, he ejected from his F-4 Phantom II fighter over South Vietnam on 27 January 1973, the last day of official American hostilities in Vietnam. Though his radar intercept officer was repatriated with other prisoners of war, Hall never returned.

When naval aviation went to war over the sands of Kuwait and Iraq, a host of former and future Blue Angels manned the cockpits of jets launching from the Navy's carriers. Today, the legacy of valor continues as men who once wore blue and gold patrol trouble spots throughout the world, ready and able when the call to arms comes again.

Top, left: *Commander Harley Hall, one of the most popular aviators to ever fly a Blue Angels jet, was shot down on the last day of the Vietnam War, the second Blue Angels flight leader lost in combat. (U.S. Navy)*

Top, right: *Lieutenant Commander Roy M. Voris (right) turns over the reins of the Blue Angels to Lieutenant Commander Ray Hawkins on 16 December 1952. The array of ribbons on their chests is testament to their combat prowess. Both men became fighter aces during World War II. (U.S. Navy).*

Above: *Lieutenant Commander John Magda demonstrates a flight maneuver to his fellow Blue Angel pilots during 1950, the year the team was disbanded to form the nucleus of Fighter Squadron 191 for service in the Korean War. (U.S. Navy)*

Above: *Affectionately known as "Fat Albert," the U.S. Navy Flight Demonstration Squadron's C-130 Hercules transport aircraft carries equipment and support personnel to show sites and also performs a flight demonstration of its own by executing a jet-assisted takeoff at airshows. (U.S. Navy)*

Right: *The Blue Angels pride themselves on the fact that they have never had to cancel an air show because of maintenance problems on one of their aircraft. Mechanics often work late into the night to ensure that the jets are in top flying condition. (U.S. Navy)*

Opposite: *All demonstration jets come together near the end of every Blue Angels performance to perform maneuvers in the Delta formation, allowing air show spectators to witness the awe-inspiring sight of six high-performance jets operating in perfect harmony. (U.S. Navy)*

have seen but few have flown. However, I also had the opportunity to inspire a child, put a tear in a veteran's eye, and relieve, however briefly, someone of the pain, tedium, and loneliness of daily life. More remarkable than anything else in the Blue Angel tour of duty was the twist of irony that this experience left indelible marks on my life as well and made me a better patriot and better man.

A DAY IN
Naval
Aviation

A DAY IN
Naval Aviation

Morgan I. Wilbur

Pages 302–303: *Sailors on board* George Washington *(CVN 73) conduct a test of the flight deck sprinkler system, creating a picturesque rainbow that frames the ship. It is rare moment of peace on board the carrier, which is more at home with engine noise filling the air. (U.S. Navy)*

Above: *Bedecked in protective gear, students at the Naval Air Technical Training Center, at NAS Pensacola, Florida, brave searing heat to fight an aircraft fire. A conflagration at sea is one of the most dangerous things that can happen on board ship, and firsthand firefighter training such as this ensures sailors are ready to respond to a crisis. (Al Audleman)*

Top: *Under the eerie glow of flight deck lighting, a catapult crew prepares an F/A-18C Hornet assigned to Strike Fighter Squadron 81 for launch from* George Washington *(CVN 73) in the Arabian Gulf on 11 August 2000. Day or night, fair weather or foul, naval aviation is a "24/7" operation that rarely pauses. (U.S. Navy)*

Left: *Maintenance personnel on the flight deck of* Abraham Lincoln *(CVN 72) surround the engines and rotor of an SH-3 Sea King assigned to Helicopter Antisubmarine Squadron 17 in 1990. Keeping aircraft flying in the harsh saltwater environment at sea is an around-the-clock operation. (U.S. Navy)*

Above: Kitty Hawk *(CV 63) (right) approaches* USNS Walter S. Diehl *(T-AO 193) in preparation for an underway replenishment. Carrier battle groups consume enormous amounts of fuel, food, munitions, and other supplies, making such moving "pit stops" a frequent necessity. (U.S. Navy)*

The first rays of morning light just barely peek over the horizon as a group of officer candidates assembles on the hallowed grounds at Naval Air Station Pensacola, Florida, under the watchful eye of their Marine drill instructor. Nearby, in classrooms across the sprawling Naval Air Technical Training Center, sailors who only months before sat at desks in high schools throughout the land learn skills that months hence, on board a floating airfield, will keep an aircraft flying. That afternoon, at the same time a father proudly pins wings of gold on his daughter, signifying the completion of her training, others wearing those same wings launch from a carrier for a patrol over Iraq. It is any given day in naval aviation.

Top: *An F/A-18 Hornet—armed with Side-winder and HARM missiles—launches in afterburner from* Carl Vinson (CVN 70) *in 1999. The heat and noise generated on the flight deck are daily but manageable hazards to the flight deck crew. (David Peters)*

Above: *An F-14 Tomcat crew stands by to man their plane on the flight deck of* Constellation (CV 64) *in 1999. "Hurry up and wait" is a feature of life in naval aviation as in any military organization, but more typically carrier aviation is fast-paced and inherently dependent on a chain of instant decisions and flawless actions. (David Peters)*

A Seahawk at Sea

The SH-60B Seahawk hovers over the small flight deck on the stern of a guided missile destroyer as it cuts through the rolling swells of the Arabian Gulf. Through the headphones in his flight helmet, Lieutenant Pete Collins listens to instructions from the landing signal officer as he begins the descent that will eventually plant the aircraft on deck, the culmination of a three-hour mission. He seems to have the world by the tail, a seasoned fleet helicopter pilot with a youthful exuberance that belies his experience and responsibilities. With the gold stripes on his shoulder and wings on his chest comes a level of responsibility unique to the profession of arms. As a helicopter aircraft commander, he carries the success of any assigned mission and, more importantly, the safety of his crew, on his shoulders. The junior officers and enlisted men under his command look to him for leadership. This climate of constant scrutiny is both daunting and satisfying.

His squadron is Helicopter Antisubmarine Squadron Light (HSL) 45, based at Naval Air Station North Island, California. This type of squadron deploys detachments of one or two Light Airborne Multipurpose System (LAMPS) Seahawks and their supporting maintenance and flight crews to various surface combatant ships of the fleet. These ships have small flight decks and enclosed hangars giving them the capability of all-weather, day or night helicopter operations. A "det" lasts six months if deployed over-seas. If operating in the Arabian Gulf, three to four months will be spent

Above: *Students at the Naval Air Technical Training Center on board NAS Pensacola, Florida, learn the intricacies of aircraft components during classroom instruction. Once in the fleet, these nineteen-year-olds will be entrusted with the care of millions of dollars worth of military hardware. (Al Audleman)*

Left: *The helicopter pad of* Jarrett *(FFG 33) is an inviting sanctuary for an SH-60B Seahawk assigned to Helicopter Antisubmarine Squadron Light 47 about to roost in September 1997. (Ted Carlson)*

actually flying missions there, while the remainder is used for side trips, liberty ports, and transits to and from the United States.

There is no such thing as a normal workday for Collins and those like him deployed on board the destroyer *John Young* (DD 973) to the troubled waters of the Arabian Gulf, where tensions always run high. His day may begin at five in the morning or at midnight. Through narrow passageways, he makes his way from his three-man stateroom to the ship's

Above: *A young flight deck crewman carries wheel chocks across the flight deck of* Dwight D. Eisenhower *(CVN 69). The faces of naval aviation most often appear hidden beneath helmets and behind goggles, anonymous to most Americans but owed a tremendous debt of appreciation from all those whom they protect. (U.S. Navy)*

Left: *Deck crewmembers tend an SH-60B Seahawk assigned to Helicopter Antisubmarine Squadron Light 45 on board* John Young *(DD 973) in the Pacific in August 1999. Servicing a helicopter on the pitching deck of a "small boy" presents challenges different but no less dangerous than those on a carrier flight deck. (Ted Carlson)*

Helicopter takeoffs and landings on a destroyer are guided from the "tower" located near the helicopter pad. A lieutenant prepares to direct the takeoff of an SH-60B Seahawk assigned to Helicopter Antisubmarine Squadron Light 45 on board John Young *(DD 973) in August 1999. (Ted Carlson)*

An AGM-114 Hellfire missile takes the first fiery steps toward its target after being launched from an SH-60B Seahawk of Helicopter Antisubmarine Squadron Light 49 during a training flight over the Pacific on 13 January 1999. Whereas first generation Navy helicopters at most carried a machine gun for armament, modern rotary-wing aircraft possess potent firepower. (Ted Carlson)

Combat Information Center, where he joins his helicopter second pilot and enlisted aviation warfare systems operator (AW). Detachments on board what World War II-era sailors called "tin cans" are small, tight-knit groups, and such is the case for the three-man crews of the Seahawks, highly trained professionals who know their jobs. In a briefing that the airmen jokingly refer to as "Who's Who in the Zoo," they receive the full weather and tactical picture, knowing the locations of, in Collins's words, the "good guys, the bad guys, the carrier, and any targets of interest."

The sounding of flight quarters announces the return of the SH-60B from the previous mission, and such is the constant nature of surveillance operations that the crews will engage in a hot turnover, meaning that the helicopter's engines will never shut down as the new crew takes over. In addition to being refueled, the SH-60B will receive tactical information via a data link, providing an electronic picture of the operational area that is literally at the crew's fingertips. Within moments, the Seahawk grabs the sky and takes off.

It is a much different kind of mission for helicopter crews in the Gulf, one that pits their skills against smugglers attempting to defy the United Nations embargo and deliver restricted materials to Iraq. In many cases, the smugglers confine their efforts to the cover of darkness, but they cannot hide from the Seahawk. Crews employ radar and forward-looking infrared (FLIR) imagery to locate targets of interest. Not dependent on visual light, the FLIR sensor detects varying degrees of heat and can provide the crew a good picture of a suspect ship even on the darkest of nights. Once they have located a ship to investigate, the pilot not flying the aircraft will attempt to communicate with the ship by radio. "Querying ships in the Gulf is always interesting. They may not talk to you. Other ships may respond over the radio just to make life really difficult," says Collins. The helicopter crew asks a specific set of questions to determine whether or not to single the ship out for further investigation. Sometimes they employ a communications relay feature that allows crewmen on board the destroyer to interrogate, via the

Just weeks removed from boot camp, sailors and Marines march in ranks in front of Chevalier Hall at the Naval Air Technical Training Center on board NAS Pensacola, Florida. The new facility boasts the appearance of a college campus, but few civilians will experience anything that approaches the adventure that awaits these young men and women in the fleet. (Al Audleman)

Lieutenant Randy Biggs (left) and Lieutenant Commander Todd Haeg, assigned to Helicopter Antisubmarine Squadron Light 43, fly their SH-60B Seahawk over Nevada in February 1998. Unlike the cockpit arrangement in fixed-wing aircraft, the aircraft commander of a helicopter occupies the right seat and the copilot flies in the left seat. Seahawk pilots must be expert tacticians as well as aviators. (Ted Carlson)

The plethora of sensors and weapons that make the SH-60B a valuable tactical platform—radar, infrared detection, electronic surveillance, sonobuoy launchers, and torpedoes—all are visible in this view of a Seahawk assigned to Helicopter Antisubmarine Squadron Light 45 operating over the Pacific from John Young (DD 973) in August 1999. (Ted Carlson)

Opposite: A rescue swimmer is pulled from the Arabian Gulf into an SH-60F assigned to Helicopter Antisubmarine Squadron 6 in 1999. Jumping into the sea from a helicopter is not an everyday duty for these intrepid sailors, but they must be ready at a moment's notice to plunge into cold water to rescue a downed aviator. (David Peters)

helicopter's radios, those on the suspect ship. This takes some of the load off the Seahawk crew, and lets them concentrate on flying the aircraft. If all goes well, the suspect vessel will make its way to a designated holding area so that it can be boarded the following day. However, in some cases, defiance makes it necessary to assemble a team to conduct a noncompliant boarding.

The Seahawks provide surface surveillance from ten at night until six in the morning. Having the sensor data-link capability extends the eyes of the ship well beyond the horizon, giving the "higher-ups" real-time images of the battle space. And the workday doesn't end after landing, with maintenance to be done—oftentimes trading spare parts with other deployed detachments to keep the birds up—and flight schedules to plan. In contrast to an aircraft carrier, where a large ready room is set aside for each squadron, work space is at a premium for the officer and enlisted members of a helicopter detachment on board a destroyer. Officers can often be seen working in their staterooms so that the enlisted personnel will have more room to work in the small squadron office. To be alone, they have to go up on deck, where they can take a deep breath of sea air and let the mind unwind.

Each day is an adventure at sea for Lieutenant Collins and his crew. It is a life he has chosen above all others and one at which he excels. Says Collins, "Our expanding tactical role is causing us to be called on more

than anyone else, with the exception of F/A-18s. Maybe I'm just an adrenaline junkie, but it keeps a smile on my face."

The AWs that ride behind pilots like Lieutenant Collins are a special breed of sailor. Their reason for being is to fly. Those assigned to Seahawks operate both acoustic and nonacoustic sensors to detect, track, and localize submarines and surface ships. They also fly as rescue swimmers, ready on a moment's notice to jump from the relative comfort of a hovering helicopter into heavy seas awash with foam in order to pull a distressed individual to safety.

Bill McClure didn't like college, so he joined the Navy. After enduring eighteen months of training, including "a month of pure pain" at search and rescue school, one of the toughest in the Navy, he was among the first group of AWs to qualify in the Seahawk. Now a chief petty officer with twenty-four years of service, he is assigned to HSL-43 based at North Island.

Bill McClure's "office" is nestled inside a 23,000-pound flying machine, his head covered by a special helmet that is a necessity to block out the intense noise generated by the helicopter's engines and transmission. Displayed before him are controls for an array of sophisticated equipment, including radar, FLIR, acoustic processors, and magnetic anomaly detection gear for submarine detection; electronic support measures used for detecting radars; and identification friend or foe equipment. Over the course of a mission in the Arabian Gulf his eyes will maintain a constant vigil on the sensor and navigation data presented on the multipurpose display, so he can give the pilots a bearing and range to targets of interest—be it a wooden speedboat or mammoth oil tanker—and guide them in for a closer look. He can also target designate for a AGM-114 Hellfire missile, utilizing a pistol grip controller to track a laser beam from a turret on the nose of the helicopter onto a potential target. Tracking dozens of targets during a mission is mentally fatiguing. Despite the SH-60B's air conditioning, he sweats profusely beneath his flame-resistant flight suit, helmet, and survival equipment.

In the one-man-show world of a helicopter AW, Chief McClure handles a variety of other duties, including maintaining survival gear,

supervising the loading of weapons and cargo, and even handling a side door machine gun to provide additional firepower if needed. He must also maintain his proficiency at tracking submarines, still a threat even after the end of the Cold War.

Bill McClure did not choose an easy profession for his life's work. Flying in combat helicopters over the unforgiving sea is not for the timid. As he likes to say, "This LAMPS stuff is a tough way to make a buck."

An EA-6B Prowler of Electronic Attack Squadron 138 off Nimitz *(CVN 68) flies patrol over the waters of the Atlantic Ocean during 1989. Requiring a four-person crew, including three naval flight officers to operate the aircraft's sophisticated radar jamming equipment and weapons systems, the Prowler leads the way for any strike launched against targets by American military aircraft. (U.S. Navy)*

A Prowler in Combat

Five miles above Yugoslavia, Commander Clay Fearnow, a naval flight officer (NFO), notes the flashes of enemy antiaircraft fire below his aircraft. With cool precision, his fingers move deftly over the switches in the cockpit of his EA-6B Prowler to prepare a weapon for its one-way ride to fiery oblivion. When launched, the 900-pound AGM-88 high speed anti-radiation missile (HARM) riding on a pylon under the aircraft's left wing will fly toward the ground at dizzying speeds, the end of its short flight marked by the detonation of its warhead, resulting in one less Yugoslav

This is the real thing for which they train. An EA-6B Prowler assigned to reserve Electronic Attack Squadron 209 fires an AGM-88 High-Speed Antiradiation Missile at a radiating emitter. The addition of the HARM to the Prowler gave it an attack as well as a jamming capability. (Painting by Morgan I. Wilbur)

A helmsman on the bridge of Theodore Roosevelt *(CVN 71) keeps the bow into the wind for flight operations. The carrier must keep a predetermined relative wind speed over the deck for launch and recovery of aircraft. (U.S. Navy)*

radar. The pilot sits inches from Fearnow's left arm. Behind them in the rear cockpit are two additional NFOs. The pilot squeezes a trigger and the HARM's rocket motor ignites in a plume of fire, searing the night sky with a brilliant flash. The missile leaves the pylon in an instant and races far ahead of the Prowler at twice the speed of sound before plummeting to earth to destroy its target.

Twenty years of training and flying experience brought Commander Fearnow to this moment of combat. His lanky build formed from years of running marathons, he holds the title to which many in the Navy aspire— skipper. One of the so-called "weekend warriors" of the Naval Air Reserve, Fearnow and the personnel under his command in Electronic Attack Squadron 209, known as the Star Warriors, were ordered to leave their stateside home in Maryland two weeks after air strikes began as part of Operation Allied Force in March 1999. Their new home was Aviano Air Base in northern Italy, where they joined elements of three other Navy and two Marine EA-6B squadrons flying combat missions for almost ninety days. The EA-6B's primary mission is suppression of enemy air defenses, using powerful jamming gear and radar homing missiles to deny the enemy use of radar that guides surface-to-air missiles (SAM) and aims

antiaircraft artillery (AAA). The aircraft has been out of production since 1991, but because Prowlers must accompany every Navy, Air Force, and NATO strike mission, each airplane is a valuable asset.

Soon after Fearnow's crew eliminated the threatening radar site, a pair of Air Force F-15E Strike Eagles, flying close to the Prowler for protection, began their attack. With the Prowler defending the Strike Eagles from radar-directed weapons, the two fighters rolled in on a strategic bridge and proceeded to destroy it with laser-guided bombs. This type of mission was typical. Other missions might have dozens of strike aircraft attacking targets within Yugoslavia or the Kosovo engagement zone.

Commander Clay Fearnow (foreground) in the Electronic Countermeasure Officer Number One seat plans a mission with pilot Commander Chuck Mingonet in the cockpit of their EA-6B Prowler assigned to Electronic Attack Squadron 209. Close coordination between the crew often will determine the degree of success of a mission. (Morgan I. Wilbur)

EA-6B Prowlers assigned to Electronic Attack Squadron 209 deployed to Aviano, Italy, in 1999. Prowlers provided electronic warfare support for every strike mission into Kosovo and Serbia during Operation Allied Force. (Clay Fearnow)

An EA-6B Prowler assigned to Electronic Attack Squadron 209 takes on jet fuel from an Air Force KC-10 Stratotanker in 1999. Tanking is a routine and necessary event for most tactical jet missions. (Clay Fearnow)

Home at last. Commander Clay Fearnow greets his family upon return to NAF Washington, D.C., following a deployment to Aviano, Italy, in 1999. Homecomings following deployments, which oftentimes feature formation fly-ins, are stirring events that bring joyous reunions. (Clay Fearnow)

Flying their first combat missions in theater produced moments of high drama for the flight crews. "When we first went in, we were engaged with AAA all the time and often with SA-6 SAMs. For us, it took a while to gauge how close the missiles were. After a few nights of hard turns and expending decoy chaff and flares, we started to get smart. It's remarkable to see six SA-6s airborne coming in your direction," says Fearnow.

With six to seven hour flights being routine, sitting on hard ejection seats becomes extremely uncomfortable. The Prowler crews developed, as Fearnow puts it, "steel butts." These long missions forced the EA-6B crews to obtain fuel several times during flight from Air Force tanker aircraft. Refueling at night, with many other airplanes trying to do the same thing, could be downright frightening. "The air controllers would direct us to the tankers, and depending on their skill level, they sometimes became saturated with many thirsty jets. You could hear the frustration in their voices, and certainly in ours, to find the tanker and get us on it."

Early in his flying career, Fearnow rarely considered the possibility of one day commanding a squadron. Focusing on each job was his main goal. As he progressed through various assignments and organizations, he decided that being a commanding officer (CO) was what he wanted. "Being a CO is the greatest job in the Navy, and going into combat builds a tremendous sense of camaraderie within the squadron."

A Super Hornet on Target

The rewards are plentiful for a young fighter pilot like Lieutenant Rosario Rausa. Like all naval aviators, walking out to a beautiful aircraft that was prepared for him to fly makes the heart beat just a little faster. Launching into the sky frees him from petty earthly irritants, while the thrill of extending his physical body with a machine that spits fire, makes enough

noise to wake the dead, and twists and turns to his every desire provides great adventure. For him, there was no thought of doing anything else with his life. As is often the case in naval aviation, earning the wings of gold is a family affair. With his father having served as a career naval aviator, attack and strike fighter squadrons have been well served by Rausas over the years.

The rumble of jet engines permeates the California sky at NAS Lemoore, California, as a pair of F/A-18F Super Hornets prepare to

A formation of F/A-18E/F Super Hornets assigned to Strike Fighter Squadron 122 pictured during a training flight in the skies over California. The Navy's newest tactical jet aircraft, the F/A-18E/F will be joined by the Joint Strike Fighter to form the backbone of carrier aviation in the early twenty-first century. (Ted Carlson)

Two Super Hornets assigned to Strike Fighter Squadron 122, an F/A-18E (right) and an F/A-18F, fly in formation with tailhooks down, over California in September 2000. Intensive training hones crew skills to the point that the pair flies as one. (Ted Carlson)

launch on a training hop. Rausa, flying Dash One, the first aircraft in the formation, pushes the throttle forward and, as the landscape around him becomes increasingly a blur, blasts into the wild blue. His wingman, Dash Two, follows ten seconds later. Rausa's task this morning, as it has been since he joined Strike Fighter Squadron (VFA) 122, is an important one—training pilots and weapons system officers (WSOs) to fly the Navy's newest fighter.

Ensuring that the radars on their warplanes are functioning properly, the pilots climb to an altitude of 26,000 feet and head toward the practice range at NAS Fallon, located in the remote desert of Nevada. Lieutenant Rausa has honed his skills near Fallon numerous times, and put them to the test over other desert sands halfway around the world. While flying an F/A-18C Hornet with VFA-94 off *Carl Vinson* (CVN 70), he and two others became the first fleet pilots to simultaneously launch AGM-154 Joint Standoff Weapons against an enemy target. He knows that training pays dividends once the shooting starts. After flying for twenty minutes, the Super Hornets begin their descent. Now the real fun begins, as the pilots increase their speed to over 400 knots and bring their jets down to 1,500 feet to begin their low-level attack.

The teamwork between pilot and WSO becomes vital, each dependent on the other for the successful completion of the mission. The backseater navigates the aircraft while correlating what he sees outside the cockpit with what he sees on his moving map display and low-level chart. He converses with his pilot in concise phrases, a skill that Rausa stresses to all of his students. Things can happen so fast in combat that overly long

Opposite: Lieutenant Rosario Rausa in the cockpit of an F/A-18F Super Hornet assigned to Strike Fighter Squadron 122, the Super Hornet fleet readiness squadron, at NAS Lemoore, California, in September 2000. Fleet-experienced aviators such as Rausa, himself the son of an attack aviator, pass on their expertise to the newly winged aviators that will follow them in operational squadrons. (Ted Carlson)

Having completed a training flight in an
F/A-18E/F Super Hornet, Lieutenant Rosario
Rausa strides confidently across the flight line
at NAS Lemoore, California. (Ted Carlson)

Where training is put to the test. An F/A-18C
assigned to Strike Fighter Squadron 137
patrols the skies over Iraq in 1996 during
Operation Southern Watch. Hornets have been
supporting Southern Watch for more than a
decade, and occasionally have been called
upon to put ordnance on target. (U.S. Navy)

communications, especially with other aircraft, can block out an important
missile alert or other tactical event. The WSO thinks ahead of the airplane
and directs his pilot to make minor speed adjustments as they head
toward their target.

"Time on target (TOT) is really important. If HARMs are scheduled
to hit enemy radars that are defending your target at a precise time,
TOT becomes critical for your survival," says Rausa. On today's training
flight, his student navigates them to the target and hits it within four
seconds of their planned attack time. Fighter pilots being fighter pilots,
Rausa then engages the other Super Hornet in a mock dogfight before
the two aircraft set course for home. Thanks to the aircraft's increased
fuel capacity over earlier models, they have time for some more training
while passing over Lake Tahoe and the Sierra Mountains. "The hardest
thing we do in combat is target acquisition," says Rausa. He conducts
some impromptu eyeball to target recognition training. Passing over
a city he will give his backseater a specific building to find. The student
must locate it on his radar and then bring his eyes out of the cockpit
and acquire it visually. Then he must guide Rausa's eyes to the correct
building, with no misunderstandings. This seemingly simple act of
communicating with the pilot forms the foundation for the WSO's
future success.

After landing, Rausa spends up to an hour debriefing his student,
dissecting any problems so they will not be repeated. Ground duties,

session, consume the remainder of his day, one that sharpens the men and women who will one day be at the tip of the spear.

Deep within the bowels of an aircraft carrier, a sailor of nineteen on his first cruise climbs into his bunk, the only place in the mammoth warship that he can call his own. He has spent his day amidst the fury of the flight deck, and even now he hears the activities of his shipmates through the curtain that provides him his only privacy. Tearing open a letter from his hometown sweetheart, for a fleeting few moments all is quiet as he transports himself 3,000 miles away before drifting off to sleep. It is the end of another day in naval aviation.

Over the Horizon

Over the Horizon
Naval Aviation in the 21st Century

Vice Admiral John Nathman, USN

The old paradigm: The battleship Maryland *(BB 46) fires a broadside with her 16-inch guns. In the twentieth century naval aviation changed forever the limited ship-versus-ship scenario, and in the twenty-first century naval aviation will dominate the littoral battlespace and areas of conflict far inland. (National Museum of Naval Aviation)*

As the 20th century dawned, war at sea, in many ways, had changed little since the days of John Paul Jones. Although steam had replaced sail, wood had given way to steel, and main batteries boasted rifled artillery in place of smoothbore cannon, dominance at sea was still largely conceived as a contest between ships of the line trading broadsides. The usefulness of naval forces to implement national policy, advance America's economic interests, and serve as guarantor of our citizens' rights and security abroad was well established. Although the coercive power of a warship in support of diplomacy was very real and often decisive, the actual ability to project power ashore—and thereby directly influence the course of events—was limited by the range of her guns, measured in thousands of yards. Naval commanders developed an understanding of the battle space either secondhand through reports from observers ashore, or through firsthand inspection, which was limited to what could be discerned from the masthead with a telescope.

Yet barely ten years into the new century, the concept of naval aviation became a reality, and the visionary efforts of a handful of early pioneers sparked a fundamental revolution in naval warfare. The revolution began quietly, for the early airmen had to overcome the technical challenges of adapting nascent technology to the maritime environment. Similarly, it was necessary to explore and refine tactics and doctrine for integrating naval aviation into existing fleet operations. Soon, a new type of combatant, the aircraft carrier, evolved to support the growing capabilities and requirements of aircraft operations at sea and fully exploit the tremendous power concentrated in the carrier air group. By the time

Pioneer naval aviator Lieutenant Godfrey del. Chevalier shows a Sopwith aircraft to the Commander in Chief U.S. Fleet and the commanding officers of several battleships at Guantanamo Bay, Cuba, in 1920. Visionary efforts of men such as Chevalier sparked a fundamental revolution in naval warfare. (AP/World Wide Photo)

Pages 322–323: An F-14A Tomcat assigned to Fighter Squadron 2 launches from Ranger *(CV 61) in July 1990. Already long in the tooth and scheduled for retirement by 2010, the Tomcat remains both an unequaled interceptor and effective attack aircraft. (Robert L. Lawson)*

Sailors position a Sopwith 1½ Strutter onto a special wooden platform erected over a gun battery on board the battleship Oklahoma *(BB 37) during experiments with shipboard employment of aircraft at Guantanamo Bay, Cuba, in February 1920. In the ensuing two decades aircraft became an increasingly more prevalent and important fixture on board ships at sea. (Wide World Photo)*

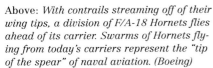

Above: *With contrails streaming off of their wing tips, a division of F/A-18 Hornets flies ahead of its carrier. Swarms of Hornets flying from today's carriers represent the "tip of the spear" of naval aviation. (Boeing)*

Above, right: *An F/A-18C Hornet assigned to Strike Fighter Squadron 37 patrols the "no-fly zone" over southern Iraq in February 2001 during Operation Southern Watch. Naval aircraft will be effective instruments of U.S. foreign policy in potential trouble spots around the world for the foreseeable future. (U.S. Navy)*

the war in the Pacific ended in 1945, the rules for waging war at sea and from the sea had changed forever.

From the end of World War II through the "hot" and "cold" conflicts of the Cold War to Desert Storm and beyond, the carrier battle group has remained the organizing principle for naval expeditionary forces. Forming the backbone of the U.S. Navy's strike capability, today's carrier air wings are organized, trained, and operated so that they deliver precise, lethal, and coherent warfighting—packing a punch far greater than the sum of individual platform capabilities.

The U.S. Navy entered the 21st century as the unchallenged master of the seas, and the preeminence of naval aviation is the major reason. From the first use of naval aircraft in combat to perform tactical reconnaissance during the Vera Cruz Insurrection in 1914, to the recent prosecution of the air campaign in Kosovo and no-fly zone enforcement in the skies above Iraq, naval aviation has time and again proven its value to the security of the nation across the spectrum from humanitarian operations to world war.

A battle group centered on John F. Kennedy *(CV 67) flanked by two Kuwaiti patrol craft (outboard) in the Arabian Gulf. As they have for the last half-century, carrier battle groups will remain the "force of choice" for U.S. presidents in responding to crises abroad. (U.S. Navy)*

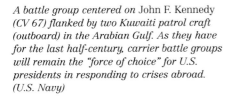

As the nation's "force of choice," carrier battle groups responded to more than fifty international crises in the 1990s alone, and the demand for what naval aviation brings to the fight is likely to continue to grow well into the new century. In addition to crisis response, naval aviation allows the United States to sustain a credible forward presence that serves to preclude crises in critical regions of the globe. When it comes to protecting American interests and maintaining stability in today's and tomorrow's dynamic strategic environment, clearly, as former Secretary of State Madeline Albright observed, "the only thing that can replace a carrier battle group is another carrier battle group."

Three strategic trends guide the Navy's planning for the future: continued regional instability, increasing globalization and interdependence, and the explosion of information technology. These trends are two-edged swords in terms of their impact on naval aviation. On the one hand, we are leveraging new technology to achieve incredible improvements in precision and lethality. On the other hand, the rapid development of diverse military technologies and a fluid global arms market make relatively cheap, advanced weaponry available to nation states and transnational organizations whose aims may be contrary to U.S. national interests. The enduring value of sea-based aviation is that it provides the nation with the capability to succeed within this increasingly complex threat environment. In the future, the coherent warfighting

An F/A-18C Hornet assigned to Strike Fighter Squadron 34 launches from the angled deck of George Washington *(CVN 73) in October 2000 as crew members ready another Hornet for flight. In the early twenty-first century various versions of the Hornet will dominate carrier decks, ensuring that the United States sustains a credible forward presence of potent force. (U.S. Navy)*

*Carl Vinson *(CVN 70) sails toward a setting sun while on station in the Arabian Gulf in 1998, ready on a moment's notice to project power against a nation that threatens it. (U.S. Navy)*

327

Above: *An HH-60H Seahawk assigned to Helicopter Combat Support Special Squadron 4 deploys SEALs to a Mark V assault craft in October 2000. Increasingly capable helicopters will remain central to many missions, including antisubmarine, antishipping, special warfare, mine countermeasures, rescue, and logistics.* (U.S. Navy)

Above, right: *A gunner in an SH-3H Sea King helicopter assigned to Helicopter Antisubmarine Squadron 5 monitors the transit of* Dwight D. Eisenhower *(CVN 69) through the Suez Canal during Operation Desert Shield. Carriers have sustained continual aerial patrols over the Middle East for more than a decade.* (U.S. Navy)

Below: *Members of the flight deck crew of* Oak Hill *(LSD 51) receive a briefing from a U.S. Army helicopter pilot detailing the basic maneuvering of the AH-64A Apache helicopter at NAS Norfolk, Virginia, in preparation for a Joint Shipboard Helicopter Operations Test. In the future naval aviation will operate increasingly in a joint operational environment.* (U.S. Navy)

Below, right: Kitty Hawk *(CV 63) alongside a pier in Apra Harbor, Guam. Permanently forward-deployed to the western Pacific,* Kitty Hawk *and embarked Carrier Air Wing 5 are influential instruments of U.S. foreign policy.* (U.S. Navy)

capabilities inherent in our carrier air wings will continue to ensure our military forces have unrestricted access to critical regions of the world and, once there, that we have the ability to exert decisive influence ashore. In short, as the centerpiece of our naval expeditionary forces, naval aviation will continue to deliver the capabilities to fully shape the conditions for success.

Within this strategic framework, the way ahead for naval aviation is defined by the answers to three fundamental questions for the 21st century: *Where is the fight? How will we fight? How must we be shaped to fight?* The answers to these questions reveal how we are building naval aviation today to be a decisive force in the years ahead.

Where is the fight?

The answer to this question is clear—we must be prepared to fight in the littorals, or the coastal regions of the world, which are home to 70 percent of the world's population and, as a result, most of the world's conflicts. Our strategy of focusing on the littorals has been validated by

the success of naval expeditionary forces in crises from Taiwan to Southwest Asia and the Balkans. As we consider potential hot spots around the globe today, we can see that sea-based aviation is essential to our ability to influence future conflicts ashore. Many of these areas present tough challenges for strictly land-based forces—island nations such as Taiwan or Indonesia are particularly daunting. Indonesia, for example, is a strategically vital nation that includes a half billion people spread over some 13,000 separate islands. It would be impossible for the United States to directly influence the course of any potential conflict in that region without the strategic flexibility that naval expeditionary forces provide.

Because its movements are not dependent upon a foreign government's permission to use land bases and airfields, carrier battle groups can guarantee access to a region by operating from international waters. Naval aircraft performing surveillance and reconnaissance missions can take advantage of the "height of eye" their altitude provides, training sensors to "see" far inland to gather intelligence and build battlespace awareness. Finally, although the air wing's strike fighters can project power hundreds of miles ashore if needed, the forcefulness of the battle group's response to a given crisis can be tuned to the precise degree required. Clearly, no other force can match the unique combination of

Coming and going: An F-14A Tomcat prepares to launch from the flight deck of George Washington *(CVN 73) in 1994 as a second goes around for another landing attempt. Modern carriers are flexible enough to keep aircraft airborne around the clock for sustained periods. (Department of Defense)*

CH-46 Sea Knight helicopters land to extract elements of the 31st Marine Expeditionary Unit from Dededo, Guam, during an urban environment training exercise in January 2001. Naval aviation may be called upon to fight in unfamiliar arenas during the twenty-first century as the face of the modern battlefield changes. (U.S. Navy)

The pilot of an F/A-18 Hornet assigned to Strike Fighter Squadron 106 braces for launch from Dwight D. Eisenhower (CVN 69) in 1987. Hornets and their Super Hornet cousins will be repeating this scene time and again for decades to come. (Department of Defense)

rapid response, flexibility, and deep landward reach provided by the air arm of our naval expeditionary forces. This one-two-three punch can be available wherever and whenever it is needed, to the farthest reaches of the globe.

How will we fight?

The Navy's success in battle relies on the physical superiority we can achieve through the sophistication of our platforms and weaponry; the superior training and skill of our people operating within a professional

Chief Warrant Officer Steve Young stands watch as tactical action officer in the combat direction center on board Harry S. Truman (CVN 75) in August 2000. Carrier combat systems are progressively modernized and all eventually will include the cooperative engagement capability as the concept of network-centric warfare takes hold. (U.S. Navy)

culture that honors initiative; and our robust, dynamic, decentralized command and control. Despite tremendous technological advances during the last decade, a 34 percent reduction in personnel and real defense outlays accompanied by a 60 percent increase in commitments worldwide have challenged the Navy to become more efficient. Although numbers of platforms will always count, in the new millennium numbers alone will not be sufficient to successfully exert influence anytime, anywhere. In order to effectively respond to regional aggression, we must ensure that we have knowledge superiority as well. Real-time understanding and awareness of the battlespace will allow our on-scene commanders to make timely, fully informed decisions. In other words, whenever American interests are threatened around the globe, while forces based in the continental United States may be *readily deployable*, naval aviation is *immediately employable*. This is a result of the responsiveness afforded by forward presence combined with the battlespace awareness and intuition afforded to our commanders through knowledge superiority.

To achieve this essential formula, naval aviation is at the forefront of two military revolutions. The first of these, known as the revolution in

Above: *A single-seat F/A-18E Super Hornet (rear) and two-seat F/A-18F (front) assigned to Strike Fighter Squadron 122. The VFA-122 Eagles are training aviators and flight officers to fly the Navy's newest combat aircraft, scheduled for its first deployment in 2002. (Ted Carlson)*

Below, left: *An F/A-18C Hornet assigned to Strike Fighter Squadron 195 drops a Joint Direct Attack Munition during a training exercise in 1999. The JDAM is representative of a new family of standoff weapons that rely on global-positioning-system guidance rather than laser designation, and therefore are undeterred by poor visibility. (U.S. Navy)*

Below: *A fiery finger of flame emanates from an AIM-7 Sparrow missile shortly after launch from an F-14B Tomcat of Experimental Squadron 9 over the Pacific Ocean in April 1999. Naval weapons systems undergo constant testing and evaluation in an effort to achieve the most lethal performance. (Ted Carlson)*

Artist's concept of the Joint Direct-Attack Munition. The JDAM is a Mark 80-series bomb modified with a guidance kit that includes the global positioning system. The weapon—used with great success during Operation Allied Force in 1999—allows crews to strike targets with greater accuracy from standoff ranges. (Boeing)

Above: *An electronic countermeasures officer pictured in front of the instrument panel in the rear cockpit of an EA-6B Prowler of Tactical Electronic Warfare Squadron 128 during a training mission. Even the precision-guided weapons of today and tomorrow will rely on skilled aircrews to get them to the launch point. (Ted Carlson)*

Above: *Aviation Ordnanceman Second Class Alejandro Montalvo and Aviation Ordnance-man Third Class Chris Tucker prepare a 2,000-pound Mk 84 Joint Direct-Attack Munition for loading onto an F/A-18 Hornet on the flight deck of George Washington (CVN 73) in August 2000. Sailors on flight decks today handle weapons that are marvels of sophistication. (U.S. Navy)*

Right: *An F/A-18 Hornet armed with four developmental AGM-154 Joint Standoff Weapons. The combat-proven JSOW has been launched from Hornets against targets in Kosovo and Iraq since 1999. (Raytheon)*

332

strike warfare, has been underway for a number of years now and is the result of innovations in aircraft design combined with the introduction of new precision munitions. The synergy between these two advances is fostering a dramatic expansion in naval power projection capabilities. The capstone event in the strike warfare revolution is the Navy's newest strike fighter aircraft, the F/A-18E/F Super Hornet. Soon to be complemented by the Joint Strike Fighter, these first-day-of-the-war strikers bring substantive improvements in weapons load, range, penetration, survivability, precision, growth potential, sortie generation, and maintainability. We will realize the full potential of the strike warfare revolution as we arm these new, highly capable aircraft with the new generation, standoff, precision weaponry already coming on line. Many of these weapons, such as the Joint Direct-Attack Munition, the Joint Stand-Off Weapon, and the expanded response Standoff Land-Attack Missile, are already combat-proven. Teaming these all-weather "smart" munitions, which are extremely accurate and cost effective, with the advanced Super Hornet and Joint Strike Fighter will result in a *ten-fold increase* in carrier striking capability less than a generation after the Gulf War.

The second revolution currently underway is designed to realize a dramatic improvement in our ability to mass combat "effects" to achieve

Top: *Artist's concept of an AGM-84H Standoff Land-Attack Missile–Expanded Response being launched by an F/A-18 Super Hornet. Standoff precision weapons such as the SLAM–ER give the carrier air wing a ten-fold increase in striking capability. (Boeing)*

Above: *An aviation ordnanceman removes caps from the tips of AIM-9 Sidewinder missiles on the flight deck of* John F. Kennedy *(CV 67) during Operation Desert Storm. Modern weapons will boast a more potent and accurate punch than those handled by redshirts in the Gulf War. (U.S. Navy)*

F4U Corsair and F6F Hellcat fighters assigned to Carrier Air Group 83 crowd the deck of Essex *(CV 9) in 1945. The Navy's air groups in the closing months of World War II were filled with fighter-bombers, just as carrier air wings of today and the future will be dominated by multimission strike fighters. Though the air wing's complement is similar, the increase in carrier strike capability since World War II is hyperbolic. (U.S. Navy)*

a desired outcome on the battlefield by implementing a concept known as network-centric warfare (NCW). To understand the origin of NCW and its potential power, one only needs to look at the amazing advances in computer processing power and communications technology. Scientists and engineers report that computer chip performance has consistently doubled

Maintenance personnel service an EA-6B Prowler electronic attack aircraft on the crowded deck of Constellation *(CV 64) in April 1997. The electronic warfare capabilities of the EA-6B, now in more demand than ever, are vital to survival of strike aircraft in a dense air-defense environment. (U.S. Navy)*

every eighteen months. Similarly, certain types of communications capabilities are doubling every year. These types of changes do not merely offer the potential for incremental warfighting enhancements—they portend *revolutionary* improvements in our warfighting capability. These technological advances will increase combat capabilities by networking sensors, decision makers, and shooters. The result of this networking will be shared awareness, increased speed of command, higher tempo of operations, greater lethality, increased survivability, and improved synchronization among widely dispersed forces.

Network-centric warfare is not exclusive to naval aviation or even naval forces in general, but sea-based air power will clearly play a unique and vital role in the implementation of this revolutionary form of warfare. Naval aviation is well suited to lead this revolution because of the range, reach, mobility, and number of platforms we operate—platforms that can all serve as nodes in the network. We are currently engaged in the process of refining the NCW concept, applying it as an organizing principle for doctrine, tactics, and concepts of operation, and defining organizational "lanes" of responsibility among planners, programmers, and policymakers.

In recent Fleet Battle Experiments and real world operations, we have taken important first steps in the transition from concept to tactical implementation. In congressional testimony following Operation Allied Force (NATO air strikes against the former Yugoslavia from March to June 1999), Vice Admiral Daniel J. Murphy Jr., Commander of the U.S. Sixth Fleet, described how tools such as secure video-teleconferencing, e-mail, and information networks contributed to developing a common operational perspective among commanders and planners ashore and afloat, allowing them to reach any area of the globe to collaborate across service and operational boundaries. Yet, these achievements are only the tip of the iceberg.

When coupled with the revolution in strike warfare, the revolution in combat effects enabled by NCW will see naval expeditionary forces,

Top, left: *Senior Chief Operations Specialist Ron Morris mans the Force Over-the-Horizon Track Coordinator station in the combat direction center of* George Washington *(CVN 73). Battle management is an increasingly difficult challenge for a carrier battle group and one that must be mastered for warfighting in the littoral environment. (Department of Defense)*

Top, right: *Seventh Fleet commander Vice Admiral John Hyland and Admiral Roy Johnson, Commander in Chief, U.S. Pacific Fleet, listen as Rear Admiral C.D. Richardson, Commander, Task Force 77, briefs them on board* Kitty Hawk *(CVA 63) about an air strike on Haiphong Thermal Power Plant in North Vietnam in April 1967. In the future, such high-level briefings will increasingly take place using modern communications technology. (U.S. Navy)*

Above: *Vice Admiral Michael G. Mullen, commander of the U.S. Second Fleet (seated center at table), speaks with President George W. Bush from his flagship,* Mount Whitney *(LCC 20) via video teleconferencing equipment in 2001. Modern teleconferencing equipment and common operational networks are enabling commanders anywhere in the world—ashore and afloat—to develop a common operational perspective. (U.S. Navy)*

Crewmen assigned to the primary flight control division don protective masks during a nuclear-biological-chemical drill on board Saratoga *(CV 60) during Operation Desert Shield. The twenty-first century brings an even greater threat of employment of these weapons of mass destruction against which naval aviation needs to remain vigilant. (U.S. Navy)*

A radome mounted on its chin, an EP-3E Aires II of Fleet Air Reconnaissance Squadron 2 pictured in flight over the Mediterranean Sea in June 1991. On 31 March 2001 an aircraft of this type made headlines when there was a collision with a Chinese fighter while on a surveillance flight. Intelligence gathering is a valuable mission that assists in the formulation of strategy and tactics. (U.S. Navy)

Lieutenant Shane Osborn, commander of the EP-3E Aries II that collided with a Chinese fighter over the Pacific, hugs his father upon returning to NAS Whidbey Island, Washington, on 14 April 2001. The twenty-four-person crew was detained for two weeks in China. (U.S. Navy)

led by carrier striking power, emerge as the decisive force in tomorrow's regional littoral conflicts. NCW is important to our future success because of its tremendous potential to accelerate the process of transforming information into knowledge. In a network-centric environment, we will be able to reduce the planning cycle from days or hours to minutes. At the next level, NCW will enable us to reduce the tactical decision cycle, greatly enhancing responsiveness throughout the battlespace, and providing real time sensor-to-shooter targeting information to successfully engage even the most elusive and fleeting targets. The overarching goal of NCW is to get inside an enemy's decision cycles at the tactical, operational, and strategic level. Then we can maximize effects from dispersed forces, defeat the opponent's scheme of maneuver, and lock out potential enemy courses of action.

How must we be shaped to fight?

The principles of warfighting balance and proportionality guide the plan for the future of naval air warfare—shaping carrier battle groups, carrier air wings, and land-based naval aircraft to take full advantage of both the revolution in strike warfare and network-centric warfare. To execute the Navy's primary missions of combat-credible forward presence, maritime dominance, and decisive power projection ashore, carrier battle groups and naval air forces will continue to be sized to sustain adequate numbers of platforms to maintain the forward presence that ensures timely access to the physical and virtual battle space. Concurrently, naval aviation will be shaped to fight and win, allowing us to rapidly capitalize on our access to directly influence the course of local and regional events.

Innovation in strike warfare and networked operations promises to give the U.S. Navy a decisive edge in a greater number of potential scenarios under a wider variety of circumstances. However, the integrated and interdependent nature of NCW means the way ahead for naval aviation cannot be focused on a particular platform, capability, or mission area. Large numbers of aircraft were built in the 1980s as the Navy expanded, but the end of the Cold War and the desire for a so-called "peace dividend" brought about a decade of depressed procurement and curtailed modernization in the 1990s. This has left the United States with a highly capable but rapidly aging naval air force, which has been flown hard in recent years to meet the growing demands placed on it. Many segments of our force are in need of critical modernization to sustain warfighting viability. Others require near-term development of follow-on platforms as the aircraft models currently in the fleet reach the end of their service lives.

Our land-based maritime patrol and reconnaissance aircraft, for example, will play a prominent and critical role in battlespace shaping, maritime dominance, and strike support. The new multimission maritime aircraft that is now under development will enter service in the second decade of the 21st century as a successor to both the P-3C Orion and EP-3E Aries II aircraft. Whether configured for specialized intelligence,

surveillance, and reconnaissance missions to build battlespace awareness, tasked to conduct antisubmarine or antisurface warfare for maritime dominance, or even as a precision strike-targeting platform, the multi-mission maritime aircraft will have the right connectivity for networked operations. Thus, it will be more deeply integrated into battle group concepts of operation, assuming a greater role in missions that are now performed by aircraft "organic" to the battle group.

The performance of naval aviation's land-based maritime forces during the Kosovo air campaign was a preview of the contribution these aircraft will make as part of a total force approach. Though the Navy provided only one-fifth of the land-based reconnaissance platforms for the air campaign, naval aircraft executed well over one-third of all reconnaissance missions during the operation. In some cases, utilization rates for P-3 and EP-3 aircraft in a reconnaissance role were as much as twice that of the next busiest non-naval reconnaissance assets. Additionally, P-3s maintained an around-the-clock armed surface combat air patrol in the Adriatic Sea throughout the crisis, which effectively eliminated any threat from the Yugoslavian navy and freed carrier-based tactical aircraft to concentrate exclusively on interdiction of fixed targets and Kosovo Engagement Zone operations.

P-3C Orion aircraft from the Japanese Maritime Self-Defense Force and Patrol Squadron 47 fly formation over a group of bilateral force ships during RIMPAC 2000 exercises in June 2000. Operations with other nations, a reflection of the alliances so important to maintaining stability in the world, will remain an element of naval aviation operations. (U.S. Navy)

Hovering just fifty feet above the waters of the Mediterranean Sea, an SH-60F Seahawk from Helicopter Antisubmarine Squadron 5 lowers its dipping sonar to search for submarines in June 1996. Even with the end of the Cold War, the threat of enemy submarines remains a very real one, prompting carrier-based helicopter squadrons to hone their antisubmarine warfare skills. (U.S. Navy)

A P-3C Orion assigned to Patrol Squadron 45 fires self-defense flares in training for a mission over Bosnia in 1997. P-3s provided valuable real-time photo and video imagery of operations in Bosnia, and in 1999 launched SLAM cruise missiles against targets in Kosovo during Operation Allied Force. Designed for open-ocean antisubmarine warfare, Orions have increasingly become more integrated in battle group operations, assuming missions once performed by carrier-based aircraft and freeing them for strike missions. (U.S. Navy)

The rotor wash of an SH-60 Seahawk of Helicopter Antisubmarine Squadron 15 creates a rainbow over the Arabian Gulf. Though designed initially as an antisubmarine platform, the Seahawk touches virtually every arena of naval aviation's operations and will continue to do so in the twenty-first century. (U.S. Navy)

The helicopter master plan is the linchpin for developing a modern, total force solution to increase fleet capability and lethality in the littorals. The plan's essence is the transformation of the helicopter community from a multiplatform force of eight type-model-series aircraft into a tightly focused force comprised of two extremely capable versions of the H-60 airframe, namely the SH-60R and the MH-60S. First and foremost, this transformation will greatly enhance the warfighting capabilities of the helicopter force—the SH-60R and MH-60S will be, without question, the most technologically advanced helicopters ever to enter the fleet. Second, by consolidating to a force of two H-60 variants, we will be able to capitalize on the efficiencies of a single maintenance, logistics, and training pipeline, resulting in significant cost reductions and better supportability..

Beyond traditional missions such as battle group core logistics and search and rescue, helicopter forces will be key enablers for 21st century warfighting, providing critical surveillance, sensor networking, and maritime strike capability. This tremendous leap in capability has compelled naval aviation to reexamine fundamental concepts of operation, community organization, and command and staff relationships for the naval helicopter force. Although formal studies and analyses are ongoing, it is already clear that continuing to regard helicopters as merely extending the capabilities of the individual ships from which they operate is no

longer appropriate. Completing the transformation of our helicopter forces will therefore include sizing and distributing rotary-wing forces across the battle group in a way that optimizes their warfighting contribution from a total battle force perspective.

The F/A-18E/F Super Hornet brings a tremendous increase in capability as well as the capacity for future growth to our carrier air wings and will serve as the Navy's principal strike fighter. The single-seat E model will soon begin replacing our older F/A-18C Hornets, while the two-seat F version will replace the venerable F-14 Tomcat. Some F/A-18C Hornets will continue in service in each air wing until replaced in the second decade of the new century by the Joint Strike Fighter, which is currently in development.

The Navy's EA-6B Prowler electronic warfare aircraft is America's sole airborne support jammer. The tremendous demand for the Prowler's unique capabilities in support of Operation Allied Force in 1999 highlights the continued importance of airborne electronic attack. In fact, Prowler availability for strike support was considered a go/no-go criterion for air strikes inside Kosovo. Currently our EA-6B fleet is being modified to a common configuration and equipped with improved jamming pods. The Prowler will also receive the Improved Capability III (ICAP III) upgrade in the near future, significantly

E-2C Hawkeyes of Carrier Airborne Early Warning Squadron 112 pictured high over the Pacific in September 1999. The Hawkeye features a multiple-surface tail that counters the peculiar airflow over the radar dome atop the fuselage. The first versions of the E-2 flew in Vietnam, and in the future it will continue to serve as an integral component of carrier air wings. (Ted Carlson)

An SH-60B flies over Essex *(LHD 2) in the Pacific in November 1997. The Navy's helicopter master plan calls for the service's entire operational helicopter force to operate variants of the Sikorsky Seahawk. (Ted Carlson)*

An F/A-18E Super Hornet assigned to Strike Fighter Squadron 122 lifts off at NAS Lemoore, California, for a training flight. The Super Hornet will be able to launch all types of precision weapons currently under development for strike aircraft, and strike multiple targets safely from standoff ranges. (Ted Carlson)

improving the aircraft's receivers, which in turn will enhance jamming performance to keep pace with future threats. ICAP III also includes increased battlespace connectivity critical to network-centric operations. The Navy is leading the effort to determine the appropriate replacement for the EA-6B as the aircraft reaches the end of its service life. The EA-6B follow-on, known presently only as the Airborne Electronic Attack aircraft, will enter service early in the next decade.

The E-2C Hawkeye will continue to perform critical airborne command and control for naval expeditionary forces. E-2C missions include early warning of approaching enemy air and surface units through area surveillance; intercept; search and rescue coordination; communications relay; and strike/air traffic control. Plans to upgrade the E-2C include a radar modernization program to improve detection and tracking capability against small and overland targets, and incorporation of an airborne cooperative engagement capability to enhance the E-2's ability to detect, track, and engage targets in concert with surface combatants.

The light of the aircraft's surveillance and radar equipment illuminates the faces of naval flight officers inside the darkened cabin of an E-2C Hawkeye of Carrier Airborne Early Warning Squadron 117. In an actual wartime situation, Hawkeye crews play a pivotal role in monitoring a wide-ranging aerial battlefield. (Ted Carlson)

A two-seat F/A-18F "traps" aboard a carrier during the Super Hornet's carrier certification trials. The F/A-18F will replace the F-14 Tomcat in fleet squadrons and assume its fighter, strike, reconnaissance, and forward air control roles. (Boeing)

The central role of our aircraft carriers themselves is another critical aspect of the vision for naval aviation. More than the "flattops" at the heart of our striking capability—which provide for fueling, arming, launch, recovery, and turnaround of our tactical aircraft—our carriers possess tremendous potential to enable operational-level command and control of expeditionary naval and joint forces. The *Nimitz*-class carriers of today's fleet will continue to serve through 2050 and beyond. Their flexibility and capacity for adapting new aircraft, weapons, and command and control systems, as well as enhanced communications and connectivity, serve as a testament to the strength of their design and the foresight of the teams that conceived and built them.

The next ten years, however, will bring the dawn of a phased evolution in carrier design to create a new generation of aircraft carrier, currently known as the CVNX program. CVNX will incorporate several major improvements over the *Nimitz* design based on today's cutting-edge technology. These include high-density nuclear reactors; an electrical-power generation and distribution system; internal redesign of spaces; an

Left: *An EA-6B Prowler assigned to Electronic Attack Squadron 138 flies over Nevada in February 1999. The Prowler fleet is being upgraded to a more advanced configuration, ICAP III, but is scheduled eventually to be replaced by a yet unidentified new Airborne Electronic Attack aircraft. (Ted Carlson)*

Above: *The Lockheed Martin X-35 won the competition for the future Joint Strike Fighter. The JSF is planned for production in conventional-takeoff-and-landing (Air Force), carrier-based (Navy), and short-takeoff/vertical-landing (Marine Corps and Royal Navy) versions. (Lockheed Martin)*

Above: *(Left to right) Aviation Structural Mechanic Third Class Christopher Kelly, Aviation Machinist's Mate First Class Octavio Balangood, and Aviation Electrician's Mate Third Class Eric Sanders perform maintenance on an aerial refueling "buddy" store on board* Abraham Lincoln *(CVN 72). The talented enlisted force that "keeps 'em flying" will always be the heart of naval aviation. (U.S. Navy)*

Left: *An E-2C Hawkeye about to be launched from the flight deck of* Carl Vinson *(CVN 70). The Hawkeye has been in production for most of the last four decades, but no replacement airframe is on the horizon. The E-2C has been upgraded continually and the newest version—the Hawkeye 2000—was rolled out in 2001. An even more capable version, the Advanced Hawkeye, is envisioned for further development. (David Peters)*

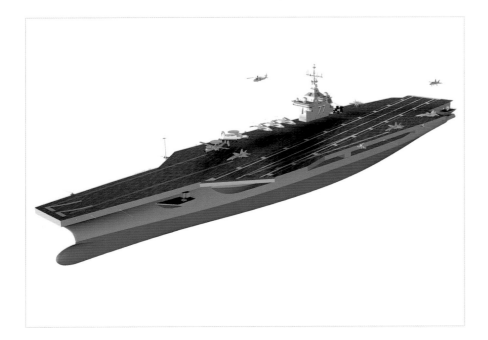

Three artist's concepts of CVN 77 and the next-generation carrier, CVNX. The last Nimitz-*class carrier, CVN 77, will be a transition platform for CVNX 1, which will feature new high-density reactors, electromagnetic aircraft launching systems, and integrated warfare systems. CVNX 2 will feature further improvements, including an electromagnetic aircraft recovery system. (U.S. Navy, above left; Morgan I. Wilbur, above right; Newport News Shipbuilding, below)*

integrated, technologically advanced island; and, ultimately, a new hull and flight deck design. This smart, reconfigurable aircraft carrier will be focused to fully support network centric warfare by maximizing its capabilities as a command platform. Equipment will be installed in modules to allow certain computer and combat systems to be replaced or modified several times over the ship's life span, giving CVNX greater flexibility and longevity than even the highly successful *Nimitz*-class.

The tools of the trade—the high technology of our carriers, aircraft, and weapons, and our sophisticated tactics and doctrine—are impressive, but they are only part of the story of the enduring value of naval aviation. Directing our battle groups, manning our carriers, and flying and maintaining our aircraft are a steady line of officers and enlisted

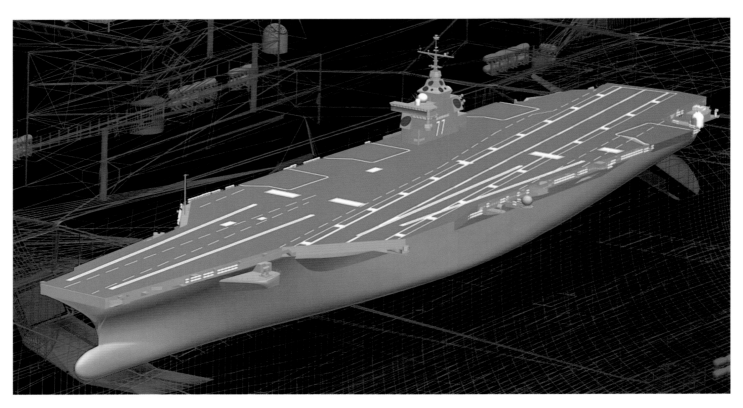

men and women who steer by the same stars of boldness, valor, loyalty, and patriotism that guided those who served with John Paul Jones. Yet those who are specially called to serve in the Navy as aviators, flight officers, or in aviation-related rates are also imbued with the pioneering spirit, desire for adventure, and physical courage that inspired the Wright brothers to take flight into the unknown.

When terrorism visited the United States with such tragic consequences on 11 September 2001, naval aviation stood ready to respond. While *George Washington* (CVN 73) and *John F. Kennedy* (CV 67) deployed to New York City, half a world away *Enterprise* and *Carl Vinson* (CVN 70) took station in the Arabian Gulf and prepared for action. From the decks of these two carriers naval aircraft launched Operation Enduring Freedom, on 7 October 2001, striking al-Qaeda terrorist camps and Taliban military installations in Afghanistan. Operating alongside carrier-based aircraft, P-3 Orions provided surveillance and battle-damage assessments while helicopter assets and AV-8B Harrier II aircraft supported Marine Expeditionary Units on the ground.

Though the United States is only beginning what will certainly be a long struggle against terrorism, the actions of naval aviation thus far prove the wisdom of one of our founding fathers. The camaraderie born of a passion for flying and dangers shared binds together the generation of Ellyson, Towers, and Mitscher to the young men and women airborne at this very moment in naval aircraft around the globe. It is in their hands, minds, and hearts, even more than in the technological innovation of the machines they fly, that America's security and the future of naval aviation lie. And although naval aviation's first century is drawing to a close, as I look over the horizon to the century that lies before us, I see we've really only just launched off the deck, climbing furiously, with open sky ahead.

Above: *A formation of F/A-18 Hornets salutes Abraham Lincoln (CVN 72) after a fly-off before heading for the "beach." The mutual respect between the air wing and the carrier that hosts it creates a synergy of teamwork that will continue to make naval air power the force of choice far into the future. (U.S. Navy)*

The pilot of an EA-6B Prowler awaits taxi signals from a handler on the flight deck of Carl Vinson *(CVN 70). The projection of power ultimately rests in the hands of the skilled men and women in the cockpits. (David Peters)*

Acknowledgments

Like the carrier flight deck that is naval aviation's defining symbol, assembling a book of this magnitude was a team effort. Editor Rick Burgess touched every facet of the work and much of the credit for the final product is due to him. Wendy Leland lent her considerable talent to the work of copyediting the words of multiple writers, ensuring accuracy and consistency throughout. The talented corps of authors, as you read, brought naval aviation alive with their words. The stunning images, whether created on canvas or taken through a camera lens, are the work of true artists and completed this portrait of naval aviation. Special thanks to Al Audleman, who focused his camera on a variety of things as he successfully captured every type of shot that popped into my mind over the course of many months. I would also like to recognize the Navy photographers, who as I write these words are currently at work in the fleet. Much of the imagery on these pages is the result of their dedicated service to our nation.

The book would not have been possible without the support of the staffs of the National Museum of Naval Aviation and Naval Aviation Museum Foundation. Many thanks to Captain J.J. Coonan, USN (Ret.), Gene Countryman, Captain Charles E. Ellis, JAGC, USN (Ret.), Vice Admiral John H. Fetterman, USN (Ret.), William Johnson, David Jonik, Colonel Denis J. Kiely, USMC (Ret.), Robert R. Macon, Frank Matson, Captain Robert L. Rasmussen, USN (Ret.), and Captain E. Earle Rogers, II, USN (Ret.). A great deal of gratitude is owed to Rear Admiral Stephen R. Pietropaoli, Chief of Information, Department of the Navy, for his support in arranging access to training activities in the Pensacola area. The public affairs staffs of the respective commands proved most helpful in this endeavor, and many thanks go to Lori Apprilliano, Commander Anthony Cooper, Kay Esty, Barbara Kelly, Lieutenant Steve Mavica, Lieutenant (jg) Allison Myrick, Lieutenant Richard Naystatt, Lieutenant Commander Ike Skelton, Harry White, and Joy White.

I would be remiss if I did not thank the crew of *Enterprise* (CVN 65), who at the beginning of this project provided me with a firsthand look at carrier aviation. It was an experience that greatly benefited this book and left me with a memory I will cherish for the rest of my life.

Finally, I dedicate this book to two special people. My loving wife, Maria, who was pregnant with our second child during much of the period in which I labored on this work, always provided inspiration and support above and beyond the call of duty. Though he's been absent from my life for some time now, I also acknowledge my grandfather, Lieutenant Commander Robert F. Goodspeed, USNR, a wearer of the wings of gold who pointed the way for his grandson.

M. Hill Goodspeed
Editor-in-Chief

Suggested Reading

General Naval Aviation Histories

Roy A. Grossnick, *U.S. Naval Aviation, 1910–1995* (1995)
Richard C. Knott, *A Heritage of Wings* (1997)
Robert L. Lawson, ed., *The History of U.S. Naval Air Power* (1985)
Archibald D. Turnbull and Clifford L. Lord, *History of United States Naval Aviation* (1950)

Pre-World War II

Thomas C. Hone, Norman Friedman, and Mark Mandeles, *American and British Aircraft Carrier Development, 1919–1941* (1999)
Charles M. Melhorn, *Two-Block Fox: The Rise of the Aircraft Carrier, 1911–1929* (1974)
Dwight Messimer, *No Margin for Error: The U.S. Navy's Transpacific Flight of 1925* (1981)
Ralph D. Paine, *The First Yale Unit* (1925)
Geoffrey L. Rossano, ed., *The Price of Honor: The World War One Letters of Naval Aviator Kenneth MacLeish* (1991)
Richard K. Smith, *The Airships Akron and Macon* (1965)
D.W. Tomlinson, *The Sky's the Limit* (1930)
William F. Trimble, *Admiral William A. Moffett: Architect of Naval Aviation* (1994)
George Van Deurs, *Wings for the Fleet* (1966)
Thomas Wildenberg, *Destined for Glory: Dive Bombing, Midway, and the Evolution of Carrier Airpower* (1998)
Robert A. Winston, *Dive Bomber* (1939)
Eugene E. Wilson, *Slipstream* (1950)
E.T. Wooldridge, *The Golden Age Remembered* (1998)

World War II

Tom Blackburn, *The Jolly Rogers* (1989)
LCDR J. Bryan and Philip Reed, *Mission Beyond Darkness* (1945)
A.R. Buchanan, *The Navy's Air War* (1946)
Hal Buell, *Dauntless Helldivers* (1991)
Robert J. Cressman, Steve Ewing, et al, *A Glorious Page in Our History* (1990)
Steve Ewing and John B. Lundstrom, *Fateful Rendezvous: The Life of Butch O'Hare* (1997)
Stanley Johnston, *Queen of the Flat-Tops: The U.S.S. Lexington and the Coral Sea Battle* (1942)
Alvin Kernan, *Crossing the Line: A Bluejacket's World War II Odyssey* (1994)
Richard C. Knott, *Black Cat Raiders of World War II* (2000)
Walter Lord, *Incredible Victory* (1967)
John B. Lundstrom, *The First Team: Pacific Naval Air Combat from Pearl Harbor to Midway* (1984)
Clark G. Reynolds, *The Fighting Lady: The New Yorktown in the Pacific War* (1986)
Clark G. Reynolds, *The Fast Carriers: The Forging of an Air Navy* (1992)

Frederick C. Sherman, *Combat Command* (1950)
Edward P. Stafford, *The Big E* (1962)
E.T. Stover and Clark G. Reynolds, *The Saga of Smokey Stover* (1978)
Barrett Tillman, *The Dauntless Dive Bomber of World War Two* (1976)
Barrett Tillman, *Corsair: The F4U in World War II and Korea* (1979)
Barrett Tillman, *Avenger at War* (1990)
Barrett Tillman, *Wildcat: The F4F in WWII* (1990)
Barrett Tillman, *Hellcat: The F6F in World War II* (2000)
William T. Y'Blood, *Red Sun Setting: The Battle of the Philippine Sea* (1981)
William T. Y'Blood, *Hunter-Killer: U.S. Escort Carriers in the Battle of the Atlantic* (1983)
William T. Y'Blood, *The Little Giants: U.S. Escort Carriers Against Japan* (1987)

Korean War

Richard P. Hallion, *The Naval Air War in Korea* (1986)
James Michener, *The Bridges at Toko-ri* (1953)
G.G. O'Rourke and E.T. Wooldridge, *Night Fighters Over Korea* (1998)

Vietnam War

Wynn F. Foster, *Captain Hook: A Pilot's Tragedy and Triumph in the Vietnam War* (1992)
Rene J. Francillon, *Tonkin Gulf Yacht Club: U.S. Carrier Operations off Vietnam* (1988)
Peter B. Mersky and Norman Polmar, *The Naval Air War in Vietnam* (1986)
John B. Nichols and Barrett Tillman, *On Yankee Station: The Naval Air War in Vietnam* (1987)
Barrett Tillman, *MiG Master: The Story of the F-8 Crusader* (1990)
James and Cybil Stockdale, *In Love and War* (1990)

Cold War and Space Age

Alan B. Shepard and Donald K. Slayton, *Moon Shot: The Inside Story of America's Race to the Moon* (1994)
E.T. Wooldridge, *Into the Jet Age: Conflict and Change in Naval Aviation, 1945–1975* (1995)
Gerald L. Miller, *Nuclear Weapons and Aircraft Carriers: How the Bomb Saved Naval Aviation* (2001)

Gulf War

Sherman Baldwin, *Ironclaw: A Navy Carrier Pilot's Gulf War Experience* (1996)
Edward Marolda and Robert J. Schneller, Jr., *Shield and Sword: The United States Navy and the Persian Gulf War* (1998)
Jay A. Stout, *Hornets over Kuwait* (1997)

MARINE CORPS AVIATION

Marion E. Carl and Barrett Tillman, *Pushing the Envelope: The Career of Fighter Ace and Test Pilot Marion Carl* (1994)

John Pomeroy Condon, *Corsairs and Flattops: Marine Carrier Air Warfare, 1944–1945* (1998)

Bruce Gamble, *The Black Sheep* (1998)

Bruce Gamble, *Black Sheep One: The Life of Pappy Boyington* (2000)

Samuel Hynes, *Flights of Passage* (1988)

Peter B. Mersky, *U.S. Marine Corps Aviation, 1912–Present* (1998)

Robert Sherrod, *History of Marine Corps Aviation in World War II* (1952)

COAST GUARD AVIATION

Barrett Thomas Beard, *Wonderful Flying Machines: A History of U.S. Coast Guard Helicopters* (1998)

Arthur Pearcy, *U.S. Coast Guard Aircraft since 1916* (1991)

AIRCRAFT CARRIERS

Norman Friedman, *U.S. Aircraft Carriers: An Illustrated Design History* (1983)

Norman Polmar, *Aircraft Carriers* (1969)

GENERAL AIRCRAFT HISTORIES

Richard C. Knott, *The American Flying Boat: An Illustrated History* (1979)

William T. Larkins, *U.S. Navy Aircraft, 1921–1941 and U.S. Marine Aircraft, 1914–1959* (1988)

William T. Larkins, *Battleship and Cruiser Aircraft of the Unites States Navy, 1910–1949* (1996)

Gordon Swanborough and Peter M. Bowers, *United States Navy Aircraft since 1911* (1990)

BIOGRAPHIES

The below listed books cover more than one era. Biographies and memoirs that pertain to only one era are found below the respective heading.

J.J. Clark with Clark G. Reynolds, *Carrier Admiral* (1967)

Donald Engen, *Wings and Warriors: My Life as a Naval Aviator* (1997)

Paul T. Gilcrist, *Feet Wet: Reflections of a Carrier Pilot* (1997)

Arthur W. Radford, *From Pearl Harbor to Vietnam: The Memoirs of Arthur W. Radford* (1980)

E.B. Potter, *Bull Halsey* (1985)

Clark G. Reynolds, *Admiral John H. Towers: The Struggle for Naval Air Supremacy* (1991)

Theodore Taylor, *The Magnificent Mitscher* (1985)

Authors and Editors

LIEUTENANT COMMANDER TOM BEARD, USCG (RETIRED)
(Guarding Our Shores)
served as an aviator in both the U.S. Navy and U.S. Coast Guard, and has accumulated 7,000 flight hours in thirty different military and civilian aircraft, from carrier aircraft to seaplanes to helicopters. Following his retirement from military service, he received an M.A. degree in history, and is the author of numerous articles and three books, including *Wonderful Flying Machines: A History of Early Coast Guard Helicopters*.

LIEUTENANT COMMANDER RICHARD R. BURGESS, USN (RETIRED)
(Editor, Sea Wings, Fight Deck)
was designated a naval flight officer following his graduation from Auburn University, and during his career flew in maritime patrol squadrons, served as an analyst with the Defense Intelligence Agency, and was a staff officer with Carrier Group Four and *George Washington* (CVN 73). A former editor of *Naval Aviation News*, he is currently the managing editor for *Sea Power*, the magazine of the Navy League of the United States. He is also the editor of the fifth edition of the *Naval Aviation Guide*.

MR. M. HILL GOODSPEED
(Editor-in-Chief, A Golden Journey, Flight Deck)
is the historian at the National Museum of Naval Aviation. A former George C. Marshall undergraduate scholar at Washington and Lee University, he holds an M.A. degree from the University of West Florida. He is the author of one book, *The Spirit of Naval Aviation*, and his articles and book reviews have appeared in the *Journal of Military History*, *Naval History*, *Naval Aviation News*, *Foundation*, and *Wings of Fame*.

DR. THOMAS C. HONE
(Flattop: The Queen of Naval Operations)
is a professor at the Industrial College of the Armed Forces. He has also taught at the Naval War College and served as a special assistant to Commander Naval Air Systems Command. A frequent contributor to the *Naval War College Review* and *Proceedings*, he is the author of *Power and Change: The Administrative History of the Office of the Chief of Naval Operations, 1946–1986*, and coauthor of *American and British Aircraft Carrier Development, 1919–1941*. He was also a contributor to *The Navy*.

COMMANDER PETER B. MERSKY, USNR (RETIRED)
(Green and Gold)
served as an air intelligence officer on active duty and in the Naval Air Reserve. A former editor of *Approach*, the Naval Aviation Safety Review, he currently serves as the book review editor for *Naval Aviation News*. He is the author or coauthor of numerous books on naval aviation, including *U.S. Marine Corps Aviation, 1912–Present*, and *The Naval Air War in Vietnam*, and his articles have appeared in many prominent magazines and journals.

VICE ADMIRAL JOHN B. NATHMAN, USN
(Over the Horizon)
served as a fighter pilot, Topgun instructor, and test pilot. The commanding officer of the first squadron to fly the F/A-18 Hornet in combat during operations against Libya in 1986, he has also commanded a carrier air wing, *Nimitz* (CVN 68), and a carrier battle group. The former Director, Air Warfare in the Office of the Chief of Naval Operations, he currently serves as Commander, Naval Air Force, U.S. Pacific Fleet.

LIEUTENANT COMMANDER DAVID PARSONS, USN (RETIRED)
(Armor of the Air)
served as an officer in both the U.S. Marine Corps and U.S. Navy. A radar intercept officer flying the F-14 Tomcat, he flew combat missions off *John F. Kennedy* (CV 67) during Operations Desert Shield and Desert Storm. He served as editor of *Approach*, the Naval Aviation Safety Review, and is the author of six books, including *Hell Bent for Leather* and *Fighter Country*, in addition to scores of articles. He is currently the vice president for Navy/Marine Corps programs with Whitney, Bradley and Brown, Inc., in Washington, D.C.

ADMIRAL LEIGHTON W. SMITH, USN (RETIRED)
(Navy Wings)
flew more than 280 combat missions over Vietnam, and held command at sea at all levels in the aviation community, including squadron, carrier air wing, aircraft carrier, and carrier battle group. His final tour of duty included command of the NATO-led Implementation Force in Bosnia during 1995–1996. An Honorary Knight of the British Empire, he is a senior fellow at the Center for Naval Analysis and serves on the boards of numerous naval organizations.

MR. BARRETT TILLMAN
(A Breed Apart)
is an award-winning author best known for his operational histories of U.S. Navy aircraft. A former managing editor of *Hook* magazine, for which he has authored over 100 articles, he is currently a contributing editor of *Flight Journal*. A private pilot, he has logged flight time in numerous aircraft, including tactical jets and an SBD Dauntless he helped restore.

CAPTAIN PAT WALSH, USN
(Angels in Blue)

currently serves as the Executive Assistant to the Chief of Naval Personnel. In addition to his tour as a Blue Angels demonstration pilot, he flew combat missions in the Gulf War and commanded Strike Fighter Squadron 105 and Carrier Air Wing 1 flying missions in support of Operations Southern Watch and Deny Flight. A former White House Fellow, he holds M.A. and Ph.D. degrees from Tufts University.

MR. MORGAN I. WILBUR
(A Day in Naval Aviation)

served in the Naval Air Reserve, flying as an aircrewman in P-3 Orions. An accomplished artist, his paintings have been exhibited at the Navy Art Gallery, National Museum of Naval Aviation, and Smithsonian National Air and Space Museum. His work has also appeared in numerous magazines, including *Proceedings, Aviation Week and Space Technology*, as well as on several book covers. He currently serves as art director for *Naval Aviation News*.

MR. THOMAS WILDENBERG
(Farther and Faster)

is a historian specializing in the development of naval aviation between the world wars. A former Dewitt C. Ramsey Fellow at the Smithsonian National Air and Space Museum, he is the author of *Gray Steel and Black Oil: Fast Tankers and Replenishment at Sea in the U.S. Navy, 1912–1995*; *Destined for Glory*; and *All the Factors of Victory*, a biography of Admiral Joseph Mason Reeves.

MS. AMY WATERS YARSINSKE
(Memories and Memorials)

is a former naval reserve officer and the author of nineteen books, including *Wings of Valor, Wings of Gold: An Illustrated History of U.S. Naval Aviation*; *Forward for Freedom: The Story of Battleship* Wisconsin *(BB 64)*; and *Mud Flats to Master Jet Base: Fifty Years at Naval Air Station Oceana*. She is a recent inductee into the Distinguished Virginia Authors Room of the Virginia Center for the Books.

Index

349

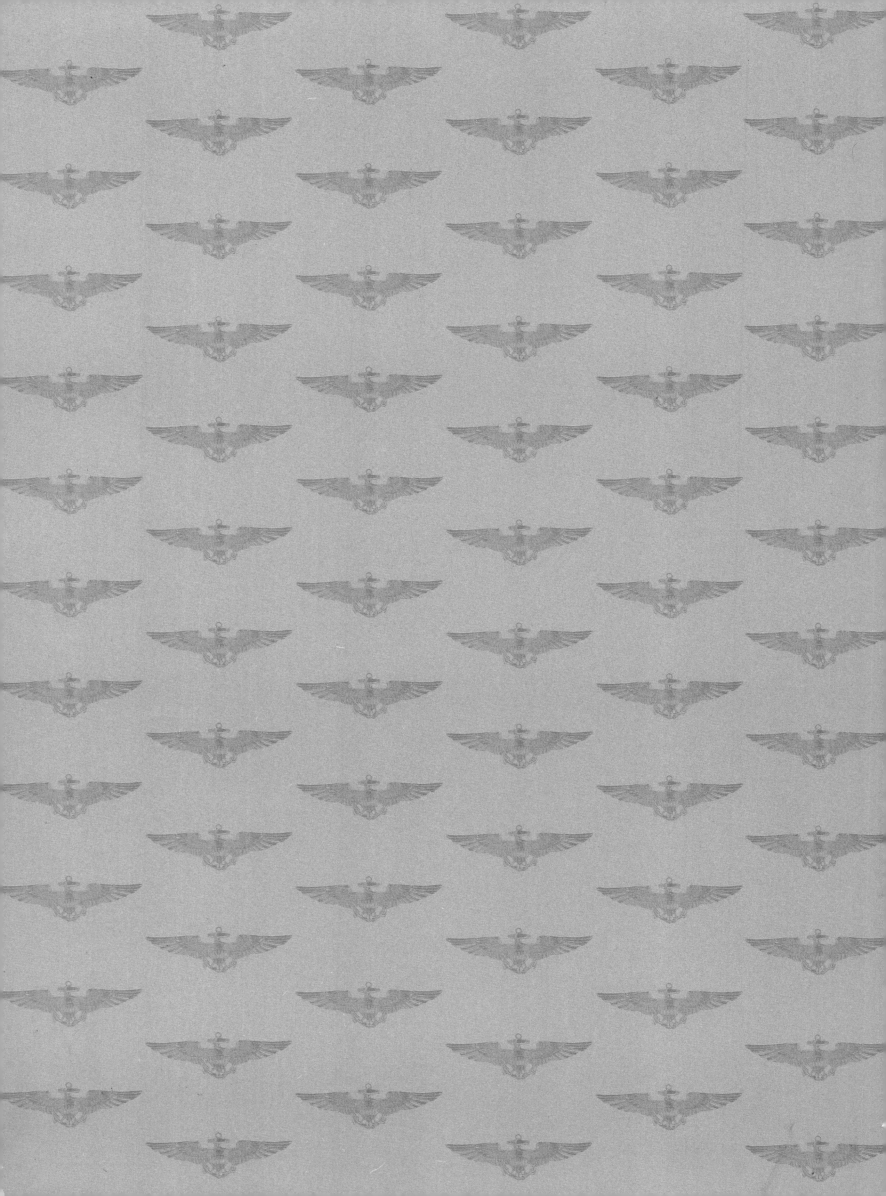